TO
SON +
Alison
much Love thankyou
L

Thank God I...™

To Jason +
Alison

"This book is a wonderful example of the age-old wisdom that every seemingly negative event contains within it the seed of an equal or greater benefit."

— **JACK CANFIELD,** co-creator of *Chicken Soup for the Unsinkable Soul*® and featured in *The Secret*

Thank God I...

VOLUME **2**

Stories of Inspiration for Every Situation

Thank God I Am Not an Ugly Duckling — Bernie Siegel, MD

Thank God I Was Physically Abused — Katana Abbott

Thank God I Went to Prison — Noah McKay, MD IN LOVING MEMORY

Thank God I Am Blind — Ben Underwood IN LOVING MEMORY

Thank God I Was Raised in Chaos — Aaron Kleinerman

Thank God I Had Postpartum Depression — Dr. Shosh Bennett

Thank God I Was Born in a Refugee Camp — Regina B. Jensen, PhD

INCLUDING STORIES FROM Dr. Doug Leher, Varant Majarian, Dr. Sue Morter, Claudia Pruett and Dr. Ramah Wagner

CREATED BY JOHN CASTAGNINI

THE PERFECT IDEA™

Thank God I . . .™, *Volume Two*
Copyright © 2009 Inspired Authors, LLC

Published by Inspired Authors, LLC
5348 Vegas Drive, Suite 1086
Las Vegas, NV 89108
http://www.thankgodi.com

ISBN–13: 978-0-9815453-1-8

Cover Design: George Foster
Interior Design: Desktop Miracles, Inc.

Printed in the United States of America

Publisher's Cataloging-In-Publication Data
(Prepared by The Donohue Group, Inc.)

Thank God I— : stories of inspiration for every situation / created by
John Castagnini.
   v. ; cm.
   ISBN: 978-0-9815453-9-4
   ISBN: 978-0-9815453-1-8 (v. 2)
   1. Gratitude—Religious aspects. 2. Life change events—Religious
aspects. 3. Adjustment (Psychology) 4. Conduct of life. I. Castagnini,
John.
BF575.G68 T43   2008

                                     158.1

TABLE OF CONTENTS

In Loving Memory

*H*umbled best described our feelings when our company assistant, **Cassandra Gatsov,** transitioned at 23 years old during the creation of *Thank God I . . .*™ Volume 1. Thank you for guiding us, angel.

Then, we felt absolutely stunned and amazed when **Ben Underwood** and **Dr. Noah Mckay** left this earth months before we published *Thank God I . . .* ™ Volume 2.

These few words are offered to honor their being:

Ben Underwood lived completely blind most of his life. This extraordinary young man made sounds and used his ears (echolocation) to play sports and ride bicycles, while using the wisdom of his heart and soul to truly SEE. Thank you Ben for your brilliance. Thank you for reminding and empowering us to LIVE beyond life's challenges.

Noah McKay, MD, was a pioneer in medicine. He represented the pinnacle of patient care—so much so that Noah went to jail for the cause. In his life, he helped heal countless lives: "Heal the patient with whatever means necessary." Thank God for Noah, the epitome for serving humanity with a genuine, healing heart.

To all of you, Thanks for your guidance.
Thank you for helping our souls to sing.

With love,
The *Thank God I . . .* ™ Core Team

Letter from the Founder

JOHN CASTAGNINI

I couldn't be more thankful for the amazing reception to date of *Thank God I . . . ™* around the world—in what we consider is really our infancy. I am most grateful for the opportunity to tour the world and carry this Work of Light.

This past year I spoke in Cancun on *Thank God I . . . ™*. Afterwards a lady ran up to me with tears in her eyes. She asked me, "How could you put on your book cover, *Thank God My Son Died?*" I shared with her that someone who had *gone through* that experience wrote this story. *Perplexed* and *enraged* is a gross understatement for the anguish written all over her face.

She screamed, "Well, my daughter *died,* and I can't possibly understand this! How could that woman write this?"

I shared that when this author—who had "lost" her son—looked deep enough, she was able to find *all* the parts that her son represented to her in her life in other people around her whom she loved. I then explained that by embracing the understanding that energy and matter could not be created nor destroyed—but only change form—this author came to honor the *new* forms of her son. When this author "missed" her son, she would simply look at what she was *missing*, and then find *that* present. When she discovered that she could find what she thought was missing *every* time, she no longer mourned his loss. Instead she carried him closer in her heart.

"Yeah, yeah—just words," many might say.

This lady then opened the *Thank God I . . .* ™ book and began to read the story right there in front of me. In the first paragraph she turned to me, her former cry of anger transformed into tears of love. She read out loud the date that the author's son died: September 3, 1999. Almost unable to speak—but with an intensity that pierced through me—she uttered, "My daughter died September 3rd, 1999."

Transformation—ya think?

More than anything I am thankful for these mystical heart-opening moments that share with us the hidden laws governing our lives.

Thank you for reading; thank you to all our authors for sharing; thank you to the *Thank God I . . .* ™ Team for working furiously to prepare these stories; and thank you, God, for the YOU we continually discover.

Please read our *Introduction*—it really helps put this *perfection series* into context.

Introduction

IMPORTANT . . .
PLEASE READ THIS SECTION.

Why this book? What makes it so different? Not only are the answers important, they are integral to your understanding of the stories presented here. Thank you for not skipping over this brief introduction in your eagerness to get to the meat of the book itself.

When I first thought to include *Thank God I Was Raped* as one of the stories for the first anthology, the concept sent chills through my spine. Could anyone who's endured this brutal, horrifying experience really embrace these words? Over the years, I've counseled countless women during their rape recovery. I chose the title after witnessing what transpires for them when *they* come to this conclusion of gratitude. What became quite apparent over the course of thousands of conversations is that we only evolve past the mental trauma from such an occurrence when we can hold *the love for it in our hearts.*

What does *God* mean?

God—certainly, the biggest three-letter word ever created. Grand Organized Designer best describes the **GOD** used in *Thank God I . . .*™.

The thousands of people sharing their stories in this series all perceive God in their own light. *Thank God I . . .* ™ is about this network of people willing to move beyond having the right "name" for God.

Even the word *God* itself cannot finite the infinite.

Rather, *God* refers to a system governing the brilliance of what *is* and *is not*.

What this book series is *not* supposed to be.

This series does not condone or promote any of the acts the writers have experienced, nor do we suggest in any way that anyone *should* either commit any of these acts or subject themselves to any of these acts. This series also does not promote or label any specific kind of behavior as "right" or "wrong"; the stories were not written and the book was not published for the purpose of anyone rationalizing these types of actions or behavior.

In addition, the *Thank God I* . . . ™ series does *not* promote or deny *any* religion. Rather, it honors the existence of *all* things as part of a *perfect creation.*

What is *Thank God I* . . . ™ about?

Our intention with this series is to convey this one key principle: *The Perfect Idea*™. Each time we fail to recognize this principle, the next lesson that comes our way will once again offer us the opportunity to see the perfection and break through it into freedom. In fact, finding perfection in the pain and pleasure of our own personal tribulations is the *only* way we will *ever* liberate ourselves from the bondage of patterns. Whether it comes in a day, a year, or a lifetime, situations will come into our lives that will *force* us to become thankful for "what was" and joyfully to experience "what is."

What does *Thanking God* mean?

During the creation phase of this series, we were fortunate to have as our ever-efficient assistant, Cassandra—a beautiful 22-year-old writer and poet. Just prior to coming to work with us, Cassandra was diagnosed with cervical cancer. A little over a year-and-a-half later the cancer spread, and she left this world before the first book launched.

After Cassandra passed, my heart was struck by the words she put to the page as she endured this experience. She wrote of her "earth angels" and her explorations as she left her body to "dance with angels." She didn't write about her "passing"; she wrote about *Thank God I* . . . ™ *living* as she moved through her life's greatest test and her life's ending. She viewed each person, each moment as precious. How fortunate she was to see God in the *now*.

Imagine, this is what she wrote about her cancer:

Tears fill my eyes daily with gratitude for every moment and every breath. It has allowed me to go after my dreams, to live from my heart, and to be truly free. I thank God for my cancer, and for allowing me to reach a place in me that I don't think would have been possible without this experience. I am now 23 and feel that I have stepped into my skin proudly. I have felt an inner peace that many don't find until later in life. I am truly grateful for all my earth angels and want to thank them for sharing with me this wonderful journey.

. . . CASSANDRA

There are four million tasks to accomplish in order to bring the *Thank God I* . . . ™ network to the standard of our vision. Thank you, Cassandra, for reminding me why *Thank God I* . . . ™ was conceived in the first place.

Thanking God is about the above. Not just what is above this sentence; it is about what is *above*, guiding us at every moment. Beyond the pain, chaos, and confusion of our circumstances exists true perfection. Thanking God is about finding this perfection. This place of thanking God might seem nearly impossible to find, but it is the only place we will find ourselves.

Thank God I . . . ™ **is true *gratitude*.**

Sure we all hear the same old wonderful things that people are grateful for in their lives. But is this gratitude? *Thank God I* . . . ™ gratitude is about a state of being. It is about a state of inspiration, non-judgment, and presence. *Thank God I . . .* ™ gratitude is beyond the illusion of positive or negative. It is beyond the lies of "good" and "evil." *Thank God I . . .* ™ gratitude is about finding God in every word, thought and deed. *In* spirit we are beyond the illusion of pain or pleasure and we are present *with* spirit. *Thank God I . . .* ™ gratitude is about *equal love* for all that is, as it is, was, or ever shall become. *Gratitude* is loving what we *don't* "like" as much as loving what we *do* "like."

The diversity of authors and experiences

The intention of this series is to reach *all* of humanity, every single unique creation. We did not base the selection of contributions to this series upon any faith or religious orientation. Each selected author took a former challenge into his/her heart, and each share the goal of the universal understanding of love/gratitude in all. The diversity of authors spans religions, countries, professions, age, race, nationality, and experiences. They range from those with disease to doctors, from ex-convicts to stay-at-home moms, and whoever they are, gratitude rules. From alcoholism to molestation or rape, the law of gratitude prevails with each of our authors. Thankfulness for whatever is, or is not, ultimately rules every one of our kingdoms.

The vision of *Thank God I . . .* ™

Little did I imagine how lightning-fast *Thank God I . . .* ™ would circle the world. Reaching diverse people, this network includes thousands of contributors sharing not only their stories but also their answers. Beyond the books, and the online community, we offer worldwide conference calls, workshops and seminars. This series provides *all* within specific communities information in order to evolve past the emotions that are holding them back. The people and the project are evolutionary.

> "All things in nature proceed from certain necessity and with the utmost perfection."
>
> . . . BARUCH SPINOZA

Making Love with Words

All too often it is common to interchange synonymous words and use them incorrectly. The *Thank God I . . .* ™ authors and editing team have done their best to clarify many distinctions that have confused humanity in the Personal Development field.

Because the *Thank God I . . .* ™ brand has so many authors, the alignment of words, terms, and expressions has become an important focus for the "continuity" of meaning.

The distinctions in the expression of language are extraordinarily important—especially with written material.

Our intent is to use terms clearly and correctly.

The following are important *word* distinctions that can assist the reader in getting a more comprehensive understanding of the *Thank God I . . .* ™ "state of mind." For making these distinctions, we give special thanks to Dr. John Demartini.

1) Passion & Inspiration

Passion is an endorphin "high" eventually attracting the opposite "low."

It is *not* heart centered.

5

Inspiration is a state of being, love, and presence.
It has *no* opposite and *is* heart centered.

2) Happiness & Fulfillment

Happiness is an endorphin "high" eventually attracting a *sadness* "low."
It is *not* heart centered.

Fulfillment is a state that encompasses happiness and sadness equally.
It *is* heart centered.

3) Peace & Inner Peace

Peace is balanced by its opposite: *war.* It is an illusion that is *not* heart centered.

Inner peace is a state of fulfillment, being, presence, inspiration, gratitude or love.
It *is* heart centered and has *no* opposite.

4) Forgiveness & Appreciation

Forgiveness implies a right and wrong—and a judgment.
In the world of *perfection*—past, present and future—nothing needs an apology.

Appreciation honors the *perfection* of what has been, is, and will be—in whatever form. It reserves *no* judgment.

5) Always & Never

These two terms have been almost completely edited out of this text. The Actual Existence of *always* and *never* in a relative universe is almost non-existent. In fact, by listening to where one uses the term *always* or *never,* one can become clear of the internal charges (misperceptions) that exist. The over-use of these terms can be indicative of stubborn positioning that can inhibit one's growth.

6) Positive / Negative & Equilibration

If you cut a magnet in half, you will still get a positive and negative "half." Each side of the magnet attracts its opposite.

Equilibration. Thank God I . . . ™ fosters a state of Gratitude. It is an *equilibrated* state beyond the illusion of positive or negative. An *equilibrated* state is also expressed as inspiration, love, being, gratitude, presence, and fulfillment.

7) Reality & Actuality

Any emotional experience has an opposite emotion. Emotional *realities* are illusive perceptions with opposites.

Actuality transcends the illusion of *realities. Actuality* is an *equilibrated* state.

Actuality transcends two complementary opposite *realities* upon their unification.

8) Emotions & Feelings

Emotions are charged realities that are illusions and have opposites.
They are *not* heart centered.

Feelings are *equilibrated actualities.* They have *no* opposites. They *are* heart centered.

Honoring these distinctions can greatly assist the reader in understanding some of the key messages that *Thank God I . . .* ™ is sharing with humanity. Honoring them can greatly increase one's experience of ACTUALITY.

Thank you,
John Castagnini

Thank God My Dad Died When I Was Six and I Became an Abused Stepchild and Wife

KATANA ABBOTT

When I was 20 I found myself lying in a hospital bed—battered by a vicious husband. My marriage reflected the suffering I endured during a terrible childhood at the hands of an abusive stepfather.

If only my father hadn't died when I was six.

I've long since emerged from the terrible darkness that marked my early life. God gave me wisdom, light, and love to transform a life of adversity into one of abundance. Today at 49 I find myself on one more new path—using my experience to help other mid-life women lead rich, blessed lives.

I thank God every day. I thank God my dad died when I was six, and that I later became an abused child and wife. God helped me survive, and the experience of suffering—and my later success—would shape my new calling.

When I was six my father was my hero. My earliest memory of him is when he came home dressed in his Army uniform. To me he looked like Elvis.

9

That same year he died in a boating accident.

I felt lost.

When I turned 10 my "tragedy" compounded when my mother married a man who verbally and physically abused my two brothers and me.

I left home at 18 and began my new life as a bright, ambitious college student—paying my tuition with the funds my father's death benefits provided for our education.

I believed in God.

I remember as a teenager lying in bed one night crying and praying in the dark. Along with the loss of my father, I also felt the betrayal of my mother who refused to protect her children against the "evil" man she had married.

I felt so alone.

But lying in my bed that night I was suddenly hit with what felt like a bolt of lightning. Overpowering waves of love and mercy filled me. I loved God and—after this night—did not feel alone anymore.

That feeling of "higher love" has remained with me to this day.

After leaving home and becoming a college student, I was desperate to be loved by a man. I was a young, needy teenager. One night I met an exotic, handsome man who was 10 years older than me. Like so many other abused children I found myself in a challenging relationship as an adult. He isolated me from friends and family, and he piled up enormous debts. As his wife I bore financial responsibility. Also because of marrying him I lost my college tuition benefits.

My mother was a dutiful wife even to my stepfather. I became a dutiful wife, too, hoping I could change him into a good man by being a "good" wife. I obeyed his commands at the expense of my own self-respect and self-love.

Just as I escaped an abusive childhood, God gave me the will to file for divorce. It was then that his verbal abuse turned physical. I ended up in the hospital—brutally beaten by this monster.

The emotional pain was as searing as the physical bruises. I was seemingly alone with no money and no hope. My mother wouldn't help me. Even a godmother I phoned responded by turning her back. I realized I had failed myself and wondered if my life was over.

Reading inspirational books guided my life, giving me that courage to file for divorce. God was my higher power, and the books I read empowered me on a practical level to discover that the person I must turn to for help was myself. *I* had the power to change *my* destiny.

Books became my role models—and reading became my life-long blessing.

The books inspired me to follow a path in which I had excelled. As a child I achieved much success at selling items to help raise funds for my parochial school and church. I began a career in sales. But I ended up in debt—overwhelmed and exhausted with the failure of two sales companies that had employed me.

Then I remembered I was *not* alone because I had God, and the books and workshops I attended motivated me to try again. It was the next job that would lead me to meet my future husband. We have been married now for 22 years and have a wonderful family.

I discovered the power of self-motivation. I discovered the "law of attraction" at the age of 22 while reading the book, *Think and Grow Rich*. I wrote down my life goals and placed hand-written affirmation cards all over the house.

I also kept motivational cassettes in my car to learn while I drove from sales call to sales call. I attended motivational workshops by nationally renowned speakers, including Zig Ziglar and Tony Robbins. I was like a sponge soaking up every anecdote and every bit of wisdom. I read and listened and applied every technique I learned to think and act with inspiration.

As a mother I gained the power to honor *my* mother. My church gave me the power to honor my abusive stepfather and first husband. My church pastor guided me to draw a circle with them inside, and to create another circle around it made up of the blessings that followed in my life. That larger circle of light transcended the darker inner circle.

There is a reason that adversity happens to us. It opens our eyes and allows us to accept the abundance there is for us in the simple, everyday joys of life, and in our own power to bring about success.

Today when I face adversity I am able to sit back, observe, and ask, *What am I supposed to learn from this and how am I supposed to grow?*

Then I give thanks.

I kept learning and growing in my professional life, and eventually had the advanced skills to create my own financial advising company that made me a millionaire. Still I was acting out of fear. I was a *superwoman* determined not to go back to poverty and loneliness.

I was successful—and exhausted.

Then an accident that confined me to being in bed for a few weeks proved another turning point in allowing me to reassess my life and my real goals. At 48 I discovered that to be truly helpful to others I was not just providing financial advice, but guiding midlife women like myself to find their true inspiration in life without fear.

My own personal journey from adversity to abundance gave me my new mission, vision, and purpose in life—to help other women reach their full potential.

After becoming a midlife millionaire I embarked on a new journey.

Essentially I re-shaped my company to run without me. Then I sold my company and started *Smart Women's Coaching*™ as my platform to inspire other women at midlife.

Thank God I lost my father when I was six because I can empathize with women who find themselves in a situation of despair and hopelessness. Thank God my stepfather and my first husband abused me because I know it is possible to survive, to empower oneself, and to transform adversity into abundance.

My love of inspirational books that empowered me also inspired me to write my own book: *Secrets from a Midlife Millionaire: How to Create A Millionaire Lifestyle While Following Your Passion.* If I had not suffered—and suffered *alone*—I would not have realized that books could become the friends and role models that empower women who *are* alone.

In creating my new company, *Smart Women's Coaching™*, I created a new circle of friends, mentors, and advisors. I discovered a community of like-minded women—all smart, inspired, and eager to share their wisdom and experience with others. Our community is a gathering place for inspiration and support of women.

I have life-long friends.

I would not be who I am—and would not have my wonderful husband and children—if I had not experienced the pain of my early years.

I love my life and I am grateful for all that I have experienced.

Thank you, God.

❤   ❤   ❤

Katana Abbott left her $100 million investment management and financial planning practice to become the founder and vision coach of *Smart Women's Coaching™*—a global online coaching, consulting, and membership resource for women entrepreneurs. Rising from a life of adversity to abundance, Katana spent 20 years as a senior financial advisor for Ameriprise Financial. In 2007 Katana retired at the age of 48 to pursue her inspiration to share her secrets for a perfect life with other women. Today she and her renowned network of experts teach midlife women how to reinvent their lives through an annual series of events, courses, and online social networking support at www.smartwomenscafe.com. She is the author of the upcoming book, *Secrets of a Midlife Millionaire: How to Create a Millionaire Lifestyle While Following Your Passion.*

Thank God
I Am Blind

BEN UNDERWOOD (AGE 16)

Thank Jesus I'm blind . . .

In 1994 at age two I lost my eyes to a childhood disease called retinoblastoma—which is cancer in both eyes. At age three I taught myself *echolocation*—where I use *sound* to *see*. I ride bikes, skate, and play video games—you name it. I do it—or at least give it a try.

It isn't so bad being blind—you just learn to *see* differently.

Others believe that blindness is a disability. I'll tell you the truth: being blind is more of an "advantage." I don't see what you see, like others being treated terribly because of the evil hearts that constantly beat among us.

All I want to do is love others and show people how to *see* with eyes *closed*—looking through the heart.

We used to care so much about others, but the number has dropped dramatically. As our hearts harden, our eyes close. To open our eyes we must soften our hearts towards others. If you soften your heart, you will see into others' hearts and feel what they feel.

14

Believing and drawing closer to Jesus is how I became softhearted—to the point where I *care*. Seeing what you see everyday, you have become used to the "torture" that others go through. I do not "see" these things. I *do* know what is going on, but not seeing these tortures helps me stay a more loving and kind-hearted person.

I thank God I'm blind because I see others for who they are by their hearts, and you see one another with your eyes, which sometimes are blinded. I remind those going through trying times in their lives that there are still people concerned about them. I thank God I am blind because I truly understand that whether no eyes, no legs, autistic, mentally challenged, or whatever the difference is, we are truly *all the same*. God loves each one of us unconditionally and wants us to learn to see one another through the eyes of God. Sometimes looking through a blind person's eyes can truly teach us to see each other as we see ourselves. Thank God I am blind.

I was again diagnosed with this cancer—retinoblastoma (this time without eyes)—at age 16. This cancer started in the sinus cavity and entered my brain, but was still the same ordeal that I endured when I was two years old. Going through cancer this time I lost my hair from the chemo treatments, and I have a scar from ear-to-ear from the surgery. Through all that I've endured I thank God I'm blind. I can't actually *see* what these changes in my appearance look like—so it doesn't matter.

I hear others crying because of their hair loss, or scarring, worried what other people will think about their looks. I don't worry about my appearance—I can't see. Thank God I am blind.

When I was 13 I went to a school for the blind for my seventh-grade school year. My mother thought it would be a good idea for me to experience being around other blind children. This school wasn't in Sacramento where I lived, so I had to leave home every Sunday in the early evening, and come home Friday night—only to be home on the weekends. They taught me a lot of technology, math, and other learning activities. We also went to the local junior high for a couple of classes every day.

As a teenager I learned how blind individuals are treated—or maybe the word is *taught*. My experience there wasn't very enjoyable. I found out that blind people are expected to "be" a certain way.

Blind students at this school traveled in groups: the guide was in front with the cane going left to right, with everyone else kind of holding onto one another, trusting the front cane traveler to guide the rest. Well, I hadn't traveled like this before. I traveled independent of a cane, or used a sighted guide like my brother or a friend.

Once I brought a big rubber ball to the school, and was told that I couldn't bring balls because someone might get hurt. I thought all kids played with balls. I called my mom and told her that I couldn't go to this school—because I wasn't like them.

I don't consider myself blind—I just can't see.

You see, my family didn't tell me there was anything different about being blind or sighted. They treat me just like a sighted person. I guess I consider myself sighted in a way because I believe anything that *you* can do—*I* can do better. I kept encouraging the staff that blind kids can play ball, video games, and other activities that sighted kids do. I continued to insist that we be treated like everyone else. After consistently pursuing equality of treatment for the blind, the staff finally softened up and began to allow the blind students to do more outside activities. One thing I enjoyed about the school for the blind was that the students didn't judge one another on their appearance—because no one could see. That was actually a very good attribute.

What a great experience.

Thank God I'm blind.

Once my mother asked me what it was like being blind. She thought that if she turned out the light in the bathroom and closed her eyes— that would be similar to being blind. I told her that it wasn't the same.

For me being blind is actually "nothingness." I don't think that a sighted person can comprehend what *nothingness* looks like. Although my sight is nothingness, my mother has described the world to me and showed me what things look like. Because of my family I actually have a "visual" of the world.

While they showed me the world they showed me independence. When my brother Derius was eight years old he taught me how to find my tags and the seams of my clothing so that I could dress myself properly. My sister Tiffany has been there for me. My brother Isaiah is three years younger than I am and he showed me everything he saw. Joe is my oldest brother—and he thought he was my "daddy." He tried to tell me what to do—so we fought all the time. I love my family because they see me the same as they are—not as a *blind* brother but as *their* brother.

My family has been there for me. They treat me in such a way that I can *echo*—and no one complains about the sound. I think they don't complain because with my echo I can ride my *own* bike—and none of them has to ride me. I think they made sure that I was self-sufficient because it gave them the freedom of not having to take care of me. I am so glad that they did what they did. Sometimes I feel sorry for blind kids who don't get the opportunity to enjoy their childhood as a child should. I thank God *I'm* blind.

I've heard from people all around the world about my echolocation. Most people are truly encouraged about me being independent and using echolocation. However, some blind people feel that I am "mocking the blind."

I just want to tell the world that I don't have anything against using a cane—it just isn't for me. I'm 16 years old and the cane sort of gets in my way when I'm "traveling."

I do understand that there are "blind" world travelers, professors, and very successful blind individuals, and I pray that as our world continues to turn, individuals are not categorized by their disability.

I feel that we should look at each individual's "difference" and not see a "disability."

As God's creation we need to learn to love and encourage one another—not discourage a person who doesn't look like you, walk, talk, nor see like you. No one deserves to be categorized and put in a disability box. Because I'm blind I don't see the appearance of a person—I see *beyond* that. I see individuals for *who* and *what* they are.

I truly THANK GOD I'M BLIND.

❤   ❤   ❤

"Faith in God." That is what Ben Underwood was about.

On January 19, 2009, after the return of his cancer, Ben's life on this earth came to a quiet end.

Like a tiny mustard seed, Ben's initial faith in life grew to incredible proportions. Like the parable of the mustard tree, he stretched out as far as possible, bearing amazing fruit. He planted his seeds of faith and, for all who came in contact with him, watered them with inspiration.

Ben was known worldwide through his creation of *echolocation*, a clicking sound created by his tongue that allowed him to visualize objects and surroundings. Speaking engagements in Germany, Japan, and Amsterdam—and media exposure across the globe—made Ben Underwood the inspiration for millions. Appearances of this extraordinary young man on CBS, ABC, CNN, the Ellen Degeneres Show, the Montell Williams Show, and the Oprah Winfrey Show amazed America.

To his large loving family, he was simply *Ben*. Never afraid of anything, Ben did anything he ever set his mind on. He rode bikes, played ball, practiced karate, danced, and loved making music—especially on the ocarina. Ben had written since the age of eight and created a children's book and a story series that may be available soon.

Thank God he shared his story with us. Learn more about Ben at www.benunderwood.com.

Thank God
I Shattered into a Million Pieces

YVONNE POINTER

Humpty Dumpty sat on a wall;
Humpty Dumpty had a great fall.
All the King's horses and all the King's men
Couldn't put Humpty together again!

Can you imagine the sight of Humpty Dumpty's crash? Splattering himself against the yoke-stained concrete? A million pieces of tiny eggshell shattering and causing a ripple effect of sorrow? Spreading a shock wave of grief?

Poor Humpty Dumpty was the thought on my mind as I watched the evening news.

One might call me a modern-day Humpty Dumpty due to the brutal rape and murder of my 14-year-old daughter, Gloria Pointer, on December 6, 1984. Gloria's brutal homicide pushed me off the wall, causing me to have a great fall.

"Little Gloria Pointer was to receive a Perfect Attendance Award today at school," said the report on the nightly local news. "Instead, her lifeless body was found savagely beaten, raped, and discarded behind a building near the school."

Her homicide sent a wave of fear throughout the community scaring little children half to death.

Who could put Gloria together again?

To date, the case of Gloria Pointer's brutal homicide remains unsolved. Like a million tiny pieces of a puzzle, homicides can rip communities to shreds, leaving behind trails of bloodstained innocence—with only committed activists following pathways in search of super-glue solutions.

Who could put Gloria together again?

Walking into the funeral home to view the body of my daughter is one of the moments in life I will remember most vividly. Standing at her casket looking down upon her, I felt I could see through generations of suffering. I wondered who could stop this violence that takes young ones away from us every day. Surely there must be civic-minded celebrities who would feel the sting of this death—even perched in their ivory towers.

The color *gray* filled my eyes.

It just seemed fitting to see life in the color gray.

My nights turned into nightmares with thoughts continually on innocent children in premature graves.

My initial plan included a massive letter-writing campaign to find an individual who would show up in Cleveland like a Knight in Shining Armor. Days seemed to blend into months as my hundreds of letters all went unanswered.

My communication with God seemed unanswered and this caused me great pain. However, how often do we learn that even the best-laid plans go unfulfilled—especially when fueled by self-will?

Who could put Gloria together again?

There was no more time to waste because children were still dying.

It was time to implement *Plan B*— temporarily to occupy the position of Child Protector—until the true individual arose. Activism became my middle name. Along with a local radio station personality, I visited schools and gave kids safety tips. I conducted interviews locally and nationally to warn communities that there is a *Killer Loose in the City.*

On the Road Less Traveled to save our children I found someone was willing to rescue the children.

Me.

Thank God I became the person I was looking for.

After all, who could describe the agony that comes *"Behind the Death of a Child"* better than a mother pushed off a wall?

Who could put Gloria together again?

Reality came along with responsibility and the fact that Gloria was not going to be put back together again.

Therefore I put more effort into finding her killer.

The pain behind the death of a child is so excruciating it was my prayer that no other family should live such a nightmare.

The media followed my every move as I grew into the role of a mother who speaks eloquently—and hides her pain along the way.

Community service and activism took center stage in my life.

I grabbed my new life's purpose by the horns.

After hearing of a proven crime-reduction program called Midnight Basketball, I eventually made a pilgrimage to Chicago

I thought, *Is it possible that basketball could be a solution to violence? Open the gyms between 10:00 PM and 2:00 AM? Swing open the doors wide enough so that every street thug can come inside? Invite in drug dealers, thieves, murderers, and gang-bangers? Dangle a basketball as a carrot or a hook to keep them off the streets?*

Yes it was.

And I launched a one-woman campaign to bring Midnight Basketball to Cleveland, Ohio. Over 1,000 young men between the ages of 18 and 25 successfully went through this program—and there wasn't a single incident of violence. Many of the young men's lives turned around as a result. I discovered that when you keep them off the streets crime rates diminish. You're not just giving them a ball— you're giving them knowledge through mandatory workshops.

You would be convinced that there is purpose in pain as you watch these young men filing into overcrowded gyms—looking for a mother. And me being there with outstretched arms—looking for a child.

Did I mention that I *did not then—nor do I now*—understand the game of basketball?

"Ms. Pointer. He *fouled* me."

"Save your breath," is all I could say to their complaints because I didn't know what a *foul* was!

Night after night—often arriving at the gym on an empty gas tank—I would leave full of hope. Hope for the safety of the children. The program was a success in more ways than one.

Honors and accolades followed that effort. I was deemed "The Mother of Midnight Basketball." I was inducted into the Ohio Women's Hall of Fame. I received the 908th Point of Light from former President George Bush, the FBI Director's Community Leadership Award, and the *Woman's Day Magazine* Women of the Year Award. I appeared on the Oprah Winfrey Show and the 2001 Essence Awards. I received the Curvation Project Confidence Award presented by actress Queen Latifah. I was honored as one of *Essence* magazine's 50 Most Inspiring African-Americans, and I was featured in several national magazines including *Essence* and *Ebony*.

I have also been able to glue my pieces back together through regular visitations to local and national prisons. Upon the request of incarcerated felons I am often invited to serve as a guest speaker inside the walls. "Ms. Pointer, your words give us hope."

Even in my search for Gloria's killer, I realize that many of those that are institutionalized also resemble Humpty Dumpty—and their lives and mine coincide in pain. Whether they were pushed, jumped, or fell to the bottom of the line—our pain is equally splattered.

I have met great minds and salvageable human beings behind those gates—but the one thing that I have yet to meet is the face of resolution in my daughter's murderer.

Support that I have received from the inmates is immeasurable; for instance, I am honored to have the formerly incarcerated Khaz Rael donate the illustrations for one of my books. His generosity and gifted artistic hands have touched an unreachable spot in the broken pieces.

Establishing the Gloria Pointer Scholarship Fund in Cleveland also helped to glue the pieces of my life back together. It was established with the unclaimed reward funds from Gloria's homicide. Any inner city young lady graduating from high school can apply. There is only one stipulation: the fund is *not* based on grades. The recipient of the annual scholarship goes to a young lady, a girl who has been victimized by violence, discarded by drugs, puddled by pregnancy, or paralyzed by pain. I am honored to have bestowed over 17 such scholarships, once again opening my arms wide to receive "daughters of hope." Through the self-publication of three books, *Behind the Death of a Child, Word from the Mother,* and *Two Dollars in My Pocket*, I have been able to maintain the scholarship.

Even with the help of God the task of saving children became a weight on my shoulders and I had to find some help. My pleas for others to follow once again fell on deaf ears because of the weight others already carried. Mothers were perplexed with everyday life, and the thought of an additional task seemed too unbearable. My solution was to form a support group, thus giving birth to Positive Plus in 1985.

Through support of each other we help one another. Then our obligation is to take that same support to the streets. Positive Plus sprouted from workshops and group meetings held in my home. The door is open for anyone who wishes to attend. The purpose is to motivate the attendees to become responsible, to plan, and to seize control of their own destiny. The mission is to reconstruct and restore that part of a woman that has been snatched and deteriorated by life, eventually benefiting both family and community.

The glue that puts things back together continued to flow. I received a letter in 2003 from a destitute 17-year-old boy named Anthony Tay living in Ghana, West Africa. In his letter, he explained that he was walking down the road questioning the existence of God. He was hungry and had not eaten for three days. He had no money for school. He thought to himself, *If there is a God, why don't the cries of the children in my village get answered?* During this conversation with God he noticed a tattered piece of paper lying on the dirt road. The frayed and yellowing paper was an article about a woman in America who had lost her daughter to violence. He felt a deep sadness over such a tragedy and decided to contact the woman and to extend his sympathy.

How did a piece of paper about a murdered girl in 1984 find its way to the feet of a boy halfway around the world?

I can answer that.

It's God's way of putting the pieces back together again.

As a direct result of that letter, Anthony began to receive financial support from other believers and me. This young man then established the Gloria Pointer Teen Movement in Ghana. I was blessed to visit these children in 2007, and am currently raising funds to build a school in Ghana in memory of Gloria.

Behind the death of one child I now have many—if not countless—blessings.

> *Little Gloria Pointer was pushed off a wall*
> *Causing her mother to have a great fall.*
> *With the help of the Lord, family and friends,*
> *Thank God her mother was put back together again!*

I looked down on death—and then found a way to look up— discovered a life and realized there is a purpose even in pain.

Yvonne Pointer is the co-founder of P.A.C.K. (Parents Against Child Killing), founder of Positive Plus Women's Support Group, and an active member of P.O.M.C. (Parents of Murdered Children). She's appeared on the Oprah Winfrey Show, was inducted into the Ohio Women's Hall of Fame, and her name was placed in the rotunda of City Hall in Cleveland. Former President George H.W. Bush awarded her the 908th Point of Light national tribute to Americans. The FBI awarded Ms. Pointer the Director's Community Leadership Award, and she received The National Council of Negro Women's Tribute to Black Women Community Leaders Award. Pointer was given the Greater Cleveland Women of Achievement Award, and was a recipient and speaker at the annual Essence Awards at ceremonies at Madison Square Garden in New York City. She's authored the books, *Behind the Death of a Child, Word from the Mother,* and *Two Dollars in My Pocket.* Contact her through her website at www.yvonnepointer.com.

Thank God
I Am Not an Ugly Duckling

AS TOLD BY BERNIE SIEGEL, MD, TO HIS GRANDCHILDREN

The other day as I sat on our back porch enjoying the sun, a bedraggled little duck startled me with a big splash as he crash-landed in the little pond I built in our backyard. As he settled down and tried to catch his breath, I noticed his feathers that pointed in all directions. I continued to watch as our rabbit, Smudge, hopped over to the pond and struck up a conversation.

"Hi, I'm Smudge. If you're looking for a place to rest, you landed in the right place. Can I get you something to eat? You look tired and hungry."

"I could use a bite to eat and a few moments to catch my breath."

When Smudge gave me the sign, I took over some birdseed and corn from our food bin, then went back and sat down so I wouldn't frighten his new friend.

"That helped. Thanks!"

"Happy to help. The humans who live here, Bobbie and Bernie, rescued my sister Snowflake and me two years ago. They have big hearts and a house full of animals that they love. We all have stories to tell; what's yours?"

"When I popped out of the egg before I was expected, my mom told me that she was disappointed in me from day one because I was so small—and had weird-looking feathers. She said she was tired of explaining things to people and hiding me. She kept telling me what a disappointment I was to her and my dad. This broke my heart—so I decided to run away. I'm an ugly duckling with no place to run to."

"Well you have a place now. You stay right here while I tell everyone about you. We'll get you moved into our bird sanctuary where you'll get to meet the other ducks and geese who live here—not to mention all the other creatures we have rescued who have learned we're all family."

"Why are you being so nice when you don't even know me?"

"Dear Doctor Bernie taught us that we're all wounded and have our share of troubles. He's a surgeon and says we're all one family with the same color inside. So we try to serve one another. I know someone whose childhood was a lot like yours, except for one thing that made all the difference in the world to him. Would you like to hear a story? It might help you understand and change how you see yourself."

"Sure. I'm definitely not going anywhere."

"Once upon a time, there was a young woman who was told not to become pregnant because she was very sick and had lost a lot of weight. Her doctor felt becoming pregnant might endanger her life. She and her husband followed the doctor's advice, but her mother wouldn't accept it. She told her daughter to lie down on the couch, and she started feeding her all through the day. Well, in time, the woman gained thirty pounds—and went ahead and became pregnant.

"Things went reasonably well until the time when the baby was due. You showed up too soon, while this duckling seemed like he had no interest in ever coming out. Weeks went by and finally his mom went into labor, but after several days he still didn't show his little head. I think it was his *big* head that was the problem—but don't tell anyone I told you that.

"His mom was going through a lot of pain. The doctor said he really needed to get her baby out. But she wasn't well enough to risk a cesarean section—so they reached way up inside and pulled the baby out! Then the fun began. His mom said when she saw him, she thought,

They didn't give me a baby; they gave me a purple melon! So she and the baby's dad wrapped him in kerchiefs and put him in a covered carriage—so no one would see him—and when they got home they hid his carriage behind the house, then covered all the mirrors."

"Boy, I know how he must have felt."

"But there was one big difference between his family and yours. He didn't consider running away from home. Can you guess why?"

"No."

"Think about it. He had what you didn't have—a *grandmother*. And he was her grandchild. She saw the beauty that his parents hadn't learned how to see. It's not their fault—and I am not blaming anyone. It's about life and what they have experienced. Hey, the next generation becomes great grandchildren, so it is definitely about what we learn from our experience.

"I'm sure you know by now that the ugly duckling with a grandmother was Bernie. Bernie's mom said her mother took him and poured oil over him many times a day. She massaged and pushed things back where they belonged. Bernie said that as he grew up—whenever he worried about how he looked—he'd go to his grandma for a hug. Finally when he was old enough to go to school for the first time, he told his grandma, 'I don't know how I look. There are no mirrors in our house.'

"She answered, 'Come over here. Look into my eyes and you will see how beautiful you are.' Bernie didn't need plastic surgery, nor did he do what the ugly duckling and you did—run away from home. You won't have to struggle to see by your reflection that you are beautiful because you'll see that in our eyes. Bernie's grandma taught us all a few things. Bobbie did insist upon having a mirror by their front door. So Bernie's grandmother hung a sign across the top of it that said, 'Come and see how beautiful and meaningful life is.'

"So whenever anyone is having a 'bad' day—and Grandma isn't around—we just go and stand in front of Grandma's mirror."

The Ugly Duckling

BERNIE SIEGEL, MD

*M*any years ago my mother—due to her hyperthyroidism—was told *not* to become pregnant because she had lost a great deal of weight, and her physician felt the added stress of a pregnancy would endanger her health and life. Her mother—my future grandmother—didn't agree, and so she had my mother lie on the couch while she gorged her with food. My mother gained weight—and became pregnant.

As the due date drew close my mother experienced an early rupture of her membranes—which she did not communicate to the doctor due to a lack of understanding. When she finally went into labor I didn't seem interested in being delivered. After several days of labor and, to quote my mom, "Screaming and tearing up all the hospital bed sheets," her doctor told her he felt a cesarean section was too risky to attempt—and they needed to get me out.

So I presume they reached in with forceps and pulled me out. My mother said, "They didn't hand me a baby. They handed me a purple melon." Yes, my mother was handed an ugly duckling. What do you do when you give birth to an ugly duckling? In the story above, we are told the duckling's mother rejects him and eventually discards him from the nest. When I read the story to our grandchildren, I thought about how rare it is for an ugly duckling ever to look at his or her reflection and accept being a swan. Even swans look in the mirror and find their faults—and not their beauty. Studies show that ugly ducklings are far more likely to become addicts and self-destructive as they grow up.

So what saved me?

My mother said that when they took me home from the hospital my father wrapped me in kerchiefs. Once home, my mother covered my carriage and placed it behind the house so no one would see me and be upset. There are photographs in our family album showing my smiling mom standing next to a covered carriage, and no photographs of me, which proves this was true. So I told my mother I wanted to know why I turned out the way I did.

My question was, "How and why did I make it?" What did I have that the ugly duckling didn't have? The answer, of course, is a grandmother. I recall reading a story where a teenager living with her grandmother complained that there were no mirrors in the house so she couldn't tell how she looked before going off to high school. Her grandmother replied, "Look in my eyes and you'll see how beautiful you are."

Well, my mother tells me my grandmother took me from her, and five or six times a day "Poured oil over you, and then pushed everything back where it belonged." I had my answer. I was massaged by loving hands every few hours. I know what that touch does to newborns of all species. They gain weight and mature faster than their untouched siblings—or the "controls" when a study of the effect of massage on infants is done. Several decades later—the first time a female massage therapist placed her oiled hands on my shaved head—I went into a trance which frightened everyone in the room because they were unable to communicate with me.

When I came out of the trance and saw all the people in the room I asked why they were all there. They said they thought I had a stroke or heart attack—because I was *gone*. I said, "Yes, I was gone. I went back to my childhood because my body remembers what my grandmother did. I returned to my infancy because of the touch of a woman's hands." That event helped me to understand why I shaved my head early in life at a time when it was definitely not in style.

So my advice to everyone—based upon my experience—is don't have children before the age of 60. Then you will be ready to love and not judge. I know this from my experience as a pediatric surgeon and as the father of five children, including twins, and as grandfather of eight grandchildren. I was very concerned regarding the physical integrity of our children—and even examined them after they were born. Yet I was only interested in loving our grandchildren when they were born. I was ready to deal with whatever came with them.

That's when I understood why we call our children simply *children*, while the next generation becomes our *grand* children, and the generation after that becomes our *great* grandchildren. The reason for the various labels, I believe, relates to our development as loving human beings as the years pass. Hopefully we will all act like loving grandparents someday. And on *this* day *all* the children will feel *loved*.

♥   ♥   ♥

Bernie Siegel, MD—who prefers to be called Bernie—embraces a philosophy of living and dying that stands at the forefront of the medical ethics and spiritual issues our society grapples with today. Bernie was born in Brooklyn, NY, and attended Colgate University and Cornell University Medical College, from which he graduated with honors. He holds membership in Phi Beta Kappa and Alpha Omega Alpha. His surgical training took place at Yale New Haven Hospital, West Haven Veteran's Hospital, and the Children's Hospital of Pittsburgh.

He retired from practice as an assistant clinical professor of surgery at Yale in general and pediatric surgery in 1989 in order to speak to patients and their caregivers. He created Exceptional Cancer Patients (ECaP), a specific form of individual and group therapy utilizing patients' drawings, dreams, images, and feelings. ECaP is based on "care-frontation," a safe, loving, therapeutic confrontation which facilitates personal lifestyle changes, personal empowerment, and healing of the individual's life. The benefits that followed led to his desire to make everyone aware of his or her healing potential.

Bernie and his wife and coworker, Bobbie, have five children and eight grandchildren. Together they have co-authored several children's books and articles. Bernie's venture into the printed word came in 1986 with his first book, *Love, Medicine & Miracles*, and so far he has written more than 10 books. His current books focus on the goal of humanizing medical education and medical care, as well as empowering patients, and teaching survival behavior to enhance immune system competency. For more information you can access Bernie's website at www.BernieSiegelMD.com; and you can access his ECaP website at www.ecap-online.org.

Thank God
I Am Not Enlightened

RAMAH WAGNER

When I was a very young girl I began my quest for enlightenment. I craved an "awakened state of being" like other children craved candy.

My mother first introduced me to spirituality by talking about the saints. She also mentioned a sort of mystic in the chiropractic field—I say "sort of" because I hadn't heard anyone label him a mystic. This *mystic*, Dr. Jim W. Parker, had a deep concept, "What you see in the universe sees you."

My mother told me things like this while we folded the laundry.

It was this idea that caused my youthful mind to run sagacious scenarios of the Universe—which to me at the time meant God: He was watching me, like I was watching him. I say *him* because I began my spiritual journey in a lively sect of Christianity called Pentecostal where God was a father figure.

I remember being told in Sunday school of saints having holy fires on their heads that only those with enlightened spiritual eyes could perceive. Or, while taking grape juice communion and crackers that these elements could turn into poison—because the Universe or God could see *if* it was taken with a *selfish* inclination. It was in this church—that encompassed all those wild and spiritual men and women speaking in tongues and prophesying—that I first was "illumined."

I remember being nine years old and sitting cross-legged—or as it's called in the east, the *lotus position*—opening my whole heart to God.

I believed at that tender age that I was embarking on a different path by this act of "totality." I emphatically promised myself to God in my path through life. At first this manifested as inner-directed messages that were not my own—as I walked down the red-carpeted halls in silent contemplation.

Then at 12—with an elucidated knowing for wisdom and beauty— I began praying at the sanctuary altar.

I promised God I would not use these gifts in vain. I also knew wisdom is "beauty" and beauty is "wisdom." I desired to be like Solomon, stories of whom I often pored over in the Bible while the pastor rattled on in the backdrop.

It was at this time that I first had visions and was cognizant of the seeds of greatness growing and glowing in my being—as if my heart were on fire for God.

In my teens—as I transformed from an ugly "bucktoothed" duckling into a lovely and perceptive young lady—my desire to be one with God continued.

I spent many of my teen hours reading about mystical saints and apostles—the great thinkers of my religion. My discontent with the ordinary took me to find solace in quietude. My illumination in God was fragmented into blissful moments here and there—like beautiful glass chips that make up a stained glass window. My thirst was for a holy vision so bright it would burn down everything inside of me and make room in my being only for God.

It was easy to see from the saints that this mystical dream was not something to consider attainable.

In my late teens and early 20s, this realization led me into other philosophies and religions. I was vigilant at delving deep into the philosophies of the wise. I'd hoped I'd find a route to enlightenment. I enjoyed the Buddhist concept of Nirvana as a state of being—like heaven on earth. It was what I was seeking in order to remove suffering and hardships.

I had my first near-death experience at that time—by almost dying from pneumonia.

It changed me forever to know, finally, that for the mind to remain pure the body must be pure as well. I learned that the mind and body are intricately connected and, like my heart, was with God. I learned how to harness the powers of the mind and to realize that the contemplative life meant selecting what thoughts to dwell on. I felt my mind was pure—until I added an impure thought that would steep like a tea bag in water infusing the whole.

The inner pull towards finding enlightenment deepened as I moved through my twenties. I shifted my studies to the esoteric world while learning about Universal Intelligence in chiropractic college.

It seemed I was getting closer—but I needed to go further.

My friends laughed at me when they would find me, again, cross-legged in contemplation—this time in the self-empowerment section of the bookstore. They told me I should change my address to that of the bookstore—because I pretty much lived there. I found great masters, gurus, and authorities on enlightenment who lent me their brilliant minds while I pondered the wisdom of their lives. Simultaneously, I was getting a nine-year education in the sciences educating me as a doctor.

When I was just ripe to finish graduate school at age 27, I traveled to India seeking enlightenment—like a man with his hair on fire seeks water. In an Ashram, wearing red robes, sitting cross-legged for hours—I still could not seem to grasp enlightenment.

I left—again feeling a familiar glow of energy—but not the life-changing experience of *enlightenment*.

Later that year I had a car accident—and had my second near-death experience.

I split out of my body and was hovering far out above my car. I felt so much bliss and so much of the deep blue inner peace of God. I understood my life and could apprehend the complex order that was *all love.*

And then—suddenly—I was back in my body.

I was back in the "samsara of life." Once again, there was the white light loving experience but it, too, was only momentary.

Why couldn't you let me die, God?

I wanted to experience that enlightened bliss forever.

I knew it was pure stupidity being mad that I had to "live." I knew I must still have something important to experience here on planet Earth, but it didn't change my apprehension towards coming back here to once again be in the struggle of life. I was close to returning to God—then slung like a rock from a slingshot back to the chaos of daily life.

This ennobled my desire for enlightenment and to be one with God.

I re-emerged into life with the willingness to do whatever it takes to become enlightened.

Not long before my 32nd birthday, I came back to the fullness of the totality of my wish.

I had spent several years in my own practice trying to "blend" as much as possible with my patients. My practice was dedicated to having the *seer* (that would be me) and the *seen* (that would be my patient) be on common ground. I laughed, cried, and experienced the fullness of each of their challenges as my own. We looked together at the divine order of how these events—rapes, divorces, molestations, abuse, cruelty, diseases, and suffering of all varieties—served their lives. The degree attained in Clinical Counseling was meaningless compared to sharing in facilitating this divine order in my patients' lives.

I felt a warm glow and fathomed the concept of *Thank God I . . .*™. I began to be extremely masterful at showing others that in their great traumas were great blessings. I explained that these challenges are the things that are the great catalysts for growth in each of our lives.

We grow with challenges, and our capacity to love and to be loved is enlarged.

Yet I still was hoping for something greater than the growth of these challenges. I wanted so badly to become an enlightened mystic. I wholeheartedly desired to be one with God. I felt I would be forever in that state of bliss, and free from life as I had known it.

I prayed that fateful night at 32 years old, with the thoughts of the many gurus, mystics, sages, and mentors scanning in my vision. I prayed to God, "Let me for just one moment have the view of the universe from *Your* eyes. I don't long for money, or a perfect husband, or children, wealth or fame—just You, God. I long to be one with *You*— for the seer and the seen to be one. That's all I want, God." My tears sprung out like sprinklers—and I fell asleep with a wet pillow against my cheek.

A few days later I sat down with my visiting parents at the kitchen nook for an ordinary dinner. I felt a familiar warm glow opening in my heart. This was a sort of wonder that I had in the peak moments of my life. I have heard these moments called white light experiences—a fleeting inner bliss I first felt at nine years old. I glanced at the roast, potatoes, and broccoli in front of me at the dinner table. I smiled at my ordinary parents and felt a strange glow in each of them—and me.

Suddenly a deep reflective thought passed my mind, and I said, "I am already enlightened, aren't I?"

They both smiled, and my father said to my mother, "She is starting to get it."

Then another thought illumined my perception, "Enlightenment is an ongoing thing, isn't it?"

My father stated emphatically to my mother, "Honey, now she is *really* getting it."

I continued, "It's these moments where we see life as it truly is." Their grins widened. I humbly bumbled on, "I've been enlightened in *this* way since I was nine. That means I've been chasing my own tail all my life." I experienced no shame—only absolute freedom. "I have been *one* with God all along, haven't I?" The thought was as lucid as their glowing faces.

Finally I understood the deep mystery of Dr. Jim Parker: "What you see in the universe sees you."

When John Castagnini, one of the pioneers of *Thank God I* . . . ™, called to discuss my contribution, I answered with an inculcated tone, "I would love to write, *Thank God I Am Not Enlightened.*"

We laughed in unison—two who were grateful to be one with the Universe.

❤ ❤ ❤

Dr. Ramah J. Wagner is a third generation alternative health doctor. She graduated from Palmer Chiropractic College in Iowa, where chiropractic was first discovered in 1895. Her clinic is located outside Orlando, Florida, where she works with cutting edge technology in the alternative healing arts—including chiropractic, specific nutrition, detoxification of heavy metals, and acupuncture. Dr. Ramah—as her patients and friends call her—is an internationally recognized author and nationally known speaker. She focuses on the belief that content energy is the key to creating an amazing life. In her recent book, *The Health of Business—How to Balance Your Life for Greater Returns,* she shares colorful stories and powerful healing methods to achieve a larger energy field. Her keen ability to read energy has recently been captured in her art exhibition called "Portraits" that depicts in line and color each subject's energy field. To see more about Dr. Ramah's work, visit www.HealthofBusiness.com or www.DoctorRamah.com.

Thank God
I Am the Daughter of an Addict

JENNIFER BARBOUR

At age 10 the only thing I understood about people who used drugs was that they were criminals who were most likely out of their minds. I imagined that they spent their days lurking around school playgrounds trying to lure young children into trying their "candy"—only to get them instantly addicted and forever ruined.

Imagine my horror the day my mom sat me down and told me that my dad was in the hospital because he was a drug addict.

I couldn't even comprehend it . . . *my dad . . . one of those men who lurked around the playgrounds?*

Then Mom handed me a book called, *My Daddy Is an Alcoholic*, and explained that addiction to alcohol was similar to addiction to drugs, and that the book would explain more.

I tried hard not to cry.

I wanted to know more—and yet at the same time I didn't want to know. The only question I could bring myself to ask was, "Which drug?" She said he was a heroin addict. I took the book to my room—but instead of reading it, all I could do was cry. I just wanted it to go away.

So I hid the book—unread.

As is often the case with drug addiction, the problem didn't just go away. Our illusion that the weeklong hospital stay "rehabilitated" my dad gave way to our "enabling" him. We ignored suspicious behavior while we tenaciously held on to the belief that he no longer had a problem. Thinking back, I'm amazed at the unwavering faith we had in a man who pushed us to lie incessantly. Every time my dad drove my brother, sister, and I to that dreaded city—where he would go to get his *fix*—we bought his lie that we were going for some practical reason.

Every single time we believed him—or at least *pretended* to believe.

He left us sitting in the car for long periods of time . . .

We often hid on the floor so that questionable passersby wouldn't see us and knock on the car window, asking us for change.

Meanwhile, Dad carried on with his "errands."

He would often return to the car with that sleepy drugged look that I came to know so well. He'd coach us on what to tell our mother regarding our whereabouts. The stories we told to cover for him sounded like more fun than our reality of singing songs to pass the time as we sat on the car floor.

We did as we were told—instead of telling of all the gas station bathrooms where we waited, we told of trips to McDonalds; instead of dump-side apartment complexes, we invented trips to the park.

We became such good liars that sometimes we almost believed our own stories.

And through it all, we desperately held onto the lie that Dad was still sober.

The hardest part of growing up with a father who revolved in and out of rehab and jail was that I had to grow up too soon. At school, classmates unmercifully teased me because Dad's name was in the newspaper's Police Log, again; or because we lost our house and had to live in a basement apartment with no windows; or because our phone or heat was disconnected . . . again.

However, the most difficult part for me was dealing with adult worries at such a young age. I stressed every day about how we would pay the bills, and how Mom was going to be able to give us money for lunch. By age 12 I had to have dinner cooked and ready, so that when Mom got home from work she could eat, and then run back out the door to go to her second job. Luckily my aunt helped a lot during these times. I don't think we would have been able to make ends meet without her.

After Dad went to prison we lost our house and Mom filed for divorce. We visited him in jails and halfway houses from time-to-time, but as the years went on we saw a lot less of him.

When I started high school I wondered more and more about why he didn't seem to want to be a part of our lives anymore. His absence—coupled with the fact that we still struggled quite a bit with money because of him—triggered anger and resentment in me.

Why did he continuously choose drugs over his family? Why weren't we his priority?

And I felt guilty—guilty for all the lies I told to protect him, and guilty because I felt somewhat responsible for it all not ending sooner. I wondered what would have happened if I'd just refused to lie and trusted my gut feeling every time I thought he was back on drugs—rather than just believing him all the time.

Could I have changed the outcome for us all?

Perhaps I subconsciously needed to release the stress and worries that I had been carrying since I was 10. Perhaps my resentment for having to have adult responsibilities at such a young age manifested itself into a desire to rebel. Whatever the reason, I cared less and less about school and grades, and thought more about having fun and being independent. I skipped school and experimented with drugs and alcohol. Before I knew it, I went from honor roll and honors classes to failing two classes—and being suspended on more than one occasion. Drugs were particularly appealing to me because of my curiosity as to why people would choose getting high over everything else in their lives. What was so amazing about drugs?

As children of addicts often do, I experimented with many drugs, but I couldn't bring myself to try the *one* drug that I felt was proven more important than I was—heroin.

I can't say that I necessarily had an *aha!* moment that brought me back to my senses and made me realize that I was making extremely bad decisions. But I *can* say that—while I don't condone the use of drugs or alcohol as a means to an end—I do believe that all of the events in my life, including those bad decisions, have put me in a place of gratitude. I'm not only grateful for my own "bad" decisions, but also for the decisions of others that have affected me—including those of my father.

Obviously, I don't have the ability to say how my life would have been different if I had a different childhood—but I do know that as a result of my rebelling and failing classes I was only accepted by one college from all that I'd applied to—and even that was on a probationary basis.

I decided to go to that one college, even though it wasn't even my *third* choice. I planned to get my grades "up" there and then transfer to a "better" school—and I did just that. But during the semester before I was to transfer, while working in a local pizza parlor, I met the man I later married.

I realize now that everything happens for a reason. Don't get me wrong, there were plenty of times that I angrily questioned why I was being "punished"—and bitterly felt contempt for those people, even my own friends, whom I envied for their loving nuclear family or their freedom from financial stress. I was angry that my mom worked two jobs and felt stressed all the time. I was angry about the childcare responsibilities I had because of Mom's work schedule. And I felt guilt for lying all the time and not speaking out.

Lying and not speaking out distressed me for years.

I blamed myself, believing that had I not been silent I could have prevented my little brother's arrest—along with my dad—when he walked out of department stores with appliances under his little coat. I blamed myself because my sister's learning disability went undetected, as schools chalked up her behavior to our "troubled" family life.

I doubt many people get through life without asking, "*Why* is this happening to me?" It's only when we truly accept the undesirable life experiences as inevitable, and view them as lessons and building blocks towards something greater, that we can accept and even be grateful for the cards that we are dealt.

I have experienced what it's like barely to be able to make ends meet—and I'm so thankful for it.

I now realize that I was blessed with very strong women in my life, including (and especially) my mother. Without these women I would likely have walked down the wrong path. Now I consider my childhood as a prerequisite toward a career in affecting change for children and families who might be questioning their own difficulties. As a graduate student in public policy, I realize that my own family's experiences with addiction, incarceration, and financial struggles give me empathy and insight, which allows me to evaluate policy issues from the ground up.

I'm particularly interested in the role that schools play in the lives of children. Many schools in our country are not only places for learning, but also environments of safety and consistency—or at least they should be. As I continue my work and studies in education policy and reform, I'm driven by my experience of having had women in my life who taught me that I could be and do whatever I set my mind to. I am so grateful for this influence as I realize that many young people are not so lucky.

I know now that my experiences have truly been blessings—even if they were often in disguise. If I hadn't lived what I perceived as a somewhat harrowing childhood, I might not have rebelliously acted out in high school. Had I been accepted into my first- (or even third-) choice college, I wouldn't have met my future husband. The more I thought about the way things fell into place for me, the more grateful I became. I soon came to be thankful for every event that led me to where I am today. As a bonus, this feeling of gratitude has eliminated the bitterness and resentment that I once felt, not only for my dad but also for everyone who I believed hurt me in the past.

Thank God I am the daughter of an addict.

❤   ❤   ❤

Jennifer Barbour was born and raised in Nashua, New Hampshire—located about an hour north of Boston, Massachusetts. Her childhood as an addict's daughter ultimately inspired her to pursue a career shaping and addressing policy related to child and family issues. She received her BS in Human Services from Northeastern University in Boston, and is currently a full-time graduate student at the University of Chicago, where she is pursuing a Masters Degree in Public Policy (MPP). She currently resides with her husband and young daughter in Chicago.

Thank God
I Lost My Sister and Brother to AIDS

DOREENE A. CLEMENTE

*T*hank God I had two very close and personal experiences with the Diagnosis, the Denial, and the inevitable Defeat of the AIDS virus. I know first hand the pain HIV inflicts and the emptiness HIV leaves behind. Nothing ever quite feels the same again. You fill the void with everyday hustle, and call upon all of your strength for survival, until days become months—and years.

You cannot prepare yourself for death.

But to watch as death takes someone slowly, you almost wish it would come sooner than later.

That's how I felt.

> *Please, God, take her*
> *in her sleep.*
> *Let her rest*
> *and be at peace.*

> *Please, Father God, don't let him suffer anymore.*
> *He deserves to be home with You.*

Then—when it does happen—you work on preparing yourself for living the rest of your life without them. I had no idea how I was going to do it at the time.

I had *no* idea.

As I think back, I wonder: *What was I thinking? How did I feel? Where was I? Why was this happening to my family?* I hadn't experienced such a family "tragedy."

What would I do?

I repressed—although I didn't know it at the time—all the anger, frustration, confusion, guilt, pain, and the questions.

I felt lost.

In my repression, I asked myself, *Why am I so calm? What does this mean?* I didn't want my family to see me so devastated. I needed to be strong for them.

Years later I discovered I'd been in physical and emotional shock.

Shock numbs your emotions . . . that is until the day it catches up with you.

I was born in New York City, raised in the South Bronx on Longwood and Fox during the 70s and 80s when our block was "hot" with crime and police activity. I grew up with three brothers: Dennis, Danny and Steve; and three sisters: Cindy, Cookie and Wanda.

And I remember through it all—we celebrated *life.*

We struggled, hustled, fought, learned, and grew through tough love, but we found a reason to play music, sing, dance, and entertain each other. I lived in a house full of creativity. Music was—and still is—our savior. Music took us away from the problems of the world and the household.

Cookie—Pablo Vasquez, Jr.—was born a male with the soul of a female.

She was a transvestite.

Early in her life my mother gave her permission to change her name to Alexis Sanchez—and live as a woman with our support.

From the start I knew Cookie to be my sister, since she made her change before I was born. So it was a challenge for me to accept her as anything else. Cookie was a very strong, inspirational energy for me.

Most people who knew our family knew Cookie was not a biological woman, so we dealt with the neighborhood talk. But with all the talk no one would ever disrespect her—at least not in her presence. There was a respect/fear they had for her.

She wasn't naive about the pressure of being different; she just didn't care what anyone thought of her.

I admired that.

I looked up to her—but my internal struggles for acceptance filled me with guilt.

I was raised Catholic—elementary school, high school, and college. I remember learning that anyone practicing the "sin" of homosexuality would be "damned" to hell. They coupled their teachings about love and acceptance with messages to judge and condemn. Their contradictions—along with my own reality—shaped my feelings about the hypocrisy in religion.

Thank God for my sister, Cookie—and her life lessons.

Cookie was incredibly talented. I sat in the living room and watched her rehearse for hours; her practice sessions taught me about performing. Cookie was a female impersonator for Marilyn Monroe, Liza Minnelli, Barbra Streisand, Evita, and Sheryl Lee Ralph in the original Broadway Musical, *Dream Girls*. She also worked as a trapeze artist at The Barnum Room.

Cookie and her fiancé, Michael, were an eye-catching couple when they went out dancing. They partied at the most exclusive clubs, like Studio 54 and The Red Parrot. They competed in disco dance competitions when The Hustle was the dance style of choice.

They were explosive together—and very much in love.

In spring 1990, I remember as if it were yesterday the day that changed our lives. It was my senior year at Aquinas High School in the Bronx. I came home from school to find Cookie and Mom together.

Mom asked me to sit down.

The last time I was asked to "sit down," I heard the horrible news that Michael, Cookie's fiancé, had died of a stroke. So I braced myself. Anxiously I sat down on Mom's bed and looked at my sister sitting across from me.

"I was diagnosed with the HIV virus. It's fatal. There are no cures. But I'm on medication to manage it."

I was speechless.

I honestly had no idea what that meant. At that moment, I didn't know what to say—because I didn't understand the deadly virus we were dealing with.

I went numb.

There was plenty of inaccurate information about HIV/AIDS at that time. So I wondered if we were all going to get it and how—*sharing the same utensils and plates, sharing a bed, or giving our daily hugs and kisses when we greeted each other?*

Her honesty and bluntness confused me.

She stood with no emotion, strong, and direct.

She waited for a response.

I was in shock. She just lost Michael, the love of her life, and now she would lose her own life to a brutal virus. The last thing I wanted to do was to react emotionally and make my sister feel bad.

So I went to my room, put my face in my pillow—and cried.

I didn't share this news with my friends. I repressed my feelings and kept it to myself. When my friends discovered my sister was sick, I lied and said it was something other than HIV.

My sister lasted a year on experimental drugs. We believe she had the virus for many years before her diagnosis—and it was now too late.

She died February 18, 1991—one year to the day that Michael died.

My brother, Dennis "Flaco" Vasquez, received an HIV diagnosis shortly after Cookie in the early 90s. He caught it early enough to take experimental drugs that helped him live longer with the disease.

Can we really call it living—every day ingesting tons of pills to forestall the spread of a disease that will inevitably take over?

His body ached; he couldn't walk without a cane, and his body slowly gave up on him. He suffered memory loss. His organs no longer functioned normally, nor supported his basic need to breathe without pain. He couldn't eat a solid meal without difficulty, walk without assistance, and he didn't have strength enough to make it through the day.

Nine years later, April 12th, 1999, he passed on.

Everyone loved Dennis.

He was an athlete who excelled in basketball and softball, and was skilled at playing pool. Smart and talented, Dennis got along with everyone. He was a helpful handyman who could fix anything. He loved to make us laugh with his jokes and entertain us with his songs and dance moves. He taught me how to salsa and hustle. We also sang many duets together. My bond with Dennis was not as intimate as it was with Cookie, but was just as spiritually connected and special. I remember him taking me to school some mornings and to church on Sundays. As I got older he wasn't around as much. He did his time for Uncle Sam and served time on Rikers Island.

In the 80s—when cocaine, heroin, and crack hit the streets hard—my brother decided to participate. His vice would eventually take his life. His habits were destructive—and he had many bad dealings with the dealers running the neighborhood.

Repeatedly he stole, lied, and broke our hearts with his addiction.

But what can you do?

He had a problem—an addiction.

I didn't love him any less; I was upset at him for what he was doing to my mother. Then I would get upset when Mom took him back. It was a crazy cycle. He tried rehab unsuccessfully many times, but it didn't stop him from trying.

I couldn't see his internal struggles at that time; I could just see my *own* suffering. I was young and naive. I couldn't take seeing another sibling deteriorate before my eyes—so I left New York.

Three months after I left—he passed.

I lived with the guilt of leaving New York until I learned how to honor myself.

Thank God for my brother Dennis.

Writing this story allows me to reflect on my childhood. I forgot so many things. And those memories I'd repressed I know need to be dealt with.

I couldn't express myself to my sister and brother while they were alive. I used to say:

I'm sorry for not being there to listen more—
for not telling you every day how much I love you.
I'm sorry for pushing you away—
or making it seem like I wasn't present.
I'm sorry if I ever hurt your feelings with my ignorance.
I'm sorry you suffered when I couldn't help ease the pain.

But now I speak to them every day this way:

You're very important to me.
Thank you for your strength to look death in the eye and not be afraid—
to live with integrity for what you believe in,
for your passion,
and for being who you are.
Thank you for loving me in return.
Thank God I have you both in my life!

As my family expands to extended families, we share old pictures and memories with new generations. It's important they know of their aunt (Titi Cookie) and uncle (Tio Dennis).

So I dedicate this story to my family.

It took time to get to this place of inner peace. But the trip was worth it. Sharing my story with the world is the best decision I ever made.

Thank God I have a life full of color, blessings, and adversity; that I have emotions, experiences, and many mountains to climb.

I appreciate it all with no regrets.

I appreciate my family and friends who inspire my life and my determination. Thank God I kept going forward and am now living my dreams. My gratitude—for the many opportunities to watch and imitate my siblings interact and entertain—taught me to follow my heart and do what I must to be fulfilled in this life.

It makes sense that I developed a life in the wellness and dance industry. I represent my childhood, family, friends, neighborhood, and culture. At an early age my life lessons with my family taught me not to take my health for granted. I live a life in gratitude and harmony as an example for others.

❤   ❤   ❤

Doreene Clemente, certified wellness coach/personal trainer/choreographer, successfully teaches people to live happier, healthier, and longer lives through wellness in mind, body, and soul. Doreene—a.k.a., Deena 'SnapShot'—and Wanda 'WandeePop' Candelario are co-owners of TruEssencia Dance and Wellness, LLC, and teach their signature Hip Hop class—Snap, Pop & Lock—combining hip-hop choreography with strength and flexibility moves, plus dance technique drills at various studios in New York. They assist in worldwide workshops promoting Hip Hop 4 Health. Their websites are: www.SnapPopnLock.com, www.Myspace.com/Snapoplock, www.HipHopMindBodySoulShop.BlogSpot.com, and http://thankgodi lostmysisterandbrothertoaids.blogspot.com/.

Thank God
I Was Fat, Ugly, Poor, Divorced,
and Live in Chronic Pain

Aymee A. Coget, PhD

What do we all want in life?

We want happiness—that deep inner sense of contentment that we think is too ethereal to develop ourselves. We may have heard of this happiness before, yet achieving it ourselves is a different matter. Most of us depend on circumstances to bring us happiness—and we project our happiness into the future.

We find ourselves saying, "I will be happy when . . . "

This type of happiness is known as 'hedonic' happiness. It's dependent on external sources—and is impossible to sustain. Hedonic happiness is a fleeting positive emotion; it is not the deep inner sense of contentment we all truly crave. The happiness we all want is called "eudaimonic" happiness, and it is developed from specific internal circumstances. Eudaimonic happiness is a sense of *being*—and it is within our control—whereas, hedonic happiness is external—and out of our control.

Eudaimonic happiness *is* possible to sustain.

As I experienced the benefits of eudaimonic happiness in my own life, I realized the benefits it could bring to others. So in 1996 I decided to devote my entire life to helping millions of people attain this sustainable deep inner contentment. When I recognized this as my spiritual mission, God or the universe had tests in store for me.

Let me tell you the story . . .

In my mid-20s I attended graduate school and worked at a full-time job. I loved my job as a happiness coordinator on a trading floor. This job was perfect for me in many ways. However, the nature of an office job means sitting long hours at a desk. After work I took a long bus ride to school, where I sat in class for another three hours. I was sitting down for at least fifteen hours a day. I had a very active mind—and a very inactive body. I noticed I was gaining weight, and I began to view my body as a grotesque and bulbous lump of clay.

As time passed I noticed my pant size increasing.

Then one day as I walked down the street, I became aware of fat jiggling on my back—like a couch potato silver-back gorilla. Dealing with my weight problem was a new experience because I grew up as an athlete, playing soccer and volleyball. I could not believe this was happening to me.

I could have fallen into depression for letting my body go down the drain, or gained even more weight (with a goal of becoming a circus elephant or a Woolly Mammoth). But instead of becoming a victim and eating everything in my grocery store's "made with 100% lard" section, I found the intestinal fortitude to become proactive—and lose the weight.

I began running, counting calories, and actively participating in yoga. The first time I ran, my body felt like scoops of ice cream melting with every step. At this point I made my body a priority and stopped ignoring it. Even though I was unsatisfied with how I looked—and a little disappointed for letting my body get to hippopotamus proportions.

My eudaimonic happiness was unaffected.

My disposition stimulated me to go into action with a clear mind and address my problem with confidence and ease. This experience showed me that no matter what my body looks like, I could still experience eudaimonic happiness.

Thank God I was fat because I know my eudaimonic happiness is not connected to the shape of my body.

In my mid-20s I developed a severe case of cystic acne, which caused a transient facial deformity. Cystic comedone after cystic comedone peppered my face like a battlefield. It appeared everywhere—on my cheeks, forehead, chin, all over.

At the onset, I realized how attached I was to my physical appearance. I ended up with so many zits on my face that it was difficult to discern where the cystic volcanoes ended and normal skin began. I looked like an alien, and did not want anyone to see me. I became introverted and, as a result of the acne, my self-esteem suffered.

I stopped looking in the mirror—altogether.

After many months of trying every aid under the sun, I went on severe cystic acne medication—Acutane. I could only last four out of the prescribed six months of the treatment because of the intense side effects. The acne cleared up enough so at least most of my skin was normal again.

Even though disenchanted with my physical appearance, my inner eudaimonic happiness stayed strong.

I kept my general mood high, despite what was going on with what I perceived as a very ugly face. Thank God I was ugly because by experiencing my beauty stripped away from me, I learned a very valuable lesson: beauty is really on the inside. I also learned to be unattached to my physical appearance, to understand the value of modesty and humility, and to experience eudaimonic happiness regardless of what I look like. I developed compassion for other people who were going through the same thing. I experienced introversion—so now I can relate with others who are shy.

Most importantly I learned how to build my self-esteem again, and realized that only I can give myself a positive self-image.

Beyond being fat and ugly, my eudaimonic happiness withstood another test: being broke.

After working for a Fortune 500 company, I decided to take a bold step and start my own business, as well as attend school full time. My initial efforts produced little income. I concentrated heavily on my schoolwork, and lived off my severance package and school loans.

Eventually the money ran out and I found myself scavenging my kitchen cabinets for canned food. I ate pancakes and oatmeal every day, and wondered where I would get money for my high San Francisco rent. I borrowed money from friends—and one month paid my rent with two cents left over in my bank account.

Even though it seemed like my financial reality was full of gloom and doom, my eudaimonic happiness remained unwavering.

I realized at this point that my eudaimonic happiness was independent of the balance in my bank account.

Thank God I was poor. I believe that my eudaimonic happiness during those struggling times enabled me to be resourceful; it gave me the wherewithal to be able to survive. I did not become depressed and downtrodden, lying in my bed having a "pity party," or allowing circumstances to worsen.

Being fat, ugly, and poor were not extreme enough challenges to defy my eudaimonic happiness. There would be more . . .

In my late 20s I experienced a whirlwind romance. I fell in love at first sight with a French man who also had a keen interest in happiness. We realized right away that we were meant for each other.

We fell deeply in love—and decided to get married just two days after knowing each other . . .

I quickly packed up my life and moved to Paris to be with my *one and only.* The man I had waited for my whole life. We had a formal engagement at the French Riviera—where every girl dreams of being "proposed to"—and had an intimate Parisian wedding at the City Hall.

The romance actually died off quickly when we started to get to know each other—and disenchantment set in.

We fought all the time.

We tried everything including couple's therapy.

It turned out that our life belief systems did not mesh.

After a roller coaster first year, filled with many ups and downs, we ultimately decided to divorce. This was a very painful experience because I had to recognize I made a mistake in marriage, and had to admit my fairy-tale romance was just that—a fairy tale.

I could kick and scream every day of my life in this marriage, or I could face the reality of my mistake and move on.

Thank God I had the experience of what it's like to find the one I was waiting for—realizing he was not what I perceived him to be—and going through a divorce. This was a blessing that showed me *my eudaimonic happiness is independent of my love relationships, and I do not need someone to make me fulfilled in life.*

I can experience eudaimonic happiness on my own.

Being fat, ugly, poor, and divorced were still not extreme enough challenges to affect my deep inner eudaimonic happiness.

I was born with a congenital disease of the spine: scoliosis. This can be a crippling and debilitating condition, where surgery or a life-long brace are the alternatives. Instead of traditional options, my parents decided to give me three chiropractic visits a week.

When I was living on my own, I realized that if I do not keep up with the care of my spine, my body becomes deformed. Not only does my body change structurally—making me hunch forward like Quasimodo—but I also experience intense pain all over my back, and get migraines to the point where I am bedridden for days.

Thank God I live in chronic pain because now I take very good care of my body—making it a top priority. I also realized *that my eudaimonic happiness remains present even though my body sometimes experiences excruciating pain from this congenital disorder.*

Thank God I've been fat, ugly, poor, divorced, and live in chronic pain because I know now that my eudaimonic happiness is not dependent on these external circumstances.

My eudaimonic happiness is only dependent on me choosing eudaimonic happiness in every moment—regardless of circumstances.

I have an ever-present sense of gratitude for *all* of my life experiences.

❤   ❤   ❤

In 1996, Aymee Coget (Pronounced Co-jjaayy) made a decision: she would devote the rest of her life to helping millions of people live happier lives. After years of studying, teaching, and experiencing fulfillment, Aymee has perfected her life to be "happy" every day, and has become the embodiment of "happiness." Aymee holds a BA, MA, and a PhD in psychology—and her area of emphasis is positive psychology. She has a thriving international coaching practice based in San Francisco, where she teaches clients how to build their own deep inner happiness. Aymee is a writer for multiple websites, including *Yahoo! Health*—where she gives tools on how to build sustainable happiness. She also hosts a weekly Internet radio show, *Friday Happy Hour,* from 4–5 PST at adviceradio.com. Aymee is also one of the founding members of an organization called This Happy Planet where the mission is to spread happiness globally.

Thank God
I Don't Believe in God

DAVID E. COMINGS, MD

For a book with dozens of authors thanking God about a range of problems, this title may sound a bit sarcastic—but I really mean it.

I'll tell you why.

When I attended grade school, my father, a professor of Chemical Engineering at the University of Illinois, did his best to get my brother and I off to Presbyterian Church Sunday school.

I could think of a long list of things to do on a Sunday morning more interesting than listening to a teacher tell us things that I found incredulous. One particular teacher stated that if we truly had faith, we could walk on water—or even on air. Half of the class immediately climbed up on tables or chairs and took a step off into space, saying, "I have faith"—only to land on their respective asses—to which he stated that the trace of *doubt* prevented success.

My father was a first class scientist, eventually becoming dean of the entire engineering department of a major university. I either inherited or adsorbed his devotion to science, becoming a science nut even in grade school. I scoured the back shelves of the local city library, consuming books on every "-ology" available.

By comparison, what they taught in Sunday school seemed to come from a different planet.

None of this, however, led me to believe that God did not exist. I just thought what I learned in Sunday school was not worth the time spent away from romping in the woods looking at birds, or hunting for rocks and fossils. Speaking of fossils, paleontology was one of my major passions. My parents purchased an entire encyclopedia set, *The Book of Knowledge*, probably the night after they conceived my older brother. Soon after I developed a love of reading, I began to devour the chapters on the different geological periods and the animals that inhabited them. Darwin's theory—one of the most magnificent works of reasoning ever produced by the human mind—beautifully explained evolution.

When I was in fourth grade, I lay in bed one night working my way backward down the geological ladder from the Pleistocene down to the Cambrian period, reveling in how the animals got simpler and simpler as time went backward. This process finally took me back to the origin of the universe. This was before the Big Bang theory, and I assumed the universe came from primitive gases. Although my Sunday school teacher repeatedly told me that God created everything, I marveled at how easy it was to get back to primitive gases using only the laws of nature without needing God's help. I then thought that since each step comes from something simpler, what makes more sense—that these gases came from something still simpler—like pure energy—or that God made them? The problem? God was the most complex entity one could possibly imagine, able to create universes, solar systems, and living beings—including man—with a wave of the hand. He was able to listen simultaneously to the prayers of billions of people and other wondrous things. To my thinking the answer was clear: the gases came from something still less complex. This principle, I later learned, was called Occam's razor—the simplest explanation is usually the correct one.

Then I thought, *If we did not need God for one of the major duties humans assigned to him—creating—why did we need him at all, and did he even exist?* I then thought, *If God created the gases, then where did God come from—a God for God?* It was infinitely easier to conceive that primitive gasses came from something simpler, than to figure out where God came from. It then occurred to me that the answer to this question really wasn't that difficult: man created God. This creation process took place several thousand years ago when theories were required to answer difficult questions such as, "What is the source of the universe, the earth, all the animals, and man?" Now, thousands of years later, better theories came along based on scientific principles. We no longer need the theory that God did it.

So from that day on, not only did I not believe that we could walk on air if we really believed, I didn't believe God really existed. This took place in the days of Madeline Murray, the militant atheist who blamed religion for everything. I thought that just because I didn't believe something, that was no reason to belittle others who did. If their belief systems brought them joy and comfort in life, why should I complain? Thus I preferred the less militant term—non-theist.

So why am I thankful for my early belief system? One of the greatest benefits of my access to other theories meant that I didn't struggle over some of the questions that tortured my friends, who remained faithful to God as the sole source for their beliefs. Questions like, "Why does such evil occur in the world?" and, "How could God let horrible things happen?" I grew up during the Second World War, one of the most horrific periods in history, with many millions of people murdered or killed. The question of "How could God let these things happen?" didn't bother me. The answer was simple.

God did not exist.

I did not have to be tortured with guilt over having fun, listening to rock music, dancing, dating, and a long list of other "do not" rules common to some religions. Most of my friends weren't bothered, either; we did not live in the Bible belt where such restrictions were a way of life. How many millions of people have gone to their graves after living an excessively pious existence, unnecessarily cut off from the many pleasurable things in life? Blissfully, I didn't have the burden of going through life thinking myself a worthless sinner.

This leads to another advantage.

I also did not believe in the duality of mind and body. This concept says that the mind—or in religious terms the soul—is independent of the body and can live on, and after we die will ascend up to heaven or down to hell. I believed the mind and the body (brain) were inseparable. Once the brain dies—*poof*—there goes the mind and the soul. No afterlife, no heaven, no hell. How many billions of people believe that God invented morality and, if we didn't obey that Moral Law, we would be doomed to hell? If we did, we were rewarded with heaven. My belief that when the mind dies, so goes the "soul," did not mean that I was free to do whatever I wanted.

Inherently, I believed I knew the difference between good behaviors and bad, and inherently believed in treating others the way I would like to be treated—the Golden Rule. Just as I didn't need a belief in God to explain the creation of all things, I didn't need God in order to behave morally. With the exception of psychopaths and a few chronic offenders, I believed the moral behavior of the human condition was built in by evolution so societies can survive.

What about a purpose in life?

Many have claimed that without God or religion, life has no purpose other than dust-to-dust. That's nonsense. There are an untold number of wonderful and rewarding purposes in life—from taking pleasure in a job well done, having a rewarding and loving marriage, raising children in a supportive and caring home, learning new things in school, finding a rewarding career, performing in a sport with class and panache, and on and on.

What about spirituality?

Isn't God and religion necessary to be a spiritual person? While the definition of spirituality often refers to God or supernatural beings, its broader definition is a wondrous feeling of connection to something greater than oneself. This can occur during a walk in the woods, or a hike to a mountaintop, or a loving relationship with a spouse, sibling, child, or even a friend. A spiritual experience can even occur at an exciting sports event in the presence of thousands of people or in the pursuit of a good golf game on a sunny afternoon on a beautiful course.

Readers can supply many examples of their own. There is enormous room to be "spiritual but not religious."

As Julie Andrews might say—"These are a few of my favorite things," reasons of why the philosophy "Thank God I Do Not Believe in God" provided me with a rich and wonderful life, free of the conflicts of logic that many believers face, free to peruse the pleasures of life within the confines of human natural laws of morality, and free to pursue the acquisition of new knowledge through the art of science.

❤   ❤   ❤

Dr. Comings—author of *Did Man Create God?*—is a physician, neuroscientist, and behavioral and molecular geneticist. Dr. Comings held the position of Director of the Department of Medical Genetics at the City of Hope National Medical Center for 37 years, before retiring in 2002. This internationally known scientist-physician has written over 450 scientific articles and three books, including, *Tourette Syndrome and Human Behavior*. His research areas included cytogenetics, as well as human behavioral and molecular genetics. He ran a large behavioral medicine clinic specializing in Tourette Syndrome, ADHD, and oppositional defiant behavior in children. Dr. Comings was previously an editor of the *American Journal of Human Genetics*, and past president of the American Society of Human Genetics. www.didmancreategod.com.

Thank God
. . . for Abusive Men

KENYA D'AGUSTINO

The story I'm going to share relates to an abusive relationship in high school. Even as I start to write this, I feel energy throughout my body—and there is a sudden jolt of emotion. I think to myself, *If my story helps even one stranger, one teenager, sooner than later, I will be incredibly fulfilled.*

I believe giving you a quick insight into my past will show you why I would have chosen such an abusive person.

When I was seven, my parents went through a terrible divorce.

My mother remarried when I was eight, and I became aware that the majority of the adults in my life—including my new stepdad—talked to me as though I were worthless.

By age nine I tried my first drug.

Signs of obsessive-compulsive disorder started at age 11.

At 15 my boyfriend started physically and emotionally abusing me, which lasted until I was 18—even though at that time, I saw light and hope when my mother took me to a therapist.

But within a year I entered another not-so-healthy (nine-year) relationship.

In my early 20s drugs consumed my life.

I was in my late 20s before true healing began.

Today at 35—I am grateful for it all.

As a child I witnessed my dad sitting in front of the door so my mother couldn't leave.

Included in many other incidents, some of my family members would continually ask my dad, "What's wrong with your kids?" That damaging question became branded into my head.

My abusive boyfriend was a representation of my family, and a representation of what I felt about myself.

Here is how it began . . .

I grew up in a very small town, and we all liked to party in the woods—actually any spot we could find. I remember at 14 years old walking into my first party that my older sisters attended. I was nervous, but I remember how excited I was to be there with the "older" kids.

I met *him* at this party.

He was 19, very well known, and drove around in big Chevy trucks. Actually, it wasn't really driving—it was racing and "burning out" all over the place. This was the beginning of it all. Soon after that evening, we met again and became inseparable. I'd sneak out of my house almost every night to spend time with him—and then sneak back in the morning. Unfortunately for my mother, I really became a pro.

It was the typical fast-paced, youthful relationship—fresh, fun, and passionate. Then one day it all changed. He became angry and jealous and tried to control everything I did. He not only didn't want me going out with my friends—he didn't even want me to go to the convenience store.

My years with him included many abusive incidents.

One of these incidents stuck in my mind for years as the saddest one—not because of the pain or injury he caused me, but because of the extraordinary challenge it was. It started when he saw me talking to another guy at a party.

He was furious.

On the way home he drove my car like a madman.

I was so relieved when we finally made it into my driveway.

Suddenly, he pushed me out of the passenger side door—and I fell right on my elbows onto the pavement.

Now, sometimes I'd fight back, but other times I wouldn't; I guess it just depended on my mood. On this particular day I just cried as I went into the house. He followed me, saying he was sorry—adding that it was my fault, and that I "made" him do those things.

Then he asked me to make him a sandwich. As I put the mayo on the bread, I was disgusted with the whole thing. I thought, *Look what he just did to me—and I'm making him food!* I broke down in tears, but still just continued on.

That incident represented great pain because it was clear that I had no self-respect, no self-worth, and was very guilt-ridden. I had put the feelings of others first—ignoring my own.

I wasn't an angel and, as I said earlier, at times I'd fight back. I'd call him names and instigate things, too. I also felt extremely jealous—and together we were simply a nightmare. Our insecurities fit like a glove.

I struggled with the thought of leaving him because of my guilt—it was a family dynamic. I believed I could help or save him, and that if I left he would feel alone. There were so many layers. Subconsciously I believed I deserved this. Consciously I found ways to rationalize and tell myself it wasn't that bad. I was almost 15, and he was five years older. I thought he was a "cool dude," which intrigued me. My dad was the James Dean type, and anyone who represented the *rebel* was the one who attracted me. Overall, I carried a lot of embarrassment and shame, but I felt trapped and co-dependent—trapped mostly with, and in, my own emotions. This combination made a wonderful recipe for an abusive relationship.

My mother recognized my pain and put me into therapy.

I'm so grateful for her.

After more than a year in therapy, trying to realize that I was important and didn't deserve this, I finally left him. It took getting a restraining order and moving away to another town. However, shortly after the move as I sat in my new apartment, one of my friends telephoned and said, "Kenya, your ex has packed his bags and is on his way to kidnap you!" One of my other friends happened to be there with me, so we jumped in the car and drove straight to the police station.

On our way there we passed by him.

I was really terrified that day.

I didn't know if he was snapping—thank God I didn't find out.

As time went on, I carried a lot of anger towards him, but there was a part of me that was grateful as well because he was the reason I began to value myself.

Years later I saw him at a mutual friend's wedding.

I had a strange, calm feeling without any rush of emotion. He still looked at me the same way he did years before, as if a day hadn't passed—and there was sadness in his eyes.

I realized in that moment that any anger or bitter feelings I thought I still held—were simply gone.

He didn't have power over me any longer.

My wounds were mending.

He became just another human being in need of love and support.

That is the day I became truly grateful for that abusive experience and my healing within it.

These events set me on a path to healing. I now strive to become my authentic self, to find my inspiration, and to gain back my selfworth. I don't think of my abuse as a "gift" because I wouldn't give it to you, but it gave me inspiration to get what I deserve and truly want in this life. It also gave me the desire to inspire others. I love that I now recognize that I'm a caring, kind person who deserves kind treatment back. I'm grateful that I'm up for the self-exploration challenge, and the incredible beauty that results.

If there is one gift I can give back to the world, it is to inspire others to take this challenge—no matter how hard it seems—to find the love, to find the lesson, and to find themselves. It can be a long road, but it's so worth the travel.

Today I experience loving relationships.

My sisters and I created a product and started a company called www.HipPurse.com. I'm in the process of writing a series of workshops for children called Kenergy Kids.

I'm grateful that my parents cared enough to make changes for themselves and for us. I'm grateful that I'm part of this wonderful, enlightening book series. I'm healthy and I can see, hear, touch, feel, and walk. I have fantastic friends and a strong bond with my family, who all supported me through my darkest days. I am grateful for it all . . .

WE TAKE THIS JOURNEY

We take this journey as we are placed on soil ground
We take this journey and there is no turning around
Some of us have no guidance and care
While others continually live in fear

We take this journey with the haunting question why
We take this journey until we humbly die
Some of us learn the strategy of the game
While others deny the truth of their pain

To take this journey and win along the way
You must confront and listen to what educators say
It may be a god, or a power greater than you
Just open your mind and the truth will find you

If you take this journey and dig to your soul
You will reach and cure your most painful hole
You will fill this hole so deep and secure
A new, magical journey begins, as you once were!

~ KLD ~

Kenya D'Agustino grew up in a small town in Connecticut, and graduated with a degree in Communications/Marketing. After graduation, Kenya worked with entrepreneurs—and then one day decided to become one. She now owns HipPurse.com. This successful business owner, along with her sisters, developed a program to empower young girls by creating a "Hands-Off" line and donating proceeds to various charities. Additionally, she is one of the founders for a women's group in Connectcut. This group of influential women is on a mission to empower young children to become advocates for healthy minds, bodies, and souls. Her business and the programs can be viewed at www.HipPurse.com.

Thank God
I Had Hodgkin's Disease

HALLEY ÉLISE, B DIV, C HT

I think I know not—and no one else does either

I wasn't feeling myself.

It started with lethargy—not wanting to do too much.

I tired easily, sometimes needing to pull to the side of the road to nap during just a 20-minute drive. Overwhelmed with weariness, it was unbearable even to hold my eyes open. Frequently a nap lasted a few minutes—other times as long as an hour—and still I felt woefully tired.

My mind attempted to process the source—*anemia, blood pressure?*

What else could this be?

Could I be depressed?

Depression didn't make sense—not for me. I awoke in a fulfilled state, meditated, and believed in transforming difficult moments.

Other then feeling poorly, all was right in my world. Home life had motion—friends in and out constantly. Our familial interaction and relationships remained sound; even our teen was doing what was needed. Business thrived; my radio ratings showed "thumbs up"; the Healing Circle enjoyed a great attendance—and it felt good sharing with the community. The *Psychic Apprenticeship Program*© gained more momentum; the column received good feedback, and there was more than enough downtime throughout my day for me to know inner peace.

So much happening in a positive way—and yet something was sincerely wrong inside.

In the past, I experienced symptoms that led to a diagnosis of Fibromyalgia. I reflected on the arduous process of finding a diagnosis at that time. Many doctors told me, "It's in your head." It seemed like an eternity before I connected with a doctor who I considered professional. He went the extra mile and gave a name to my experiences. I used breath work, meditation, stretching exercises, and some constructive dietary changes—which rendered the symptoms virtually unnoticeable.

While contemplating an answer to my current fatigue, a new interruption to my relatively healthy and usually relaxed life emerged—an unusual, irregular oval bump horizontally positioned at the base of my neck. It felt tender one day—then not. It appeared—then disappeared—then reappeared in the same place, or on the exact opposite side. It was large—and then it was small.

It was perhaps an over-active gland?

Maybe a little virus running through my system?

I asked my physical therapist friend and my chiropractor about it, and their agreed consensus determined that it was my body's way of ridding itself of something—no worries.

The next peculiar change was by far the most disconcerting. You cannot imagine how incredibly horrid pruritus can be. One symptom is an insatiable itchiness, like a dog that cannot escape the attack of a dense blanket of fleas. I also experienced what looked like hives that later became a mottled discoloration of my skin. Behavior modification (mind over matter) was the only way to get through my day in public.

When alone, I'd dash into a closet or lavatory to scratch.

Sleeping was nearly impossible.

But when sleep overcame me, I inflicted myself with war wounds—which I discovered in the morning.

My skin was scratched, discolored, and bleeding.

No recommended medicine, herbs, baths, or teas prescribed or suggested by the dermatologist, the naturopathic physician, the pharmacist, or friends gave me relief. What I didn't know was that symptoms of this severity—not responding to conservative therapies—need evaluation for an underlying systemic disease.

I was incredulously frustrated.

In a less aggressive manner other symptoms arose—restlessness and occasional nausea. My encounters with doctors became more trying and, at times, extremely disturbing. One doctor said the bump must be a thyroid gone awry; but many test results showed no thyroid problems (so said the automated message on the phone with no follow up suggestions or care).

When it came to the lethargy, the response was, "You're getting older." Older! (What? My 40s?) Or, "You're over-doing it—take a vacation." Or, "Your blood work is just fine."

The dermatological consultation was less then assuring; the knife whipped out and a biopsy taken before I could say anything. Results were most amusing; the doctor determined that my condition was due to an *adverse reaction to drugs*. This might have been right—with the exception that *I do not even take aspirin!*

When challenged that the results were flawed, the diagnosis became an Id-response. Yes, Id. What is Id? *It's an allergic, physical manifestation to some unknown factor, and your body freaks out all over.* (Yes, this was the medical description given to me. It IS what the medical professional said.)

That was it.

I would have no more silly "specialists" and the occasional well-meaning practitioner. They would not acknowledge that they didn't know what was wrong, nor did they make any constructive suggestions as to where to go from there. They didn't attempt to put the symptoms together. Even the Medical Intuitive (with a doctorate degree in medicine) could not give an answer. None of the doctors compared notes; they did not research beyond the basics, and some called me a hypochondriac.

I took it upon myself to research the different symptoms looking for a corollary relationship, any possible explanation, and then investigate natural approaches. I determined to leave doctors out of it.

That's when the first car accident happened. What was going on? I began treatment for my spine for the whiplash and was supposed to get an MRI. Treatment was going along fine and the physical therapy eased my pain.

I was dealing with my other physical distresses when accident number two occurred.

An MRI became an immediate necessity. In addition to seeing the vertebrae injury on the MRI, they spotted an irregularity believed to be a soft tissue mass. Whoa! All of a sudden people are calling and saying, "You've got something that needs attention!"

I'm sitting here laughing as I share this with you.

The Universe works in strange ways. I say, "Enough." It says, "You're not done yet."

Sadly there's more of the same indifference. Though now at least it was undeniable that something was causing havoc with—and in—my body.

More doctors.

One, who had unkind-heartedness down to a skill, said, "It's not your thyroid. Why don't you just go to someone and let them cut you open?" But blessedly shortly thereafter, the perfect, honestly concerned and forthright doctor tested me. After analyzing the results, he recommended a specific surgeon/teacher in the Otolaryngology (ENT) department of UM Sylvester Comprehensive Cancer Center.

Seeing this surgeon turned into an all-day event, over two hours of travel and a three-hour wait for my scheduled appointment—but so worth the wait. In about a month this doctor had things going in the right direction. Thank God I found him and his staff. These compassionate human beings listened, investigated, compared, deliberated, and were intelligible. They restored my faith in the medical community.

More tests, Sonograms; MRI/CT scans with and without contrast; X-rays; Mugga scan; Gamma Ray scan; PET scan; blood tests, etc.; some invasive—some not; then surgery to biopsy the area in question.

More tests—*then finally an answer.*

Prior to the biopsy, while initially reviewing and comparing all test results, my doctor conjectured that the culprit might be an unusual virus because so many of the tests were coming in with a negative result.

Let me mention, here, that through all of this, my faith in God didn't waver—no blame and no feelings of being singled out. There was just a knowing that something needed to be uncovered; something had to be learned.

The final pronouncement was Hodgkin's disease—a less familiar, rare type of lymphoma cancer.

Finally, an answer.

Thank you, God.

Angels, Acupuncture, and Soup

It's very interesting how gratitude can sneak up on you unexpectedly. My belief system often keeps me in a state of grace in daily life. But this . . . this was gratitude in a new light, and a real opportunity to walk my talk.

The diagnosis created a combination of simultaneous thoughts and emotions, overflowing as they ensconced my brain. First, I experienced enormous relief and gratitude finally to identify the "what." Then, I felt sadness simply because the "it"—known as cancer—could wreak so much turmoil, coupled with concern for my family and their reaction.

Yet the most profound thought of all was, *Do I want to be here?*

My answer of "Yes!" came instantly.

Once diagnosed, I plunged myself into researching all the history, nuances and professed cures of Hodgkin's disease. I experienced gratitude for my practice and knowledge of the healing arts. Thank God I had friends who were knowledgeable healers. I contacted a nutritional doctor whose specialty was healing cancer patients—what an incredible gift she was. I found Louise Hay's material helpful (she's an authority on the mind-body connection).

It took me approximately six months to make the decision to use a holistic/alternative approach in tandem with some conventional treatment.

In advance of accepting the chemotherapy treatment, I felt that it was necessary for my body to strengthen its immune system through multiple strategies. I got clear on diet, supplemental herbs, and vitamins. Along with physical advances, my mind built a mutable barrier for the chemo and reprogrammed my entire system for health. My usual sensitivity became even more acute as I worked with intuition and meditation in each situation.

Often I felt like an observer studying the Oncologist, the nurses, and the patients—watching how people responded to me and around me. Watching myself, I did what I could to stay grounded.

I learned so much.

My friend the acupuncturist (an "angel") became indispensable to me, coming to my home to give treatment when called. Another angel brought me homemade chicken soup each time I had a whim. Other friends sent pink roses to symbolize their love and support. Another friend gave me private Reiki sessions. Within a short period, it became apparent who could stay in this experience with me, and who needed to run away. One of myriad blessings included having the right people with me at the right time.

Another blessing was a new awareness of *unconditional love.*

Help me be cognizant

Hodgkin's disease came into my life to teach me—and those in my life—lessons of love, awareness, patience, and healing. In part it helped me be more cognizant so that I may know how to give value to my *self* and have presence in each of my moments.

Being in service to others will be a great part of my life.

When the occasion occurs that sharing my experience with another is of value to them—I do so.

But pushing myself too hard is not the way to honor God, or myself, because that behavior uses up my life substance.

Through the challenge of a life-threatening illness, I found more of myself.

Being present in my own life is now a natural occurrence, and my gratitude is boundless for love expressed and love received.

❤   ❤   ❤

Halley Élise, B Div, C Ht, is a Spiritual Entrepreneur and Intuitive. She facilitates spiritual guidance, harmony, wisdom, health, and personal increase. Halley is a UB Minister, graphologist, meditation facilitator, speaker, artist, and holds a certification in Clinical Hypnosis. Accomplishments include the *Treasures Within©* meditation book, *Table of Love©* newspaper column, OurBestIdea.com spiritual/personal development website, *The Psychic Apprenticeship Program©*, *The Now Manifest ALL Program©*, Conscious Sex radio show, and being the Quantum Life Hour radio host. Halley's life is a testimonial to knowing your Divine purpose and pursuing it with love. Please contact Halley for more information on programs, services, community work and projects. Be sure to ask her about her lecture series for your corporate events. 561-755-2166 or 954-584-8812, http://www.MysteriesLady.byregion.net and MysteriesByHalleyElise@Juno.com

Thank God
I Was a Runaway Child

JOHN JOSEPH

My father was a prizefighter.

As a result of his violence, our family was broken up. My two brothers and I were placed in foster care in New York State. We were separated, but after several foster families gave us up, we were finally united in a house of "horrors" on Long Island where, for almost seven years, we were starved, and were physically, emotionally, and sexually abused.

We had to steal just to get food in our stomachs, while the foster parents' two children got whatever they wanted. We found out they were getting a lot of money for our care—and that made things hurt even worse. Our foster parents told us constantly that no one loved us, and that we should be thankful they took us in.

We were tormented in the neighborhood and at school because we were the foster kids who lived at "The Crazy House."

After the home was shut down by the State—and all six foster kids were removed—my brothers and I were bounced around to other foster and group homes.

Finally in 1977—at the age of 14—I'd had all I could stand of the State's idea of "childcare."

I ran away.

I ended up in the mean streets of New York City. I swore daily I would be someone, become something, so I could throw it back in the faces of the people who had turned their backs on me. Then I could say, "See? Look at who you didn't want anything to do with. Look at who I am now!"

I had so much anger and hatred toward the world for what was done to me.

I was angry with my father for busting up the family. I hated what the foster parents had done. I really resented my mother for not taking us back. I lashed out against everyone. I was as violent as they came, and in NYC in those days—as a kid on the streets—you had to be. I was a heroin mule, a hustler, a scammer, a drug dealer, a drug user, and a thief. I did a lot of things I'm not proud of—but I had to in order to survive.

After almost 18 months on the streets and several arrests, I was sent upstate to a juvenile detention center. I thrived in the program, and later joined the Navy. I thought everything was going well at that point, but the problem was I hadn't faced the demons of my childhood. I hadn't dealt with the ticking time bomb that was inside me. I used alcohol and drugs to self-medicate, and after a year in the Navy I went AWOL.

I was on the streets again with warrants for my arrest—and no place to turn. I was lost. I didn't know where to go. I prayed to God.

Help show me the way.
Direct me.
Take away the pain I have inside me.

My prayers were answered. While I was stationed in Norfolk, I met a musical group called Bad Brains. They talked of love and peace, and were surrounded by people who were into yoga, meditation, and vegetarianism.

Months later I ran into them in NYC when I was AWOL, and we developed a very close bond. They offered me a job as their roadie and I took it, seeing it as a blessing to be surrounded by such amazing people every day. The Bad Brains and their entourage became my family. We prayed, talked, and had great times traveling around the country, living out our dreams. I gave up drugs, meat-eating, drinking—even sex. I got into hatha yoga, and got a side job in a health food store in NYC. Great. All the food I could eat.

My life was truly amazing at that point.

I eventually joined a group called The Cro-Mags, and we put out records, toured, and were even filmed in a Hollywood movie made by the famous producer of *Taxi Driver* and *Close Encounters* . . . —Julia Phillips.

I had a great spiritual foundation.

It was then that I joined the Hare Krishna religion, and lived as a monk for two years—only to be betrayed by them, as I found out they were molesting children, and stealing millions of dollars in the name of God. The leaders even murdered devotees who spoke out against them.

I was completely sickened by that.

Even now, one thing I don't tolerate—as a result of what was done to me as a kid—is people who harm children.

I believe God creates a special hell for them.

Eventually, my band broke up, and once again I struggled with homelessness, drug addiction, and a life of crime. I couldn't believe the place in which I found myself.

How did I get here?

I was doing so well.

I had so much promise.

Now, I was a crack head who ripped everyone off, and had no place to live. See, I didn't understand until I was 40 years old that my life, my healing, wouldn't be complete unless I got out the deep, dark secret of my abuse as a child. In 2000, with my writing partner and girlfriend at the time, I began writing a screenplay based on my childhood. I used a lot of the stories of my childhood—some were even funny—but I wouldn't dare bring to the surface all the things that happened in that "home." Actually, to this day my two brothers and I haven't talked about that.

Then the "Turning Point" of my life happened.

One night I had a nightmare about it all—and woke up sobbing uncontrollably. My girlfriend asked what was wrong, and I told her. I told her EVERYTHING. It was like a huge weight was being lifted off of me as we talked.

It all poured out.

All my stories.

It was so healing.

Eventually, at her urging, I wrote a book that was recently published. *THE EVOLUTION OF A CRO-MAGNON* is out now, and it's getting praised by literary and film people alike. Writing for me is therapeutic. I have several screenplays in the works, as well as a second book on health and nutrition—and I am releasing another album this year.

As a competitive marathoner and triathlete, I have remained drug and alcohol free.

I've returned to Spottford, Lincoln Hall, St. John's Home for Boys, and other juvenile centers to talk to the kids. I show them that I was there—right where they're at now—and that they, too, can make it.

Just ask God for help.

We may have the deck stacked against us, but if we try and don't give up, we can make it through anything life throws our way. My belief is that these kids don't want to listen to people with PhDs—they want to hear from people who have *been* there, and are going through what they are going through.

In 2000, I opened and helped run the Bhakti-Yoga Center at 93 Saint Marks Place in Manhattan. We teach yoga for "free" to people who don't have the money to fit in fancy classes that charge $40, or a $200 lecture series, but who would like the benefits of what yoga has to offer. It's maintained completely by donations.

We also have a free Sunday Love Feast, and run a vegetarian food distribution program for the homeless out of the Center. Weekly we feed hundreds at Tompkins Square Park on Manhattan's Lower East Side.

Having been homeless myself, going hungry many a cold night on the streets, I know a little hot food in your stomach can make a world of difference. We even got other health food stores to donate produce and dried goods to the program. My philosophy is that if a needy person is only going to get *one* meal—let's provide a *healthy* one. No ring-dings and dry bologna sandwiches here.

I thank God every day for how I grew up. Had I not led such a crazy childhood, I wouldn't have become the person I am now. I would not have the ability to help the next generation, or the homeless receive the many gifts that I have been given by God.

I have also learned about appreciation. I appreciate anyone who did anything to me as a child: my father, my abusers, even my mother. She then confided in me that because of my father raping her—two of the three of us were conceived.

As the book, *The Four Agreements,* says, "DON'T TAKE THINGS PERSONALLY." That may be the most difficult thing to do, but it's made me a stronger person—a person who can make it through anything life throws at me, even the Ironman Triathlon I'm now training for.

I was told of this *Thank God I . . .* ™ project by a friend who knows about my book, and who said that I should go to the website and check it out. I was moved to tears by some of the video clips. God bless you guys for doing this.

I hope my story can reach ears that need to hear it.

Namaste and love to all—John Joseph.

John Joseph has had a truly amazing journey through life. From foster homes to the mean streets of New York City, from a homeless runaway to a rocker touring the globe, and now a soulful healing celebrity, John continues to bring his message and gifts of endless giving to the masses.

With his music of The Cro-Mags, who became one of the most important bands in the underground punk/hardcore scene, having major tours, movie parts, videos on MTV's Headbanger's Ball, and magazine covers—his message began to spread. John then wrote his book, *The Evolution of a Cro-Magnon*, as a way to exercise the demons that haunted him. He held nothing back. Putting in subject matter previously untold, he hoped that someone struggling with personal demons could see that there's light at the end of a dark period. The response has been overwhelming. John's longtime friend, Adam Yauch (MCA—Beastie Boys), has said, "A lot of people talk about coming from the streets; when John says it, the shit is real."

It seems for John Joseph that life truly has been an evolution. As of late, he's writing for film, playing music, and embarking on a worldwide Spoken Word tour—having performed in Europe, Canada, and now the U.S. Stay tuned for dates in a city near you.

Visit John at www.myspace.com/jojomag to learn more, and get Bloodclot's latest album, *Burn Babylon Burn,* at www.bloodclotnyc.com.

Thank God
... for Silent Tears

JULIANNA JOYCE FEHÉR

I'm a second-generation American raised "old country" in a very traditional Hungarian family. Mom taught us to take what life threw at us, with our backs straight and our heads held high. And our tears? They're the silent kind. The kind you lock in your heart away from the world. That was the mode of survival for the women of a few generations back.

Dancing—one of Mom's passions—was probably a safe outlet for freeing herself of unwanted emotions. From infancy, I spent many evenings in the orchestra pit while she danced. I worked my own way to the dance floor by the time I was four. Unfortunately, her dancing days ceased shortly after my twin brothers were born, as my dad, a decorated World War II Veteran, suffered greatly from what we now call severe Post Traumatic Stress Syndrome, which led him to severe alcoholism. When I was a child, he'd have his "spells," which we only knew as "shell shock," and we just tried to keep out of his way. Ever upbeat, Mom would find fun to divert the situations. She could spin the most rancid sugar into the most delicious cotton candy. Dad wasn't the happiest of men, and Mom no longer had the outlet of "the dance."

Women labeled as strong and resilient know all too well the double-edged sword of life as a stoic. We conceal our hurts and wounds and appear unaffected. Granny and Mom brilliantly modeled "the world is fine and nothing bothers me" role. At other very brief moments, flipping to the opposite of stoic, heart-felt emotion burst forth so strongly that it viscerally affected anyone in the room. The dichotomy of human nature rarely renders a person dimensionless; we just sometimes "appear" that way.

Granny and Mom loved people, and everyone considered them mentors and friends. We were the "safe" people. We also had an uncanny way of "knowing." We seemed to tap into a realm that didn't require traditional communication. But, when it came to acknowledgement of sorrow between us, we'd give a brief glance revealing our deep pain, receive an even briefer nod of acknowledgement, and then we would quickly seal-over any untoward emotion. Stoics do feel deeply, love passionately, but express themselves awfully when it comes to intimate communication, so the world misperceives us at our own invitation.

My granny transitioned when I was only 11, so I considered it a great blessing that Mom was right there to help raise my babies. We delighted in their growing up, in their weddings, and as they started their new lives. At that time, I switched careers from psychology to writing (my inspiration). It took me away for long periods; but when I returned home, Mom was there waiting.

Then came the call.

My brother was the harbinger of the bad tidings. "Mom's in the hospital. It doesn't look good."

Driving to Los Angeles I held onto the irrational thought that it had to be a mistake. *Mom will rally; she'll be fine. She's the matriarch and she knows how to survive.* I held on to that denial until I walked into her room. There she lay, frail and unresponsive. Tubes connected her to oxygen and wires connected her to monitors.

It stunned me to see her like this.

The doctor matter-of-factly stated that she only had weeks to live and that we needed to discuss "the next step." He advised a nursing home. In unison, my brother and I both said, "No." The doctor pushed on . . . we wouldn't be doing right by Mom if we didn't place her in the hands of professionals. My brother looked to me for direction. My heart pounded, as I responded with a very weak, "Okay." Then I turned away from him to stare out the window, holding back my tears.

After the doctor left, I looked over to Mom. Her short, soft curls framed her round face, and her clouded eyes were open. She didn't say it aloud, but I heard her in my being . . . *Please don't send me away.* I could barely breathe. The doctor walked in with a social worker. I looked back at Mom, her gaze now fixed on the window.

At the nursing home, instead of healing, she slipped into a comatose state. The nurse wanted to discuss funeral arrangements. Again, the voice screamed in my head . . . *This is all wrong.* I could *feel* her inside that dysfunctional body trying to communicate—and knew I was missing something.

That night I returned to the nursing home and found her on the floor, unconscious. I yelled out for help. When a staff member finally came, he refused to call an ambulance, saying that my mother was a *No Code* patient.

He told me to let her go in peace.

At last I listened to that inner voice that persisted in haunting me. My "take charge" persona kicked in. I called the ambulance from my cell phone. The Emergency Room doctor listened to my account of the past few weeks, and immediately ordered a very specific test. Those results proved his suspicion—these past few weeks, as her body shut down, and as she suffered hallucinations, none of the medical staff recognized the well-known symptoms of overdose.

The doctor didn't think she'd make it.

My brother and I stayed at her bedside.

Then the miracle.

She rallied, but remained fragile. I convinced her to put a temporary hold on her advance directive so we could shoot for a full recovery. I quit my job and brought her home.

After three weeks, she gained strength, and was strong enough to spend several hours a day enjoying quality time with those she loved most. I knew her time remained short, but at least we helped her regain an ability to participate in life again, before that time came.

I let Mom believe she was once again "in charge" of the family, while I feigned the role of dutiful daughter—but secretly made decisions and ran things behind the scenes. (You just don't mess with the tradition of a Hungarian Matriarch.) Now I *knew* how she wielded her own power all those years making my dad think he was in charge.

Then one fabulous day I caught her looking at me.

We connected in that non-verbal way, not just for the brief second of connection . . . it went on and on.

I ran to her, dropped to the floor by her wheel chair, and laid my head in her lap. All that elusive love that I knew surrounded me became tangible, palpable.

The next few months we talked, laughed, and shared. She trusted me with her emotions . . . and her truths. She told me of her life before my father. The Hospice Social Worker even brought polka music and swung Mom's wheel chair to and fro. Grandchildren and great grandchildren played at her feet. My kitchen table could seat fifteen plus her wheel chair, and it was usually full. Mom became the Sitting Queen of all the Hospice volunteers, neighbors, and friends.

The day came when Mom could barely hold herself up in the wheel chair. I walked into the room to transfer her into bed, but she held her hand up to stop me in my tracks. She grabbed the walker, pulled herself to a standing position, and started to shake and tremble. I ran to her. "Mom! What's wrong?"

She smiled the most beautiful toothless grin. "I'm dancing!" she proudly announced as she leaned into my open arms. I was about to chastise her for exerting so much, but then we both looked at each other and broke out in giggles.

Then her coloring paled and she gasped for breath. I reached for the phone, while easing her into her bed. The doctor agreed to come right over. As we waited for him to arrive, I took Mom's hand. She spoke in such a weak voice I had to bend close to hear her.

"Promise me one thing. Promise me that you'll dance."

At first I didn't understand. Then I recalled the many conversations of the past weeks as she told me to experience life on my terms, and dance my dance. The ring of the doorbell brought me out of my reverie. I filed her words away, knowing that for the next several hours I had to get her, my family, and me through her death.

As the doctor finished his exam, I called everyone. "Mom's in kidney failure; come as quickly as you can." They took turns saying their last goodbyes. I stayed busy tending her and comforting them.

Morning came.

She motioned me close.

She pursed her parched lips. She couldn't speak. But her mouth remained puckered, so I bent down and kissed her gently. Our eyes locked, and so many images filled my mind that I still haven't sorted through them all.

Then—a swift and instant knowing as the gaze suddenly broke— my mother was no longer there.

Before anyone else in the room realized her death, I had a moment to stand in the silence, as the spiritual world opened to receive this amazing soul.

While waiting for the mortuary hearse to come for her, my brother and I dressed her in a favorite dress, brushed her hair, and placed a lilac in her hands.

When finally alone, I sat down on the floor of Mom's room, my arms wrapped around my knees.

I stared at Mom's empty wheel chair.

The image of Mom proudly dancing that last dance came to my mind. She looked so fulfilled for those few moments, doing exactly what she loved to do.

Then I recalled those weakly whispered words on her deathbed.

Now the room sat vacant and silent.

A tear rolled down my cheek.

I didn't wipe it away.

Others tentatively flowed out.

Suddenly it seemed all the unshed tears of my lifetime came forth in loud wails as I pounded the ground with my fist. There—all alone on the floor—I sobbed, until there were no more tears left to cry.

Spent, I lay my face on the cool tiles and fell asleep.

Upon awakening, my world had altered—the light brighter, and the colors more vibrant. I felt an unaccustomed calm. I envisioned my mom healthy and whole, dancing with all those who had gone on before her.

Then gratitude flooded in.

Gratitude for our love.

Gratitude for our journey.

I realized the new and wondrous legacy she left for me to pass on to my daughters . . . gratitude for the life-sustaining *dance*.

Thank God for those silent tears because now I deeply appreciate the real ones.

I hold the position of matriarch with a twinkle in my eye, grateful that the old family tradition has a new meaning.

I share Mom's legacy by teaching my children, my grandchildren, and any willing friend—the meaning of Grandma Rose's dance.

❤   ❤   ❤

Julianna Joyce Fehér connects with people at a depth that offers them the ability to discover their own passions and talents. She holds workshops, seminars, and retreats for women of all ages, teaching, and equipping them to participate in loving, fulfilling relationships. She is a writer, editor, and writing consultant for television, film, stage, and the publishing industries. She is a member of The Writers Guild of America and Women in Film. She is grateful for having had an active part in the *Thank God I . . .* ™ Community, and for helping with many of the stories in this book. For more information, contact her through her website at www.writtenby.net.

Thank God
I Was Born in a Refugee Camp

REGINA B. JENSEN, PhD

Would you like to be born a third girl, with the second one still in diapers, and the first one toddling along in a refugee camp out by the northerly German forest—no running water, and hardly any food, surrounded by the ravages of World War II?

Mom tells me how she taught herself—while pregnant with me—to fall down "carefully" when she realized she would lose consciousness from exhaustion while walking up the icy hill to get water to wash out my sister's diapers.

I can't imagine, coming from her fine, privileged background, that Mom had been taught any kind of survival moves. Although she *had* learned—not out of lack but from appreciation for the gifts of the forest—to tell edible mushrooms from poisonous ones, and how to gather berries, nuts . . . and now added firewood to her list of gatherings. "Ja," she still says gratefully and with a wistful smile, even after so many decades, luxury once more firmly in hand, "the woods gave us many a good meal."

89

I still see Mom using a match over and over to light the gas-range—from flame to new flame.

"Why strike a new one?"

To this day I have a strange sense of matches being very precious. And to this day she will rinse out a dish-sponge in a little cup rather than under running water, and then share it with a potted plant, or save it for some other small but noble purpose. Would we all have driven our planet to the brink of destruction had we learned, instead, to cherish each little blessing so devotedly?

And Dad.

Oh, how he used to irritate me with his Pollyannaish preaching: "Ach, ja, Gott sei Dank . . . " he would say, "Thank God (this or that misery) befell us . . . who knows what might have happened otherwise."

Oh, I thought, *must I endure one more childish refusal to look at life's negative, darker side—that of loss, betrayal, terror, grief?*

But Dad knew—and I now understand much more clearly the *how* and *why*—how to invoke the powers of the Universe. Those powers had saved Mom and him miraculously, many times over, even when they found themselves separated by the war.

"Karl wrote," she told her father back then. "He says it may be safe if I could somehow cross the border immediately before the Russians lock us in, and get across Germany and up north. Shall I go Dad—or stay here at home with you?"

Who knows what my grandfather must have felt when he said to his beloved young daughter, "Go now!"—then watching as she and her guide, who was to take her as far as the border, left, knowing he might not see her again.

As soon as she arrived at the border she was promptly arrested, along with several others in the same desperate attempt to reach the open side of the West.

The borders were closing quickly as the Russian powers moved in to secure their newly obtained territories. There, a young officer carefully examined each face, especially Mom's strikingly beautiful features, and picked her for his tent.

Why did he take her there—only to let her go miraculously on her way, again—unharmed?

I have often wondered why homelessness didn't frighten me, or old age or handicap. But another silent enemy did—*terror*, which had been bred into my bones. Terror was conceived into my marrowbone—a nameless terror of a different sort than the fear of hunger or losing one's home. The world of Nature stood by powerfully, and so did the presence of loving, unseen forces, ready to protect and embrace me.

But terror was a different kind of companion—like an invisible, looming threat: the inherited trauma of *war*.

Dad's incredible stories of invincible faith abound.

Or was it sheer stubbornness?

He rode for several hours on his bicycle for each round-trip from the forest to the seat of the provisionary county government 22 times—not once taking their "No" for an answer.

This denial kept him tied to receive the meager government subsistence support, just enough to keep some potatoes and grains on the table for his hungry family.

An unmoved, bureaucratic face across the counter repeated each time, "You can only receive allotments for food as long as you are personally present."

No one could replace him.

But on trip 23—by courageously asking for yet another supervisor—a miracle happened. He received a special permit, which allowed for a 10-day absence without loss of support for Mom and us three girls. He was unstoppable—and those gates of heaven opened with a "Yes" at last.

It was 10 days of hard-earned freedom to ride the old bicycle all the way down through Germany, hoping that somehow, miraculously, he would find employment. He knew he had to feed a large, hungry family—but so did countless others looking for work. Then he had to pedal back up north by the end of those 10 ominous days. What madness . . . senseless, rigid regulations, which only give way in the face of "unstopableness," in the face of that energy which becomes engaged when a human being—against all odds—keeps facing down the laws of matter, invoking the transcendent power of Grace.

Would you believe that he had to endure a similar travesty again? He had to ride over 20 *more* times—still on that old bicycle for many hours each time—to the next big city and back, hoping for a residence permit for a job application.

But he couldn't get the residence permit without a job—and no job without an address.

And so—very weary and scared, now, because it was day number nine—he tried one last time. He knew hunger would threaten his far away, overwhelmed young wife, who was without running water or much food at the edge of the forest.

But grace descended again in the form of a woman he had met weeks earlier.

"You work here?" he asked.

"Oh, yes. Let's take care of your problem right now."

This woman—just walking down the hall to her office at that moment—had met Dad at the local American Military Base. Right there and then she had the idea to find this young father employment on foreign ground—American—that also gave him an immediate address.

The Army chaplain promptly appropriated Dad to become his personal assistant. I actually grew up very close to this Army base from which Dad brought home our first dollar note—worth five German Marks. Did the familiar energy of that island of America call me later as a young woman of 22—ready to leave home for the West?

America.

A dream my father was not able to realize. Twenty-some rides twice—until Dad hit the jackpot. Two 20-something-year olds, fierce young women—first mother, then daughter—setting off for the West to find their new home.

DNA is strong.

It has me sitting here now with tear-streaked cheeks—maybe the tears my parents didn't allow themselves to cry back then—memories firmly embedded in those powerful strands of ancestrally transmitted proteins. But so is modeled behavior very strong. I benefited from both.

One wonders why the gods of fate pick certain circumstances for their earthly wards. In tens of thousands of sessions in my function as a health professional, I have helped clients come back into full power and vitality—sometimes with "death" already looming. I have a natural gift to facilitate physical and emotional healing. They say spiritual propensities are actually inherited. These—along with my hard-earned gifts and an amazing amount of grace and divine guidance—have exposed me to the finest training and professional experiences for almost four decades. All of it has seemed to present itself seamlessly.

The hunger didn't assert its deadly grip; neither in reality, nor as a fear for a child who saw how Mother Nature really does nurture each of her own. The forest stood by to fill up the food baskets, which would have been dangerously empty otherwise. But the terror stood by, too—ever ready to flood me, it seemed, in the most unexpected moments.

One learns to build one's whole personality structure around profound affect-states. Terror is not quite an affect-state; maybe it is better described as an *enormous energetic event.* I didn't know the name of these energetic experiences, but had learned to make careful allowances for them while still functioning as a successful young professional. Now I know they are called Annihilation Terror. I am capitalizing these words gladly. They are big events in a human soul sometimes triggered by the smallest events—someone turning a little too quickly, perhaps, or looking at me unexpectedly, when I felt perfectly fine only moments before.

The gods of fate served me well, guiding me by way of my suffering to a very privileged professional path, helping others find inner peace again—especially from traumatic experiences. It all has been second (or should I say first?) nature to me. So is my work as an executive coach and consultant to the entertainment industry. Creativity is a great asset in a world that needs to learn how to re-conceptualize itself moment-by-moment. The world seems to be learning that *gratitude* is the easiest and fastest way to be woven back into the fabric of creation—from which we seem to have fallen like tumbling, thoughtless children.

Suffering has also blessed me with a natural capacity for empathy—obtained from seeing my parents struggle so hard to love us in the best way they could.

Terror was my first teacher and guide in learning to sense the subtlest layers of Shamanic energy—in myself and in others. More than any other skill, that is what I am sharing at this stage of my life.

Shhhhh . . .
Come back to Nature.
Come sit down here on the cool grass . . .
Taste a few of these dandelion blossoms . . . chewy?
Some miner's lettuce . . . sour?
See, the little animals are coming already—fearless of us.
We are so woven into Nature, now; they don't even know we're here . . .
Can you feel it in your heart?
Paradise.

❤   ❤   ❤

Dr. Regina Jensen holds licenses as a psychotherapist and physical therapist, and certifications as Master Executive Coach, as well as various certifications in somatic and trauma therapies, and has more than 35 years of professional training and experience. Dr. Jensen has developed an approach to dealing with the dangerous and ultimately deadly modern-day trauma of sensory over-stimulation called *Autonomic Balancing™*. Regina works as a consultant to the media, as a metabolic counselor, and is co-author of a forthcoming book with Dr. Wayne Dyer and others, which is part of a best-selling series. She is a writer and independent researcher with a commitment to finding intelligent, expedient, and joyful solutions for the predicaments we have co-created for each other on our Mother Planet. Dr. Jensen practices in Santa Barbara, California, and can be reached through her website: www.fullyalivewellnesscenter.com.

Thank God My Friend Died of Cancer

LOIS TIEDEMANN KOFFI

*A*re you sitting down?"

I paused briefly, not understanding—or maybe not wanting to.

"Uh, I can be."

I sat down with a queasy sense of unease in my stomach.

"Mikey died this morning."

Cancer.

This mystery word entered my life at the tender age of 20. Much like a marathoner hitting a wall at mile 21 of a 26.2-mile distance race, my life seemed to stop that split second on April 5, 1998.

That was when I heard a disease took the life of my friend, Mike—leaving me changed forever.

Hitting "the wall" in marathon races is like finding your feet completely imbedded in cement—and yet the rest of your body doesn't get the memo that your feet have stopped. You keep moving forward—yet the weight on your legs, and the pressure, *demand* you STOP. The throbbing pain radiates up and down your legs as your mind and body attempt to reconvene—or perhaps intervene—with one another in that moment of indecision—that fated moment—as to whether or not it is worth it to keep going.

Who is going to win?

The body?

Or the mind?

This is not just a physical pain but a mental anguish that dukes it out within your brain cells to a point where you think your head might explode. You actually wish it would. But in a marathon the third element—your Spirit—wins out and gets you to that finish line.

The day is usually saved—the "wall" is usually destroyed.

Yet this was different.

"Mikey died this morning."

The words cut to the depths of my heart and tore my soul apart. There was an inner battle going on in my mind and body. This was no marathon wall. This was a demolition of my mind, my body *and* my Spirit—all at once.

I was completely crushed and broken.

I had been spared a close encounter with death until that second year in college. It was a blow like the bombing of Pearl Harbor—or the day President Kennedy was shot.

The first blow was when I learned Mike was diagnosed with acute leukemia. I was in Boca Raton, Florida, during my college spring break, one of my first real trips away from my home state of Iowa. I had been enjoying one of my greatest memories as I entered my second decade of life, seeing the world for the first time outside my usual box.

The second blow came when I heard the words that *Mikey* had succumbed to the disease that he had been diagnosed with just 14 days prior. It was a cool and damp spring day in the north central Iowa town of Forest City, and I thought it fitting that the sun was not out to honor my friend's departure.

Mike and I had a circle of friends who grew up in Hull, Iowa, a small country town with a population of nearly 1700 people. I could help direct a party at Mike's house, or one of the other kids' homes—with as short a notice as 15 minutes or less. We were like brothers and sisters, and were inseparable—especially those last three years of high school as we all slowly acquired our driver's license, fortunate enough to have our own cars or pickups.

It was an amazing life to lead.

Mikey, as I lovingly called him, had experienced complications with the leukemia that he only knowingly had for two weeks.

Then the realization hit me.

I would not see Mike again—wouldn't get to laugh at his jokes—wouldn't get to rub his fuzzy, almost bald head, and tease him about getting old—wouldn't hear the desperation in his voice when he talked about *not* being married yet.

Most importantly, there would be no more teaming up with him to plan an event with our circle of friends. Even though we had been hundreds of miles apart, we were still committed more than ever to keeping our group together on breaks and through regular communication via e-mail.

For the first time in my life, I pretty much lost all control of my emotions.

Once I realized that Mikey would not be there for me ever again, the tears fell.

The floodgates opened up.

My heart broke within my chest and I immediately dropped to the floor, phone still in hand. My roommate, Brooke, was out of town, so I dashed down to the second floor of the dorm looking for my friend Beth. I clung to her as I sobbed uncontrollably. Beth could barely understand what had happened as I attempted to explain, but I simply held onto her as hard as I could—not wanting to let go.

Mike had so much life left.

My tears went on for hours, days and months—until my first blessing from his death came in my mailbox. It would be one year later in the summer of 1999 that my first blessing of many would come to restore my sadness and begin my journey of gratitude.

It also began my marathon transformation.

They say God works in mysterious ways—and I would have to agree. I could not have authored what took place over the next several years of my life any better.

A postcard from the Leukemia Society of America showed itself as I searched through my mail, and I was able to find out about an informational meeting roughly 90 minutes away from my college town. This tiny gift allowed me the opportunity to learn about the non-profit organization (LSA) that would grant me the honor of training for a 26.2-mile marathon distance race, a dream I had been inspired to pursue in the last year. It also granted me the right to fundraise thousands of dollars to go toward cancer research to help those who were still battling the disease.

That informational meeting was all it took.

I was hooked.

I signed up on the spot and began the journey of becoming a marathoner and fundraising devotee—in honor of Mikey. I felt in my gut that my choice that night was pivotal and would lead me along a path of a road less traveled.

In the Spirit of giving for a higher cause—and pursuing something that is outside of oneself—I went on to raise over $32,000 over the course of the next several years—running, biking, and swimming thousands of miles—all in honor of an amazing man who died—and for those who were *still* living.

I won first place in my age division at one marathon with a time of 3 hours 29 minutes in Anchorage, Alaska.

I also finished first in the Maui Triathlon.

I got to experience many "walls" in those races and in the race of life—yet nothing seemed to compare to the pain of losing Mike. Every time I crossed those marathon and triathlon finish lines, I knew I was continuing his legacy and making a difference for others who would yet be diagnosed with the disease.

I was able to grieve throughout all those miles and hours of fundraising and feel Mike's Spirit was still with me at all times. Those miles on the road of my life spent in training were transformational. They provided me the time to find gratitude in that healing process and to be more open with God.

God—at that time—was considered simply my Heavenly Father, provider and source of all things in my life. I prayed to God daily and was taught to have a conscious duty of love and respect for Him—even above my earthly father.

Yet it wasn't until Mike's death that I truly understood the power of God and how the old adage of *everything happens for a reason* really plays a HUGE part in the Universal Laws of Life. This realization became a large tool for me.

Everything *does* happen for a reason, and the transformation takes place once you can see it.

Many people, including myself, struggle to understand why painful things happen in life. They wonder, *Why wouldn't God stop me from experiencing such heartache?* This question plagued me for a while after Mike died. Many people interpret that seeing things as "good" means that God will keep them from difficulty.

But God allows "pain."

Sometimes God even orchestrates it.

God understands the "hurt" while looking into the deeper meaning of the situation. Trials often strengthen our faith and give us compassion for others. At times God may even use difficulties to keep us from living mundane lives or wasting opportunities. Again—in the metaphor of what the marathon wall was for me—once someone can break through and be transformed in the process, anything is possible.

With God's help we profit immensely from walking through the "pain," breaking through the cement of that "wall," rather than avoiding it or giving up. When our heavenly Father knows it is best, God doesn't keep us from the pain; instead, God enables us to endure the hardship by giving us wisdom and strength. And when we get to the other side we can often see—with great gratitude—how God guided us through the whole situation.

After that self-realization (a.k.a., *aha!* moment), I was transformed, had a renewed Spirit, and could keep running the *marathon* race.

Every facet of my life was interwoven from that point on. People, places, and things that came my way as a result of LSA, marathon training, and even in this story I am writing now, were a result of a victorious mind/body/Spirit *shift*.

Now I consciously thank Mike—every time I think of him—for being there for me in his lifetime—and the next. I pursue life with a fearlessness that epitomizes a Spirit that values each day and looks forward to many more finish lines to come.

I can thank God I had a friend die of cancer.

❤   ❤   ❤

Lois Tiedemann Koffi is a professional speaker, author, and transformational success coach. She started early in sales at age 22, experiencing many successes and life lessons as a sales professional. She's a multiple-time marathoner and Ironman Triathlete. She is most passionate about her several years of coaching and training business professionals, mentoring youth, and helping to lead thousands of athletes to cross their *own* finish lines in endurance races. In 2007, she founded Transformation TriSystems, which is a personal growth and development company designed to help people create balance between their personal and professional lives in living the life of their dreams. She now lives the life of her dreams near the ocean. Website: www.LoisTiedemann.com. Blog: www.triathlonbook.com/blog. E-mail: Lois@LoisTiedemann.com.

Join the *Thank God I...*™ Community online to share your story and chat with the authors at **www.thankgodi.com**

Thank God
I Came from a Dysfunctional Family

NINA ROXANNE HOWARD

Often we understand our lessons in hindsight.

As I turn back the pages of time, I see I've created a journey of triumph over prejudice, ignorance, poverty, sexual abuse, subservience, shame, disease, and low self-esteem.

My dysfunctional family experiences included a mother with mental illness, and an unfaithful alcoholic father who emotionally and physically abused my mother and, for the most part, neglected his children. As I've matured I've realized that overcoming the adversity of my childhood stands as the most significant thread in my life leading to my growth. It molded and developed my strength, courage, and ultimately my gratitude for the lessons.

Most of us come from dysfunctional families.

Recently I spoke at a gathering of 650 people. I asked the question, "Who does *not* have dysfunction in their family?" As I looked across the audience and counted raised hands, I counted around a dozen. That's 12 out of 650. I chuckled to myself and thought, *These 12 people are in denial.*

We "humans" are here on earth learning lessons.

Every generation experiences its unique set of challenges as we spiral upward towards higher understanding and growth. Duality challenges us from the start—the duality of good/bad, right/wrong . . . How we deal with these lessons of "duality" can bring us out of the "victim" mode into ultimately *mastering our lives.*

My dysfunctional family set me on my own path, just as your family presented you with your own personal struggles and lessons for growth.

I offer to you my story of gratitude from those lessons to inspire you, and to help you gain mastery over your own struggles as well.

I was a teenage single mother with a baby on my hip and three dollars in my pocket. At the grocery store, I looked around pondering what to buy for the two of us that would last the week. That week we lived on milk and bananas, and I lived on the inspiration of Scarlett O'Hara. Like her I swore I wouldn't go hungry again.

I knew—although no one had ever told me—that I had power within myself. I dared to imagine that I had enough power to find a better job and a better life. At the time, I couldn't have imagined that I could start my own business and land in the top seven percent of women-owned businesses in America—whose yearly revenues exceeded one million dollars. I didn't imagine that I could grow up to be the woman I wanted to be—or that one day my story would be of any use to anyone else.

The bananas and milk incident taught me that scraping the bottom of the barrel built character, strongly defining for me what I did *not* want. All around me for years I saw what I did not want.

But that day pushed me to figure out how I could do better.

Before I became the teenage mother with three dollars in my pocket, I'd been a little girl in segregated Birmingham, Alabama, sitting at the back of the bus *because I was told to*, and drinking from "colored" water fountains *because I was told I had to*, and hearing angry shouts of "Jap go home!"

My heritage includes English, Irish, Cherokee Indian, Filipino, Spanish, and Chinese. Because of the Filipino/Chinese heritage, I was not valued or accepted in the Deep South; and I had no one to tell me differently. I hadn't yet come to understand ignorance or prejudice, nor that I was okay regardless of anyone's attitude.

I was born an asthmatic and treated like a handicapped child because I couldn't run and play. I spent many nights in hospital emergency rooms with severe attacks. Whether Mom reacted from being left behind while Dad went out "honkey-tonking," or due to his antagonizing her when he was at home, I was the emotional barometer of the family; my asthma attacks took the focus away from the distress and the conflict, putting focus on my illness and me.

In a strange sort of way my illness brought us back together as a family.

My father was a "good ol' boy" from Alabama with an eighth-grade education. He raised cotton on their farm—and then joined the Navy. He served 13 years, several of which were in the Philippines where he met Mom. My mother, a schoolteacher from the Philippines, spoke five languages, was valedictorian of her class, and became one of the early females who graduated from college in her third-world country in the 1930s. When she immigrated to America and settled in Alabama with my father, he treated her much like a "mail-order bride." She catered to his every whim, believing it her duty to serve her husband.

Dad ruled the nest.

When Dad drank he terrorized Mom, sometimes physically abusing her, but more often emotionally punishing her. One time as he sat in a chair, he raised his foot to Mom's stomach—and kicked her across the room. Her back hit the wall, and she slid down to the floor.

I was horrified.

I picked up the broom and smacked him on the head with the handle—trying to stop him. He chased me to the bathroom and choked me. Mom pulled him off me using the internal strength of mother lifting an automobile off her child.

I was five years old.

Dad had his own "still" where he made "100-proof white lightening"—and drank until he passed out.

I felt shame watching him.

Dad's drinking buddies visited often, and so did the "family clan." Some of these men saw "cute little Asian-looking girls" as opportunities for their own personal sexual excitement. As a result, I endured being kissed, fondled—AND MORE. This happened more often than I care to remember.

One time my sisters and I tattled on one of these men. The anger, emotions, accusations, and denials flew through the air from my parents to the perpetrator. After much yelling and anger—they concluded that we made it up.

We received the blame and scolding.

We coped with the "grown up" behavior by thinking that's just the way men are. We learned it wasn't safe to tell, so we protected ourselves by staying in our room or leaving the house when there was a knock on the door.

At the same time that my childhood turned to puberty, Dad left for another woman.

He left Mom—but it felt like he left *me*.

Mom's coping mechanisms ran out, and she developed a chemical imbalance—known then as manic-depressive syndrome (now called bipolar disorder).

At age 13, *I* became the mother to *her*.

I turned to *boys*—both to fulfill my need for love, and to retaliate against my dad for leaving. With my emotions jumbling, I remember thinking: *You're not a good dad, so why should I be a good daughter?* I became pregnant at age 15. Soon after a "shotgun wedding" and the birth of my daughter—I divorced.

Then came two more marriages and divorces in rapid succession.

My second husband wasn't a drunk, but he carried on the familiar abuse patterns of my father.

I coped with the abuse fairly well, but finally drew the line the day he beat my daughter for spilling her milk at the dinner table.

The fear of what he would do next moved us away from the situation—and my daughter and I escaped.

The theme for the third marriage was "infidelity." I caught him cheating many times but took him back—mirroring my parents' behavior.

Interspersed with his infidelity was my own. Retaliation seemed the only relief valve I could find.

Many years later, I learned I was trying to resolve and work out my parents' relationship as I matured as an adult. I repeatedly drew situations and men to myself that compromised the core of my being. I relived the past with shame, guilt, and blame. Somehow I knew I deserved better, but I didn't know how to change it. It was then that I understood that the only way out is *up*, and a major turning point in my life occurred.

The *aha!* questions came to mind.

Who am I?

Where am I going?

What am I doing?

Looking back to my scary and humiliating childhood, I found seeds of hope and strength. Even as a five-year-old child and protector of my mom, an inner voice with a quiet indignation brewed inside of me. I used that same energy to catapult me away from my station in life.

So what had changed in my world as I matured into an adult?

I built a successful, creative, and fulfilled life with wonderful relationships.

I created my own path and put an end to being a "victim."

What constitutes a *victim?*

A victim is someone who has not awakened to his or her true nature. Victims continue to re-live the nightmare of their worst fears—repeatedly—because they haven't learned to create their own reality. They're not even aware that it is possible to step out of the social consciousness that influences their behavior to create the life that they love to live.

Making the changes from *victim* to *master* is the theme of my life. I had to learn a new reality, a new truth, a reality based on the love of *self*. I created a world that radiated from that point.

I developed a process to recognize difficulties and turn them to possibilities. When feeling "fear" I used the fear to assist me. Fear can heighten awareness with a bio-chemical charge to instill movement.

Fear causes the fight or flight response and kicks the adrenals into high gear. Along the way, I somehow learned to flip that feeling of fear into strength and courage, to rise above the disparity instead of buckling, cowering, or otherwise becoming immobile.

For me fear became the fuel I used to make changes.

Now I'm constantly filled with gratitude.

I look for the good and bad in everything; I look for the gifts and blessings in every single aspect of life.

By becoming grateful for every experience in our lives, we discover that we are not, in fact, VICTIMS of circumstance but MASTERS of our destiny.

We love ourselves and receive love from others—living a life filled with drive, purpose, inspiration, and gratitude.

Thank God I came from a dysfunctional family.

Nina Howard has been inspiring others to "overcome adversity" through her life experiences and with her charismatic leadership style. She's able to show how to rise above seeming limitations, expand understanding of how to change lives, and experience gratitude for the situations that shape them. Since learning meditation in the 1970s, Nina has applied metaphysical principles and a positive attitude to her life. In 1978, Nina graduated from the Fashion Institute of Technology in NYC in Interior Design. As a master artist and feng shui inspired designer, her paintings and designs have been incorporated into many institutional, corporate, and private homes. As the 90s approached, she changed careers to massage and esthetics, and ultimately created the Bellanina family of businesses: Bellanina Institute, an international spa training school; Bellanina Day Spa, a successful million-dollar spa; and Bellanina Naturals, Botanicals, and Cosmeceuticals skin care lines. Visit www.bellaninadayspa.com, www.bellaninainstitute.com, and www.bellanina.com for more information.

 Join the *Thank God I . . .*™ Community online to share your story and chat with the authors at **www.thankgodi.com**

Thank God
We Were Within an Inch of Our Lives

SHARON F. KISSANE

Sheba—a friendly Blue Merle Collie—loves to chase geese.

One frigid day in January of 2000, Sheba and I were taking our customary walk along our street, which winds around the Lake of the Coves in South Barrington, Illinois. We spotted a gaggle of geese making themselves at home in a common area of the frozen lake.

Sheba tugged on her leash, anxious to send the geese aloft.

The leash slipped from my ski gloves—and off she ran in pursuit of the geese.

The snow-covered ground made it hard to see where the land ended and the lake began. Watching Sheba run at top speed, I noticed a large hole in the ice some 20 feet from where she began her run.

I called out, "Sheba, Sheba!"

The wind carried my words and she finally responded. She skidded on the ice, the momentum from her run propelling her towards the hole. Failing to gain hold of the slippery surface of the lake, she plunged right into the gaping hole.

Valiantly, Sheba swam around and around the edges of the hole. At times she would leap up and grab onto the edge of the ice—only to be repelled back into the water. After 10 minutes of watching her struggle in vain—I decided I had to act.

But how?

Luckily the lightness of my gym shoes would allow me to swim. I hoped my long down coat would keep me from freezing. Judging by the stinging pain in my face, the temperature had to be just above zero. I hesitated, trying to estimate how long the thin sheet of ice would hold me before it broke.

Cautiously I made my way towards Sheba.

About 10 or 15 feet from the shoreline, the ice cracked and split into shards as I slipped into the water . . .

Using my legs and arms I chopped at the sheets of free-floating ice, attempting to swim towards my beloved pet. Her soft brown eyes were trustingly focused on me.

I called out to assure her I was coming.

But my body slowed down as my legs and arms felt the effects of chopping through the icy water. A voice—which I believed to be that of an angel—said softly, "You must go back or you will die." I looked at my dog that paddled harder and harder in an effort to free herself.

Could I let her die?

Then the thought struck me—*If I die, so will Sheba!* With great sadness I turned around to head back to shore. By now the cold pierced though my coat—now stiff, heavy, and weighing me down. My lips trembled and my legs were rubbery. It seemed to take forever to get back to the shore. As my feet touched the sand, I laid my head down. My feet could no longer move, as all the energy drained from me. I knew I had but a few moments to live.

Then a light came from out of nowhere. I raised my head and could make out a headlight. It was an SUV. The vehicle stopped quickly and a young man jumped out. He headed towards my still-struggling dog. I tried to call out—but my voice was too weak. I merely waved in his direction. Stunned, he turned around and ran towards me. He came up to me and dragged me further up on the land, as I had no strength left to move.

He had me lean on him as we made our way to his vehicle. I looked down at my ice-covered shoes. I feared my feet would have to be amputated.

Inside the SUV, he encouraged me to drink his hot coffee, and then he called for help on his cell phone. He went down to the lake to check on my dog. My heart beat quickly; and I felt my soul leaving my body. The thought came to me that we merely lease our bodies until it's time for our souls to ascend.

A tap on the side of the door brought back my attention.

I saw our local policeman.

"Norman, I'm dying," I said to him.

"You're going to be all right," he assured me. "The ambulance will soon be here. I'm going to check on your dog."

Within minutes a series of bright lights shone down on the windows. The ambulance stopped alongside the SUV. As they transferred me into it, I advised the paramedic as to where the land met the shore because the mounds of snow made it impossible to distinguish.

During the short trip to the emergency room the paramedic could *not* read my temperature; it was below what could be recorded.

Later, awakening in the emergency room, I asked if they saved Sheba. The nurse said that the policeman and the young man, who turned out to be a neighbor from the next subdivision, had taken the emergency boat anchored at the common point and rowed out to where Sheba continued to fight for her life. Once they got her aboard, the policemen broke all speed records to get her to the nearest animal hospital. The doctor used a newly purchased special warming vest on her—the same type used on me—to stop the chills.

For weeks after the incident, as I walked my dog along the street surrounding the lake—I felt like a ghost.

Was I really alive?

It was the strangest feeling.

Despite my weakness, I thanked God for giving me a new start. I no longer had the slight nervous condition I had suffered before this incident occurred. It felt like God had saved me from the ultimate fear—the fear of losing one's life—so nothing else could ever seem worth worrying about again. I had appreciated my neighborhood, but now—due to the tireless effort of my young neighbor and the dedicated police officer—I realized South Barrington truly is a caring community.

An animal lover, I have a new appreciation for the geese that hovered above both Sheba and me while we swam for our lives. I recently rescued a goose with a broken wing that I found hobbling around my backyard.

It was a small way of giving back.

❤   ❤   ❤

Sharon Florence Kissane, PhD, earned a BA in both English and Speech from De Paul University, holds a Master's Degree in Communications from Northwestern University, and received her PhD in English Education from Loyola University of Chicago. She's authored five non-fiction books, and hundreds of newspaper and magazine articles. She has been a columnist and writer for the *Daily Herald Newspaper,* Contributing Editor of the *South Barrington Life Magazine,* a business writer for the *Chicago Tribune,* as well as a technical writer and editor for Commerce Clearing House in Chicago. Kissane Communications, Limited, of Barrington is a public relations agency and specialized writing firm. Kissane holds membership with the Authors Guild and the Writer's Guild of America. Recently, she received the Executive Professional of the Year award in the Public Relations category by Swathmore Publications, and was a professional poet for the Martin Luther King Celebration at North Central College in Illinois. She lectures on graphology and gives seminars on journaling. She can be reached at Kissanecom@SBCGlobal.net.

Thank God
I Wished I Had HIV

BRANDON RUD

July 1994

I wish I had HIV.

Then I might stop all this . . .

Wait a minute. That's crazy. I don't want HIV.

That would ruin my life!

But if I had something *like* HIV, I would have a reason to *stop* smoking, partying, and doing this stupid teenager stuff.

I'm only 16.

Maybe I'll just grow out of it. Maybe I can stay in school. Why do I feel like I need a kick in the ass? Why can't I just do it myself?

Maybe I can.

I sit here in the car with my friends on our way to another party. After an entire day of smoking pot and eating junk food, I have this revelation. I feel stuck in this lifestyle that really doesn't suit me.

I want a way out.

I want *any* way out and a reason to stop.

October 1995

I have a doctor's appointment tomorrow.

I had an HIV test two weeks ago—just to be sure that I was "clean." I mean, I had sex only *once* for real—but it wasn't exactly "safe." He seemed clean. He couldn't possibly have had HIV.

I'm a little nervous about seeing the doctor because why else would he make me come in for the results? He could have just told me over the phone, "It's negative."

I'm only 17—there is no way I could be positive—I'm too young.

I only had sex once!

I'm kind of nervous.

My gut is telling me what the doctor already knows.

I have HIV.

I drive back from the doctor, gushing tears, smoking what is to be my last cigarette. Waves of pain and relief flood my body.

It's so weird.

One second I think I'm "doomed"—and will die in a few years— and the next second I know an inner peace, knowing that this is what is "supposed" to happen.

Why *is* this happening?

Is this really what I *wanted?*

Is this for *real?*

I have *no* idea how, but for some reason I know it is "right"—and that someday I will be cured.

I'm only 17 years old, and I have a huge challenge ahead of me. I have HIV. Not only that, I have just been kicked out of high school. I am stuck in West Chester, Pennsylvania—a bum-boring town where all you ever hear about HIV is that it's "Evil" and it "Kills."

At times I forget—or simply push the thoughts out of my mind.

I am reminded by the doctor visits. I am *not* sick; I just *have* this virus. It really doesn't make sense to me.

I have this terrible virus that is supposed to kill me—yet I feel fine.

It is more of a mind game than anything else.

The messages I hear about HIV on TV and in the media emphasize staying "safe" and "clean."

This makes me feel like I was "unsafe" and "dirty."

This only makes things worse. I am now the embodiment of what everyone is supposed to be avoiding. At 17 I start to believe that I am "damaged goods"—and that no one will ever want me.

Eventually I move into the city: Philadelphia, the city of brotherly love. It's lovely and helps to brighten my life. After a few years I've made lots of friends, but no one who really *knows* me—I mean knows about my HIV status. My very close friends know about me, but somehow I can't be free and open with *everyone*.

I still let this thing somehow define me and lead my existence.

I start to feel lonely.

I have plenty of friends, but finding someone to "love" feels impossible. I feel like I'm not deserving of a relationship. It's not a logical existence—just a deep emotional trap.

I don't allow myself to get close to anyone because I am so afraid of rejection—and at the same moment I yearn for a real relationship.

During these developmental years it is impossible to make sense of it all.

I feel worthless.

I feel like I want to die.

So instead of boys—I turn to school. I enter The Restaurant School where I study culinary arts and restaurant management. In part I go because I want my own restaurant, but I also need health insurance. School seems to be an obvious tool for survival.

For many years I forget about the HIV—and do whatever I want. At the same time I become much more physically active. I start to rollerblade a lot, join the gym, and work out at least three times a week. Working out becomes a way of life—and remains so to this day.

With the help of my parents, I research various alternative therapies to help fight this virus that is basically *in* me—but that has *no* real effect—so far.

If I am going to keep my immune system strong, I need to change my diet. All of a sudden I have to go from eating pizza, beer, dough-nuts, and coffee—to what? I don't even know. I start to learn about healthier ways of eating. This is a whole new world that my mom had insisted on, but as teenagers we went for the junk whenever we could. Now I am relearning everything that I was taught as a very young child. My mother's granola-grubbing lifestyle has become a source of great strength for me.

Then my dad dies. He falls out of a window 24 stories above Philly. I am 21 years old. This opens up a whole new world of hurt. The entire time my dad was alive he was on my side—he was pro-gay, pro-HIV, and pro-Dad.

I know that his charm and wit are still in effect.

I quit smoking cigarettes, cut way down on the amount of alcohol and caffeine, and try to stay away from sugar. This takes really about six years to sink in. By the time I am 23, I have figured out what foods agree with me—and what foods don't. Now out of culinary school, I start a real career in the restaurant business. I am now a "foodie" with a rich and varied background of culinary knowledge.

This is when I decide to move to California. For a long time I feel like death—and I learn that *life* can feel the same as *death*.

My dad transitioning felt like the lowest point in my life.

It is also the beginning of the climb out of this hole.

I go to LA looking for something—a new beginning. We lived in San Francisco when we were kids and I had a great kinship with the west coast.

I feel like I am home.

I am now in a place where I can build a life that will flourish, pro-vide abundance, and hopefully someday include true love.

What a strange thing HIV turned out to be.

I'm sick—but I'm *not* sick?

I have a disease—but *no* real symptoms?

What is a person supposed to think?

I don't know how things would have turned out if I had *not* had HIV—maybe I would have died in a car accident?

Who knows—maybe this little virus saved my life.

I can only be sure that it picked me for a reason.

And I am grateful for all the things I have learned because of it.

Brandon Rud is now 30 years old living in Los Angeles and running a property management company. Currently he is undergoing Ozone Therapy—and his viral load has dropped by HALF. He eats well, now, does yoga twice a week, rests, works—and plays hard, too.

Thank God
My Mother Died

DR. JEFF JENKINS

The most chaotic time in my life just kept getting more insane.

Just three weeks after asking me for a divorce—my wife was hospitalized in a coma.

I juggled caring for our children while trying to run a practice that was 100 miles away.

It seemed everywhere I turned things just kept getting worse.

I felt as if life laughed at my misery.

Of course, my story starts years before . . .

One of the most amazing things you can realize is the Universe *pushing* you toward a certain direction.

Do you know the feeling?

It appears as if everything in your environment funnels you to an unknown and inevitable dynamic. I remember seeing my life triangulating to some end—more unconsciously chosen than fateful.

How did my slippery slope begin?

How did I get through my extremely painful time?

Some say you don't know where you are going until you know where you've been. When I look back at my life, so many things make sense today that I could not explain at the time.

In 2005, before we moved from Capitola to Oakdale, California, I genuinely felt like my life was borderline perfect. After a very successful career teaching competitive basketball, I found myself married to a beautiful woman, and working in a career I loved. The difficulty of balancing multiple demands while going through chiropractic school allowed me to develop an inspiration for both hard work and helping others—traits I witnessed in my parents.

Family is extremely important to me. So I supported my wife's desire to move 100 miles away in order to live closer to her parents. I got along with my in-laws well enough, and agreed to sacrifice the drive time for my wife's well-being. I didn't know if she was going through a mid-life crisis or a more serious existential dilemma, so I committed to doing whatever my family required. Still, doing the "right" thing can feel painfully "wrong" sometimes.

Instead of helping the situation, it seemed the new living arrangement only made matters worse for my wife. Stress really seemed to punish her—especially the financial stress that ensued from a practice that I could now only run four days a week, coupled with the pressure of paying two mortgages until our home in Capitola sold.

I left early on Monday mornings and returned late on Thursday evenings.

I spent less time with my family—and less time with my patients.

Our practice suffered.

Eventually the bills, financial stress, time apart, and overall frustration led to an abscess in my wife's brain—which resulted in a coma.

I didn't have time to indulge in any self-pity, although I was killing myself trying to be "Super Husband" and "Dad." I felt consumed by attempting to keep up with my commitments to my wife and to my chiropractic practice, while financially providing for family—and maintaining some level of sanity.

Adding to the pressure, my father-in-law, who is also one of my best friends, felt I should spend *every* waking moment in the hospital.

Although he grew to resent my time away from his seriously ill daughter, I truly appreciated that *he* stayed by her side, as it allowed me the freedom to take care of my family the best way I knew how. We just did not see eye-to-eye on this issue, but honestly—how could we?

I was on a learning path triggered by the death of my mother.

When I was nine I wanted to run away from home.

I remember thinking, *No one loves me but my dog.*

After my mother and I talked, I didn't feel this way again. Even after I grew up, her love and support allowed me the space to pursue my basketball coaching, and to gain the strength to juggle chiropractic college, and life's challenging surprises. However, the greatest gift she gave me—besides her love—was the gift of her death.

Throughout my life, my mother had been my rock—my rudder. Amazingly, she continued to do so long after she died.

My beautiful mother had a generous spirit. She dedicated her life to nurturing children and their creativity. As a media personality, her 25-year career of reading to children on both radio and television impacted many. My mother was the walking embodiment of service and unconditional love. She seemed to define herself by focusing on others.

In 1995, at age 59, my mother passed away from stomach cancer. I struggled deeply those last three months watching her connected to all the tubes and monitors. I couldn't understand why someone so generous would suffer with such a disease. It depressed and confused me. I felt like I was losing my source of unconditional love.

Even then, my mother was my guiding light.

Watching her waste away in those last moments of her life taught me many things. I learned that we are all dying; therefore, we must appreciate all that life has to offer for as long as it's offered. I remember the hundreds and hundreds of people who came to my mother's funeral—clearly her giving to others had made a profound difference. I missed her dearly and felt alone—despite having married my best friend earlier that year.

Of all things, cleaning out the garage changed my life.

I came upon a book called *Love You Forever,* by Robert Munsch. My mother had given me this book years before—but I had forgotten about it.

When I opened the book—I wept.

I didn't appreciate the depth of my mother's legacy of love until I read the inscription inside this little book. My life, my mission, and all future events are forever filtered through this unconditional inscription.

Inside the cover of this treasured piece of literature, she wrote: *"To Dear Jeffrey Sean, This is just how it is . . . Love You Forever!"*

It wasn't until I read this that I really understood the nature of unconditional love.

Everything became clear—as if my mother still whispered in my ear.

Through this little love note, my mother taught me to take nothing for granted, and not to let anything send me over the edge of sanity. Through her message, her life, and the gift of her death, she actually taught me how to appreciate myself. I remember the times she looked at me with this adoring smile I could not explain. However, it wasn't until she was gone that I understood how life's challenges are necessary. One cannot truly appreciate until one has a reference for wanting—and being unable to find—something valuable. Without a doubt this lesson gave me the strength I use to manage life's challenges since that blessed day.

THANK GOD MY MOTHER DIED.

Through her death she gave me the opportunity to live a life of gratitude and service. Through the loss of my mother I gained so much. It was the love and perspective of my mother, passed down to me through a thousand looks and a little inscription, which allowed me to rebuild my life once my wife got out of the hospital. I literally learned to value "struggle," which enabled me to support my wife and repair our relationship. Undoubtedly, I'm a better parent having understood the unconditional patience parents have for their children.

In truth, the blessings of her passing go much deeper.

Losing my mom didn't result in my losing my rudder; instead I found a new one in my wife. My mother didn't really value herself financially, and the stress led to her demise. Should I be surprised my wife was re-enacting this dynamic for its invaluable and necessary lesson? My wife and my mother both taught me about valuing ourselves and the service we provide to others. I now experience my clients and appreciate my practice at a deeply spiritual level.

THANK GOD MY MOTHER DIED.

I didn't lose my connection to unconditional love, but merely found it in the eyes of my children. I understand that life does not take without giving. Dark clouds not only have a silver lining, but all "great days" have the seed of challenge.

I have fallen in love with the YIN/YANG symbol as I have fallen in love with the person in the mirror.

Life is full of opportunities and choices. We get to choose whether to judge and react or expand our awareness. We get to choose a life of service—or "do the minimum required" along a selfish agenda. We decide how long we will indulge in self-pity. Are we going to be a victim—or value ourselves today?

There is more to the picture than we see.

Through apparent "loss" and "tragedy," I am now living AND APPRECIATING a life I didn't think possible.

I am building a solid financial foundation for my family doing exactly what I love—helping others.

As I look at my beautiful advocate wife who now works with me part time, I am awestruck with gratitude.

As I watch my children getting ready for school, I feel connected to the Divinity of Family.

I now clearly understand the convergence of my life, my mother's passing, my marital and financial challenges, and my life's mission.

Everything happens for a reason.

I am eternally grateful for it all—even the "gray" days.

❤   ❤   ❤

Jeff Jenkins is a Doctor of Chiropractic, a teacher and philosopher in San Jose, California. He inspires people to find the light within every "dark," the terrific in every "terrible," the blessings in every "tragedy." By example, he emulates the principals of love and gratitude so people can love themselves and their lives at the deepest levels possible. Dr. Jenkins can be reached at Jenkins Chiropractic—The Pain Relief Clinic, 1165 S. DeAnza Blvd., Ste A, San Jose, CA 95129, phone 408-873-7154, www.jenkinschiro.com.

Thank God
Mom Had Cancer

HER HAIR IN MY HANDS

LORI DAWN

I have to go in for a biopsy."

Mom called me after her mammogram. This had become routine after each exam. As usual we all expected everything to be fine—normal.

"I have cancer."

The words rang in my head—and at the same time flew past me as if I hadn't quite heard them right. A battery of questions flooded my mind like an army brigade.

Do I dare voice the questions?

Do I remain silent knowing she has the same questions?

Of course, I tell myself, *everything will be just fine.*

This is nothing.

People come through this all the time.

Right?

I remember that moment well.

The doctor notified my mom that she had cancer on a Wednesday. By Friday she had the surgery. Divine Timing. None of her children could make it home to help with such short notice. Only her fiancé and sister were there to care for her. Divine Intervention—though I wouldn't realize it for almost a year.

Although the surgery was a success, the doctors requested she do a series of intensive-strength chemo treatments, followed by experimental radiation used in Europe.

Wait a minute.

That's going overboard if they got all the cancer.

My little knowledge of chemotherapy made me wonder why the doctors wanted to put her body, mind, and soul through all of that. At the time, I didn't know my mom's breast cancer was the most dangerous, life-threatening kind you can get. Wow. Had she waited any longer to get her mammogram—she definitely would have been gone in six months. Double wow. Miracles do happen.

Some years prior to this, life took a drastic turn for her. Her husband had an affair; her oldest sister died of leukemia.

She stopped caring about living.

It had been three years since her last mammogram. Fortunately, Joe, my mom's fiancé at the time, overrode her objections and dragged her—complaining—to the doctor. He wanted to make sure she was healthy. If Joe hadn't come into her life when he did—she'd be gone now. More evidence of God's perfect timing.

Aunt Marg willingly shared the constant responsibilities of my mom's care when Joe was farming. Not only did she make the six-hour round trip to the breast-cancer facility in Denver on numerous occasions, not including treatment time; but she was also there through the vomiting, the sleeping, even through the smell—the smell of death I called it. Through this care, Mom got to know the devotion of her future husband and confirmed the compassion of her sister. My heartfelt thanks go out to Joe and my aunt—particularly my aunt.

Mom finally experienced unconditional love.

Being a hairdresser, Aunt Marg prepared Mom for her imminent hair loss—the most frightening thing for her to face.

Mom didn't fear surgery, was fine with chemo, and thought radiation would be endurable.

The possibility of losing her hair, though, truly terrified her.

With even the mention of hair loss—she cried.

With my own 15-year career as a hairdresser I understood that hair loss is traumatic for many people. I figured, though, if there was a choice between losing your hair or losing your life, hair wouldn't be that big a deal. It just seemed ridiculous to me. After all, Aunt Marg specialized in hairpieces and wigs. She knew how to fit them and where to get them.

She would help Mom.

I dismissed Mom as being dramatic and vain.

Since finding out about my mom's cancer, I reflected on our own relationship.

For as long as I could remember, even as young as three years old, our relationship was volatile. We just clashed. Back then I saw myself as a free spirit, and saw my mom as domineering. I thought I was independent; I thought she was controlling. If she said black, I'd say white. I remember saying things to hurt her on purpose. Even as an adult, there have been many times I haven't understood her.

I tried—but to no avail.

I prayed for a relationship of love and understanding between us.

Now look where we are.

Will she make the journey across this delicate bridge of healing safely to the other side?

I pondered these things on a flight home to visit her after her second chemo treatment.

Mom told me she had lost most of her hair, so I prepared myself mentally. I remember seeing her without her wig for the first time. It didn't scare or shock me. The sparse head I saw was close to the vision I had in my mind.

Mom had very little hair left—but she wasn't completely bald.

She said she needed to scrub her scalp but couldn't bring herself to do it. I think touching her head made everything more real for her.

I offered to do it for her.

No big deal.

I'm a hairdresser. I do this for people all the time. I'd washed Mom's hair before. I did realize this time would be *different*. She hadn't been this vulnerable before. We weren't a touchy-feely family—hugs were nearly forced—so I felt a bit uneasy.

However, it was a pleasure to do something I knew would help.

I began to contemplate hair loss—*her* hair loss.

For many people hair focuses their identity. For girls, entire events are planned around their hair. Birthday parties, continuations, first communions, graduations, proms, and weddings are all important hair events. For men losing hair sometimes tests their masculinity.

A woman's self-esteem, however, can be wrapped up in one place—on top of her head. Let's face it—if a woman has a bad hair day, everyone in the house knows it. She doesn't strut her stuff like she normally would.

Hair for a woman is like the beautiful plumage of a peacock.

Like all women, my mom was no different—her hair was an adornment she wore with pride.

When she bent over the sink she commented that the water was *cold*—yet it was *warm* to *my* touch. How I had taken for granted the warmth hair provides.

I applied shampoo and gently rubbed her scalp.

I hadn't prepared for this.

Oh, my God!

Her hair came out of her scalp by the handfuls.

Now I felt shock and fear.

Instantly tears welled up in my eyes.

She asked nonchalantly, "Is it coming out?"

I fought to choke back tears that threatened to fall, steadied my hands that wanted so badly to tremble, and swallowed the lump in my throat before casually answering. "Yes."

As she talked I continued to wash her delicate head. Tears flowed down my face onto my chest. I wiped my eyes on my shoulders—not wanting her to know I was crying.

I felt I needed to be strong for her. I now understood. Losing hair suddenly became a "big deal," *real*—and the cancer became real.

I prayed, *God, please make this stop.*

At that pivotal moment our relationship forever changed.

I saw my mom for the first time.

I saw her not just as "Mom." I saw her as a person with "pain" in her heart, with vulnerabilities and aspirations. I looked deeper; I now fully understood that my mom actually loved me the entire time I was growing up. Maybe in all those difficult years she didn't do the things I needed or wanted. But I finally realized that it didn't diminish her love for me. She simply did the best she could with the tools she had.

I also realized in that moment that she could die.

Everything seemed so real and surreal. God gave me this time to look at our relationship and myself. What was my part in this? I had the divine awakening of choice.

Appreciation is a choice. I could choose appreciation at that very moment or carry anger in my spirit and body—and quite possibly develop the same monstrous cancer.

I chose appreciation.

Our relationship has been different from that moment on.

Now I see my mom through *light* instead of "darkness." When she says something I don't agree with or understand—or says something "hurtful"—I can laugh or merely let it go.

I get it now.

In this lifetime she's my mom—always has been, always will be. She doesn't mean to hurt my feelings, anymore than I'd mean to hurt my own children's feelings. She's a person alive and breathing just like me. Even though we still have differences, I now recognize the joy and beauty in our relationship.

I recognize the joy and beauty in *her.*

God doesn't make mistakes—ever.

My heart changed in that year.

I now look at all relationships differently.

I look at my dad differently.

I look at my brothers differently.

I look at my children differently.

This experience taught me to look inward to see the world around me *differently*, and to look from that place of *light*, seeing people and circumstances fresh and full of potential. This makes life better—not only for me but for everyone around me.

I no longer look to my parents to fill those crevices created in childhood. Only the spirit of God heals and fills those places.

My prayer for years used to be, *Please God, let my mom truly live before she dies.*

Thank God for answered prayer.

It was an amazing year.

That year she and I both married the loves of our lives. In addition, her granddaughter married and Mom had her first great-grandson.

She has been cancer-free for more than two years and has known an abundance of laughter and fun—more than I've ever seen before with her.

She actually found God, instead of just "playing church"—and is so much more in tune with God's spirit.

Thank God my mom had breast cancer.

It woke me up to the person I was and to the person I've become. It woke me up to deep appreciation and taught me gratitude on many levels—from being thankful for my own hair all the way to being thankful that God strategically placed this woman in my life.

Nothing happens by accident. I'm grateful for that.

Miracles still happen.

I love you, Mom!

♥　　♥　　♥

Lori Dawn is an author, creator of the *Thank God I'm Naked Tele-Seminar,* and a *Thank God I . . .* ™ Core Team member. Her commitment is to help women learn to connect *with* and be comfortable *in* their own bodies, minds, and souls. With her husband, Stan Grindstaff, she helped create their company, Hope Springs Eternal. Together they clear negative subconscious memories, trauma, and habit patterns in couples and individuals for personal renewal and self-discovery. Lori Dawn's mission is to brighten lives, inspire beauty, and encourage ALL people to live life with passion. Connect with Lori at thankgodi.com or loridawng@gmail.com.

Thank God
I Wasn't Who I Thought I Was

KJ

One morning when I was five years old, I stood warming myself in front of the living room heater.

Then—like an animal sensing an earthquake—my heart raced as I looked over my shoulder to see my father's hand flying toward me.

He slammed me against the wall behind the heater.

I collapsed to the ground.

Before a thought or a word could materialize in my head, he crept close and, in a low, fierce voice, said, "You were in my way!"

He pulled back.

The stench of morning breath and old coffee hung in the air in front of my face as I watched him walk outside to his truck—and drive away.

A few months later on a springtime afternoon my parents held a lawn party by the pond surrounding our property.

My mother stuffed me into a frilly Easter dress with matching slick-soled shoes.

Wanting to play—in spite of my outfit—I crept off and hid amongst the thick tall grass and cattails that stood guard around the edges of the water. Crouching, I gazed at my reflection on the watery brown mirror beneath me, patting the water lightly with my palms.

Suddenly I lost my footing, slammed face down, as my body slid toward the water's edge.

I clawed at the mud with my fingers in a desperate attempt to stop.

The next thing I knew my body disappeared into the water.

I thrashed about, sinking farther and farther away from the surface.

Then hands grabbed me—and yanked me from the water.

I felt a jolt as I was dropped to the ground beneath a huge tree. As I regained my focus, I saw many tear-streaked faces in the gathered crowd looking down at me. Their shrieks and sobs filled my ears, as my body wretched and I vomited pond water.

The strong hands lifted me again and threw me into my mother's arms.

She clutched me to her body as if I hadn't left her since the moment of conception.

I glanced up and saw the backside of a soaking-wet figure walking away . . .

It was my father . . .

I stared at him until he was out of sight.

I know he could have used this opportunity to be rid of me forever—but he didn't. Instead he saved me. I thought I had crossed the bridge from "rejected" to "rescued"—only to land my feet once again upon the frightening fields of my dad's internal demons.

In the years following that day at the pond I came to know that he was throwing those angry fists against his own life.

I represented something quite painful—but *what* was the mystery. In self-preservation, however, I continued a phantom-like existence for the next 13 years. I would calculate when my father would leave the house in the morning before I came to breakfast; I would eat most dinners early or in my room; I bought a mini-television and watched evening shows in my room to avoid "living room family time." It was a simple recipe for "out of sight—out of mind."

One life-changing day during my late teens I was in the kitchen preparing a sandwich.

I heard the refrigerator door open behind me.

I turned and saw my father rummaging through the drawers.

My body tensed and my heart leapt.

Fear gripped me.

Soured from not finding what he wanted, he shut the door and headed for the cookie jar on the counter. I averted my eyes and tended to my sandwich. I sensed his approach behind me. I forced myself to breathe in a rhythmically calm manner. My father began to poke me sharply in the neck with his index and middle fingers.

I didn't respond.

He then furiously stabbed his fingers into my head, neck and shoulders.

I looked for an escape.

He dashed to block the doorway. I swooped down and under his blocking arm and ran into the hall. His hand clamped down around my neck. Squeezing my throat he spun me around. I choked, kicked and clawed—trying to tear his hands away. He thrust me upwards and slammed me back against the wall—my feet no longer on the ground.

Face-to-face, spit flying, we grunted and snorted at each other.

With my last amount of strength, I threw my fist with everything I had—right into the side of his head.

Stunned, he dropped me.

I scrambled away—only to feel his hands once again around my throat as he threw me onto the dining room table.

Seconds later—seemingly from out of nowhere—my brother arrived and threw my father off me.

My dad thundered, "Make her apologize for making me angry!"

In a rage I moved towards him, shouting in a voice I didn't recognize, "The only thing I've ever been sorry for is that *you're* my father!"

I prepared for a deathly lunge from him.

Instead his face softened into a sad expression.

A guttural sob escaped his lips.

He stared at me.

I watched as in slow motion he walked out of the house.

Was that it?

Was that all it took?

Were those the magic words to make it all stop?

Relief and resentment co-mingled inside me. A desire to throw my arms around the big sad man whispered into my conscious. From despising to empathizing we were reflecting from the same mirror of pain.

That very day I left the house—and didn't return.

I walked future-forward leaving a metaphoric steaming pile of memories on that welcome mat—feeling a lifetime lighter.

But now who would I be?

Being "that" girl in "that" home was all that I knew.

In the years to follow on my journey of self-discovery I tried on various superficial suits for the façade of empowerment—a bitch, a virtuous best friend, a prude, a slut, a one-day lesbian, a recluse, and a boisterous know-it-all.

But only one thing was certain: I was spinning further out and away from the *light*.

I was a free-style puppet doing all the things I was supposed to do—going to college, getting jobs, laughing with friends, keeping a calendar full of events and lovers. It was all for easy distraction. I returned to my room every night feeling a bellowing void deep in my existence.

Only one event could bring me into the family ring again—my sister's bridal shower.

The morning I woke up in my sister's house she crept into my room with our mother's high school yearbook in her hands.

Her fiancé had told her that he had had a random conversation with a man he met at a work meeting.

"Then he asked about you."

"What? Who? What are you talking about?" I asked.

"Listen. This guy at work asked all sorts of questions about our lives. Then he asked about you. He knew where you lived. Then he said how it breaks his heart to know how Dad treated you all those years." My sister said that the man continued with precise information.

She opened the book to a marked page—a page that had my reflection staring back at me. My bones went cold and my eyes filled with tears for a moment. There before me was a photo of a boy from the past who had been unknowingly setting up my future.

My sister explained how she wasted no time in phoning my mother to ask her if she knew this gentleman.

"Mom sharply replied, 'Never mention that man's name again!' And then she hung up on me."

My sister and I simply stared at each other as the possible truth slowly sank in. I needed more than the choppy bits of this story—so I decided to go to the source.

At the Wedding Dream Central Bridal Shower, I focused only on Mom's head, wondering what exactly filled it. After the event I asked her to walk me to my car. In the midst of her goodbye I interrupted with, "Mom, have you ever slept with another man while you were married to Dad?"

Awestruck and gasping, she wheezed out, "I wouldn't do such a thing!"

But I insisted and persisted—until words broke away from her lips and formed the sentence, "Well only once—but it didn't even really happen. He was too drunk."

I broke her trance by shouting, "Mom! Something happened!"

As I pointed to my face, we both stood staring at the unveiling of a secret bundled in lies for 26 years. I reached for her and told her I loved her, but the moment was too awkward for my mother to accept it. We agreed to speak later and she returned to the party.

On my drive home I felt more connected to my life than ever. I could honor and love my mother and father from a place deep inside. I was free from the thoughts that I had done something to deserve the abuse. I could solidify the reality that all those years of abuse really had nothing to do with me.

A profound healing arose as I realized that in every moment everything is exactly as it should be in its divine order. My awareness awakened to the course of the life I was given. It presented situations to look at and to listen to—and I did. I didn't take anything as a coincidence.

I am thankful for those brought into my life as tour guides on this most incredible journey—the journey within myself.

Now coming from a place of gratitude I revel in my savory experiences.

My journey inspired me to create a loving space within my life where people on the path of gratitude can connect. I've met many magical souls who have danced and shared with me.

I'm inspired by visions of gratitude gathering into dominant widespread consciousness—especially in the area of love and family. I've created a way for people to come together who already practice these principles. Knowing that I can believe in myself—and that I am ultimately all the family I need—frees me to be intimately involved only with those souls I choose to have in my life.

That abyss—which was laid in my heart and in my hands—
was the compass I came to embrace.
It led my life on adventures
following an emotional and spiritual map of treasures.

~ KJ ~

KJ walks a path of gratitude spiritually and socially, and enjoys being a facilitator with the *Thank God I . . .* ™ Community.

Join the *Thank God I . . .* ™ Community online to share your story and chat with the authors at **www.thankgodi.com**

Thank God
Suicide Didn't Send My Son to Hell

REVERAND ALIAH MAJON, PhD

*A*s I sit to write this story of healing and empowerment, the first things that come to my mind are the same thoughts I have held in my heart and soul for as long as I can remember:

What's good about death?

Why does death exist?

What don't we know?

As human beings we face death and all that it brings everyday; yet the reality of death is very much like the saying regarding "an elephant in the room"—it's there, but no one wants to talk about it or open its doors to see where it takes us. Instead, we passively wait—almost in secret—for what many of us consider the "awful" reality of death. For the large majority of people in our society, death simply arrives. We're left to *react* to it—while we do everything that we can to *manage* all of its unpleasantness. We know that it exists, but we don't care to examine or embrace it—even when we are in the midst of its circumstance.

We grieve.

We hope to get over "our loss."

And we wait for the passage of time—at least until the next death comes along—and it will come.

I didn't have that luxury when my son's death happened to me. I knew that I had to do something.

My only child, my son Sean, committed suicide on July 2, 1994.

The news was delivered by phone, spoken as half inquiry and half notification by a police officer—a stranger.

In that moment, my world stopped—then I involuntarily shifted into slow motion, as if the news with the power of a cyclone had turned my senses up to maximum alert.

In the next moment the "blare" of my feelings became so loud that I could barely hear myself think.

"What?" I heard my voice say, as if it was disconnected from me and coming from a loud foghorn far away. He was only 24 years old and had just had his new baby daughter six months before. In a state of screaming numbness I became silent—and absently turned to look out the window of my skyscraper hotel where I saw a wisp of a cloud slowly drift by.

How could I not know that Sean was in danger?

Why didn't I feel that something was wrong?

How could this happen to my son with all that I know spiritually?

When Sean died, I had diligently been practicing spiritual principles and walking my spiritual path with an enormous inspiration—both studying and teaching for about 18 years.

If anyone on this planet was "tapped in" to a Higher Power and in touch with the Universe—it was *me*. After all, I hadn't merely explored the reality of "Spirit" and read a few enlightening books—I'd given my life *completely over* to what I called Divinity. I had been transformed again and again—and had been taken higher and higher with every new "awakening" upon my quest.

My story of spiritual illumination might be considered amazing because the way I started out in life was very different. When I speak in public, now, I often astonish people by reporting that I was a high school dropout, a teenage mother, the wife of a drug dealer, and a wayward girl. Spirituality became my most trusted friend. I had been changed by it, and I was blessed, protected, aware, over-lighted . . .

So how could MY son have killed himself?

Definitely a burning question.

But—even more than that fiery inquiry—something burned considerably hotter. I almost didn't believe that my mind was going to Christian beliefs I'd been exposed to in my childhood.

I knew the real truth about life now.

Didn't I?

Like a goblin from my past I found myself wondering, worrying, and even terrified: *Is it possible that my son will go to what people call "hell" because he had committed suicide?*

Is there even a slim chance that my son will suffer damnation—like the people who go to church talk about?

I was like a protective mother lioness whose precious cub had been threatened—I had to do something. I had to make sure that my son didn't suffer this unacceptable fate.

And it did NOT matter that I didn't know what to do.

I would find a way.

This was my son—and I so loved him.

I have come to the most important part of this story—the *Thank God I Worried That My Son's Suicide Would Send Him to Hell* part—and I imagine that all of you, my beloved readers, are curious about what I will say about such a reason for gratitude.

Here is my message . . .

Every transformation teaching that I've encountered speaks about developing your "inner strength" (your soul force), and cultivating a genuine relationship with your Higher Power (God). I invite you to take this information to heart, assimilate it, and on a daily basis diligently do the following:

- Practice *meditation*—and ask via heartfelt prayers to be enlightened.

- Look deeply at your core beliefs and fears—and seek to "master" them.
- Learn to discern your own higher feelings—and listen to your *inner guidance*.
- Avail yourself of advanced teachings—and actually "apply" the sage wisdom.
- Make sure that you are exposed to *illumined teachers* and their energy.
- Explore *diverse* traditions—and embrace what specifically speaks to you.
- Make a "commitment" to honor God, life, yourself, and others at all times.

To make myself absolutely clear this is what I wish to say: When Sean died I had already *LEARNED TO LIVE MY LIFE PREPARED*.

It's like living in California and knowing how to be prepared for earthquakes; or living in the Midwest and being thoroughly informed about what to do when there is a tornado; or living in an area where there are hurricanes and floods, and being trained to act the moment the call comes to respond . . . There is nothing like it. Nothing. I found myself both girded and "guided" by my God-connection and the powerful support of my Soul and Spirit, as I faced the seeming "tragedy" and tremendous emotional blow of my son's death.

And I knew that I was blessed.

But what mattered even more than that was when I experienced the enormous and gargantuan "worry" that Sean might end up dammed and be in some kind of "hell."

I was already *SPIRITUALLY CONDITIONED* to figure out how to proceed.

When I arrived at the apartment that had been Sean's home, I built an altar and began praying for his transition to be good and for him to have Divine support on his way. I drew upon both my inward and outward intention and meditated for long periods. I made it a point to listen for inner guidance. The altar was simple—only being made up of a candle, a pair of Sean's shorts, my crystal, and some family photographs. But the channel created was made very strong from my prayers, my years of spiritual practice, and all of my love.

This time of prayerful focus was not in vain. At first I felt the presence of Sean's energy—and then I became aware of our exchange on an intuitive level. I was now sure that I could hear his voice saying that he was okay—and that he could hear me speaking to him. I asked him telepathically if he had seen the *light*—and when I experienced his answer of "Yes," I encouraged him further to look for the HIGHEST light, and to get clear in his heart of hearts that the light of God was what he desired.

I held a prayer vigil the whole night that he would move easily and deeply into still more light, and that he would not have to encounter the shadows of regret and guilt, and/or suffer with the longing for what was no longer possible.

I fully understood that I was moving beyond an earth-based frame of reference, and that I was accessing some form of the Soul's values and intelligence, but this all felt very natural. In fact it was not weird in any way—our exchange was just simple, deliberate and focused, and extremely profound, like a conversation unfolding from Soul to Soul.

Sean assured me that "suicide"—like all earth experiences—is a way to *LEARN TO DO BETTER*, and that he was being supported by Angel Teachers to learn his lessons. And—most importantly—that he was not in hell.

My . . . was I inspired to hear *that*—and my mother's heart rejoiced . . . *Thank God I learned that hell ONLY exists when people refuse to learn, and do not care to do better—and even those "hells" are temporary.*

The next day, we began looking together at why he had made the choice to end his life. I determined to support him as he uncovered the *SPECIFIC* lesson that he had created for himself.

He saw it right away—his earth self had been convinced that he was in life all alone, and he had believed that he must do everything all by himself without help or grace or the divine support that other people talked about. And even more specifically that God had deserted him and that his life was hopeless—and would stay hopeless forever—so there was no use and no way out. In other words, he had felt disconnected from the goodness in life and was unaware of any blessings or possibilities. He therefore had no trust in anything—including God. He saw, and so did I, that to him his dying was a way of confirming what he had felt already about his reality—that he was dead.

Yes, my son died from earth's experiences, but I knew that he was in another place where his existence would continue. I thank God that I can envision my son restored to his full mastery and see him with my Soul's sight, reclaiming the beauty and power that he really is—not just in death—but also in life.

Teaching about the truth of existence is my work—to assist others to reclaim their mastery and beauty as well, and to promote *evolution*, and to help expand *TRUTH* to every corner of the universe. I am satisfied and inspired.

Thank God.

I still cry my cries and have my mother-lost-her-child moments, but I have them in inner peace—a transcendent inner peace—because I truly know . . .

Once more, "Thank God!"

❤   ❤   ❤

A product of inner city Detroit, Reverand Aliah MaJon, PhD, DD, is the founder of the *International Association for Spiritual Coaching*® *(IASC)*, created to realize her lifelong goal of "bringing spirituality into the mainstream." Her work ranges from an "unadulterated" spiritual methodology—known as *SOUL TECHNOLOGY*™—to a quietly revolutionary system called *Full-SELF*™—developed for the corporate sector. Both approaches experientially explore how human potential results in life mastery. Aliah offers transpersonal courses, and regularly conducts specialized training, and experiential learning opportunities on the two topics of self-mastery and "grief recovery." She has a PhD in Metapsychology, and holds a Doctor of Divinity in the Science of the Soul. Aliah offers a downloadable handbook and audio program of more than 50 exercises, entitled, *SOUL TECHNOLOGY*™ *Book I, From Grief . . . To Growth*™ (www.fromgrieftogrowth.com), which has come to be known as "coaching-in-a-box" and which outlines a seven-step roadmap to healing. Also, please visit her at www.joiniasc.org. E-mail: aliah@joiniasc.org.

Thank God
I Went to Prison

Noah McKay, MD

Some children are born with a calling.

Though I didn't recognize it at the time, the hand of God had been at work in my life from my earliest days, shaping my interests and experiences in ways that were preparing me for a destiny I couldn't have imagined. Most children are curious about the human body—I was obsessed. I wanted to understand it—what it is, how it works, and why sometimes it doesn't. Most of all I wanted to know how to fix it when the healing process that we so often take for granted—broke down.

I studied.

I observed.

I experimented.

Much to my mother's chagrin, I fished chicken hearts out of the stew and dissected them at the kitchen table.

I patched injured friends back together on the playground.

I promised my older brother that I would one day invent a machine that would cure every disease in the world. He laughed and told me I would forget to plug it in . . .

Undeterred, I doggedly pursued my dream of becoming a doctor through high school science competitions, through rigorous pre-med courses at Tufts University, and through med school itself. I honed my skills, working brutally long nights in ERs in the Bronx—one of the bloodiest war zones in America.

It was dangerous and exhausting—but it was great training.

In 1983 my hopes, dreams, hard work, and stubborn persistence paid off the day I received my diploma from the Albert Einstein College of Medicine—*that* day I became a doctor.

The celebration didn't last long.

Young, idealistic, and determined to help my patients, I began a rigorous dual internship in surgery and internal medicine with stars in my eyes and a fierce determination to bring healing to the world. It didn't take long to realize that modern medicine was in as much trouble as its patients. Doctors and patients alike spent long, stressful days in windowless rooms, deprived of fresh air and sunlight.

It was as if the building itself had been designed to make people sick.

Hospital nutrition was anything but nutritious—and it was barely palatable.

The routine administration of antibiotics and sterilizing agents was breeding a deadly new class of pathogens—super bugs—whose appearance on the scene called for even stronger measures of control, which in turn bred even more virulent strains.

I completed my internship and entered private practice armed with a clear understanding of how medicine "should not" be done. At first my ideas didn't carry much weight with the senior physicians in the clinic, but in time they listened and eventually made me a partner in the practice. Life slipped into a gentle routine. I got up, went to work, cared for my patients, came home to my beautiful bride, got up the next morning and repeated the cycle.

The morning of September 21, 1989, began much like any other with the clamor of my alarm clock signaling the start of another busy day.

But this day something was different.

When I reached out to silence the noise—nothing happened.

I couldn't move a muscle.

The attempt to move my arm left me gasping for breath—and the sound of the alarm was slowly drowned out by a deafeningly loud thumping sound coming from inside my chest.

I lay frozen in bed—utterly helpless—my mind racing in a thousand directions at once. Something was seriously wrong—but what?

The only thing clear to me about my situation was the fact that I was in desperate need of help.

With a Herculean act of will I reached for the phone and arranged an emergency visit with a cardiologist.

I arrived at the hospital and began the usual gauntlet of tests. The results brought bad news: an unknown viral infection had caused extensive damage to the muscles of my heart—and left them too weak to function.

I was in acute congestive heart failure.

The cardiologist and I both knew that the chances of full recovery in a 33-year-old male—diagnosed with acute viral cardiomyopathy— are extremely low. My life expectancy plummeted to just 24 months.

I was filled with despair but refused to give up.

I lay in bed tethered to an oxygen tank, reading, learning, and grasping at any straw of hope offered by new discoveries in the field of quantum physics. As the weeks passed I began to feel a deep, instinctive craving for sunlight. I wanted to spend whatever time I had left relaxing on a beach.

So with the help of my wife we traveled to Mexico.

Soon after I arrived in Mazatlán I had a chance encounter with a yogi who had, himself, recovered from a terminal illness.

He shook off my grim prognosis, taught me a simple breathing technique called the "Breath of Fire," and challenged me to put into practice the hopeful theories I had been reading about in the physics books.

I tried his advice—and within a few days was healthy enough to swim in the ocean unassisted.

Within a few months I had recovered and returned to work as a practicing physician.

Inspired by my own "impossible" recovery, I began investigating healing modalities that had previously been dismissed by conventional medicine as "unscientific." I incorporated the best of these into my medical practice, and in doing so developed a new integrated model of healthcare that united dozens of practice modalities under one roof. This proved to be a highly successful and affordable healthcare model and patients loved it.

Before long, my little neighborhood clinics had become the largest integrated health care practice in U.S. history. At its peak the practice logged over 90,000 patient visits a year, with 150 healthcare professionals including MDs, acupuncturists, nutritionists, homeopaths, herbalists, chiropractors, naturopaths, massage therapists, hypnotherapists, biofeedback practitioners, and more all working together for the benefit of grateful patients.

We began offering a managed care plan that matched the hospitalization coverage provided by standard insurance policies, and also covered the full range of conventional and alternative therapies offered at the clinics. Our emphasis on proactive care and the integration of simple, low-cost treatment strategies kept our patients healthier—and that meant lower costs. We were able to offer our comprehensive managed care plan for just $115 per month—roughly one-third the cost of policies typically offered by major insurance companies.

Things were going so well that we decided to take our new healthcare model nationwide. But our plans were interrupted when the FBI turned up at my doorstep late one night. Their arrival marked the beginning of a devastating legal battle that would consume everything I had worked so long and hard to build.

Major insurance companies—with whom we were now in direct competition—had leveled accusations of fraud against the clinics.

Determined to prove my innocence, I took and passed a lie detector test.

But innocent or not—legal fees continued to mount. We could do little but watch in numb disbelief while lawyers wrangled behind closed doors—and everything we worked 20 long years to build crumbled around us.

One by one the clinics closed, leaving 150 doctors and staff members unemployed—and 30,000 active patients without access to their doctors.

When everything was gone, we had no choice but to declare personal and corporate bankruptcy.

Panic attacks, anxiety, deep depression, and poverty became a way of life.

After four exhausting years, my wife pointed out that even prison would be better than what we were going through—and she was right. She urged me to accept a plea bargain agreement with the U.S. Department of Justice.

Four years of unremitting stress had already taken a horrific toll on my health. I also had to admit that no matter how much I wanted to continue the fight, we had nothing left with which to fight. If we fought on without resources and lost in court, I could be facing as many as 10 years in prison, and our two small children would grow up without a father.

I consented to the plea bargain and began serving my 35-month sentence in a federal prison camp.

It was a difficult time.

Not long after my arrival, a veteran inmate who'd just heard my story looked me in the eye and said, "Doc, you're not going to survive in here with that much anger."

Although I didn't see the man again, something in his words rang true.

I was angry—and justifiably so—but I decided that day just to let it go.

A profound sense of freedom swept through my soul. For the first time, I truly understood the Buddha's teaching about "detachment." I had lost "everything"—and yet I was perfectly *content*.

From that day forward things changed. Colors were brighter. Food tasted better. Despite my prison surroundings, daily life took on a richness that remains with me to this day.

A few months later, one of my attorneys came to see me. "Doc, I just wanted to let you know that you've won."

I didn't feel much like a winner sitting there in a prison uniform, but when he finished his story I knew that he was right—in some small way *I had won*. Patients outraged by our situation had joined in a class action suit against Washington State Insurance Companies for denial of services. Several insurers paid in excess of $30 million for failure to provide coverage for complementary and alternative medical care—the kind of care I'd been sent to prison for providing.

This costly lesson ensured that hundreds of thousands of patients would have access to the kind of integrated health care I believed in.

In ways we could not have imagined, we changed the face of healthcare.

I was released from prison after 13 months.

By the time I left I understood why my heroes—men like Gandhi, King, and Mandela—had all spent time there.

"Suffering—whether in a hospital room or a prison cell—allows us to confront fears and overcome them, to find within ourselves the courage and heroism to become an inspiration to ourselves and others."

The calling of my childhood remains strong.

I am a doctor at heart.

Since my release I have traveled to more than a dozen countries helping people overcome the challenges in their lives, and laying the foundation for a new kind of healthcare.

The future looks bright.

I love you,

Dr. Noah.

❤   ❤   ❤

Dr. Noah McKay graduated Magna Cum Laude from Tufts University with a Bachelor of Science in Biology, and in 1983 was awarded his Doctorate Degree in Medicine at the Albert Einstein College of Medicine in New York. Lessons gleaned during his own "impossible" recovery from heart failure at age 33 revolutionized his understanding of medicine and helped him establish the largest private integrative medical practice in the state of Washington. He spent a year in federal prison as a result of his pioneering efforts to expand patient care options, but his efforts changed the face of healthcare. Since his release, Dr. Noah's inspired approach to practical quantum healing has touched hearts on every continent and helped thousands of individuals access the infinite healing potential hidden within their own cells. To preview his book online, *Wellness at Warp Speed,* and to learn more about the international Q Health Retreats program, visit www.wellnessatwarpspeed.com or www.QHealthRetreats.com.

Thank God
I Was Raised in Chaos

AARON KLEINERMAN

For many years I searched for reason and understanding to the confusions and tragedies of my past. My mind swirled with memories—some resonating with truth, and others living in a frenzy of haze and confusion. I was once filled with illusions of trouble, chaos, dysfunction, alcoholism, drug addiction, and abuse.

Were these memories real?

As a young boy—compared to the rest of my friends—I felt *life* was a bit "different" for me, as I was the one Jewish kid in school—even though I didn't know what Judaism meant. I was the "boy" who was made fun of as I walked about with a "naked vulnerability." I was the boy referred to as "shady," as I spent my high school years in the low-income project community of an extremely well-to-do suburbia town outside of Boston.

Besides these conflicts, I have memories of an inspirational and well-respected father organizing the youth basketball league. My siblings were both graduating at the top of their classes and going on to academically astounding universities. My mother owned and operated her own private law practice.

From the outside world, life appeared to be "cake and cookies"—but it was *within* my internal walls that massive turmoil and bewilderment stirred deeply inside me.

I recall my mom spending countless nights "studying" at the library, but upon investigating with my delirious and confused father—not finding her there.

I recall my father heavily drinking himself into tears, trying to find reason for my mother's unfaithfulness, and my young 10-year-old self simply trying to figure out why . . .

Upon completing fifth grade, my childhood struggles escalated. My parents were evicted from our pleasant and "peaceful" home, and the divorce of my parents stung me like a hive of bees. I remember being an 11-year-old sitting on the front lawn of our home—as the movers started to tear everything away . . .

I recall the confusion of these adolescent years, and the turmoil of moving from one place to the next for many years.

I recall my mother being forced to collect food stamps on welfare because she surrendered her right to practice law—due to allegations of embezzlement. For me as a child, buying food at the grocery store with food stamps was both vulnerably tragic and honorable.

I recall my middle-school friends asking why my mother's name had been in the newspaper for "bad" news.

I recall my father sleeping out of his car, working three jobs, trying to stay fed.

I recall observing bruises over my mother's body—and wondering in shock at the cause of such pain.

I recall my parents losing their income to my father's gambling—and to my mother's bankruptcy.

How does a growing, maturing child become thankful for all these challenges and struggles through life? For as I share these intimate family truths, my heart and body have tears of gratitude flowing for both parents.

My initial feat was attempting to understand why my life was so "messed up." I prayed countless nights through all this turmoil—just asking God for a "normal" family. At the age of 14—when my siblings were off at colleges, and my father was living out of his car—I stepped forward and discovered a new path away from the pain.

In a three-hour father-son trip to New Hampshire, I was presented with a situation that once again left me in confusion. My father had a gambling habit—and yet in this short trip, I received inner guidance and wisdom to ask him the "right" questions to *eliminate* his lifelong gambling addiction.

I had no conscious understanding of what I was doing or how I was doing it. I was simply listening to divine guidance—a skill that I later learned had immense benefits.

I began to see life from a different perspective.

I came to appreciate the "faults" of my parents, and really started to see the other side of the experiences I had previously viewed as negative.

My new relationship with my dad was one where he supported and counseled me—and I did the same for him. I no longer judged him as an "inferior" or "bad" father. I simply recognized and appreciated both his strengths and weaknesses. His girlfriend at the time told me I had a natural gift for persuasion and counseling—even though I was still unsure . . .

However, by no means did I then become a "saint," for it was only a few months later I learned the pleasures and pains of having young teenage sex. I loved the pleasure, but I was continually filled with the pains of "almost" impregnating women—along with normal teenage emotional bewilderment.

I began drinking heavily with my young friends, and started to become a recluse with both alcohol and marijuana.

This careless and complacent behavior continued for the rest of my high school years. There were many nights spent getting blacked-out drunk—and waking up in strange places. I had experiences of almost getting charged with grand theft larceny, but connived my way out of them. To the outside world I was an "A" student who was a "star" on the soccer field. So while I was promiscuously sleeping with many women, smoking pot and drinking heavily, I was getting excellent grades, awards, and winning championships on the soccer field.

I was following the same paradigm I grew up in.

I was living in the precarious balance between chaos and order.

I was on the roller coaster of highs and lows—just waiting to sink to the bottom . . .

During my senior year at high school, I came to realize how thankful I was for all this seemingly negative behavior. An opportunity was placed before me to attend the United States Merchant Marine Academy—or one of the many top level soccer and academic Division One programs out of the New England area. Since my life at that point was basically living in my own apartment—with the accompaniment of my best friend in our own "bachelor pad"—I knew there was a "different" route than just college. So I listened to the inner voice and made the decision to attend the Service Academy.

When I weighed the pros and cons of the Academy, and realized the potential to live free from the "corporate world" after graduation, I took a plunge that forever changed my perspective on life.

For the next four years I wore a Navy uniform and saluted my superiors. I found myself on board a military pre-positioning ship in the pre-Iraqi war—wondering how in the world I ended up there. It was difficult to find gratitude when I was alone in the middle of the ocean, wondering when I would return to a "normal" life. However, the miraculous "writing voice" of my future displayed itself . . .

Alone I sit
Away from the world
Searching for my path
Trying to speak with the God who has led me to this moment
Allowing me to surface these thoughts . . .
Which way will she lead me now?
I am open for change
My bags are packed

My car is ready
Is he willing to show me the way?
Or must I be willing to listen some more?
Sometimes the "muck" is just too much on the surface . . .
And it's hard to let myself go free

This "writing voice" from within my soul began to ask AND answer so many of the confusing questions of my childhood. I asked for understanding—and this inner voice began to speak its wisdom and share the other half of the "traumatic" situations of my childhood.

And as time progressed through the Academy, I found myself enduring a summer as a Drill Instructor. Once again my careless, complacent, confused, and drunk behavior created this situation. But once again my spirit led me PERFECTLY, for it was within those shoes where I learned some of my most powerful lessons as a leader.

Upon graduating from the Academy, my journey led me to a worldwide ride of both "highs" and "lows." As I was backpacking across the far stretches of Eastern Europe and South-East Asia—searching for that place of "order"—I was again drinking myself unconscious in my international travels.

A few years later, after navigating and backpacking the world, I once again had a moment of inspiration. I walked into a seafarers' Union Hall in Boston, after completing a four-month cruise-liner job in Hawaii. I had just upgraded my license and tentatively signed up for a new Second Mate job on board a ship in Africa. I was ready to take the job—until the following morning when I woke up and my body and soul would not let me finish the paperwork. I was presented with a decision: I could either travel—and continue as a recluse—or immerse myself deeply in the highest levels of personal development and human consciousness in Los Angeles. I listened to that same inner voice that had guided me as a child—and I took action. This prudent and wise choice led me to the warm waters of Southern California—instead of to the streets of Kenya and Israel.

My spirit made my decision, knowing that I would travel again in the future but with a more meaningful mission.

After just a few weeks in Los Angeles, the *Thank God I . . .* ™ Book Series and Community landed in my lap.

Over time I realized I had found my purpose.

I would dedicate my life to teaching and awakening the true genius that resides inside every human.

Through further education and studying with some of the greatest minds in human development, I came to realize that there would not be a time where "darkness" does not exist *equally in balance* with the "light." I came to comprehend the dynamic *equilibrium of complementary opposites* that exist inside every moment of my life. Within this understanding I developed a powerful transformational vision for humanity and myself.

In retrospect, it was through some of my greatest internal struggles as a child that I learned to love and see within myself all the characteristics of my parents—both the "good" and the "bad." I realized that when I judged them for these challenging experiences, I was not honoring the immense blessings that these situations were offering for my personal growth. Through space and time, I learned to love, honor, and appreciate *all* of their characteristics—for they served as a mirror, helping me "own" every part of my own consciousness.

Once I found love for both my parents, I let go of the vices that had been holding me back.

I *equilibrated* my past emotional charges and activated the true wisdom that was residing deep within my soul.

I now stand up across the world sharing my natural genius, inspiring the divine love that rests within each of us—for that is the purpose activated inside of me.

❤   ❤   ❤

Aaron Kleinerman is a speaker and transformational educator for all ages. He has walked in many shoes—and has seen life from many angles. Aaron captivates his audiences with his heart-warming and soul-quenching stories of both joy and personal struggle. Just like you, Aaron dances daily on the line between chaos and order, challenge and support. He speaks his powerful messages of love and wisdom all over the globe, teaching people to see the perfection in every situation. He releases the unconditional gratitude inside us all, bringing every individual to recognize that absolute love resides "inside." He is a Core Developer and teacher within the *Thank God I . . .* ™ Community. You can find and interact with Aaron at www.AaronKleinerman.com.

Thank God
I Am a Little Person

PEGGY O'NEILL

I'm not sure exactly when it was—the day, the weather, if I was wearing my brown plaid Catholic school uniform, or who I might have been talking to—but somewhere in the middle of fourth grade I had my first really big *aha!*

That day I had the alarming recognition that being a *little person* was not a Halloween costume; it was not a temporary situation; there would not be a day when I would be *like* the other kids, be *like* my family members, or blend in and be *like* everyone else.

No.

For my lifetime I would be a "little" person.

This was a big surprise to me.

I couldn't imagine why I deserved it, and I certainly couldn't accept that I would have to go through this for the rest of my life.

Being a little person isn't easy.

We endure innumerable difficulties.

Physically, for most of us little people, it's a challenge every time we go to wash our hands, flick on a light switch, or get a plate out of a cupboard—not to mention walking my 40-pound dog Keesha!

Yes, indeed, mingling with a standing crowd, shopping for groceries, lifting a suitcase, and preparing a meal all carry challenges.

And the emotional challenges?

They're even worse.

As a kid I was teased and called many nasty names.

As I walked by, kids belted out—without an ounce of reservation—"Midget, midget, midget," as if chiseling their supremacy in stone.

As a teenager and young adult I wasn't asked out on dates.

From the sidelines I watched others "sparkling" from the thrills of "romance"—desperately longing for my chance at being the "special one."

And as a fresh college graduate, potential bosses invariably saw my height before my talent.

Unrequited love, however, became my mother ship of anguish, the pain I could not bear. During my 20s and 30s I tried again and again . . . and again . . . with men both my *own* size—and the much larger "average" size—to create a lasting love connection.

But to no avail.

Each failure pulled me farther into the whirlpool of despair. By my mid-30s, everything inside of me had gone "dark"—despite the fact that "paradise" surrounded me on a gorgeous fruit and flower farm in Kona, Hawaii.

When I'd wake up in the morning I despised the light; I hated getting out of bed, and I loathed having to face another day.

I just wanted out.

Life had become too painful.

One night gazing at the silhouetted palm trees outside my window, I lay in bed sobbing—not an unusual occurrence at that time in my life.

But this night something unusual happened.

From the quiet deep inside me arose a prayer. During that period, prayer was not part of my daily practice. I had been meditating since my mid-teens, but conversing directly with God was not part of the program.

This night, however, I said, *God I need help. I know fulfillment is possible. So, please either take away this pain by letting me go unconscious and die—or send me someone wise who can help me make whole my shattered heart.*

A few months later I moved to Boulder, Colorado, to join an in-depth program for personal and spiritual growth.

I sensed the founder to be a man of profound wisdom, possessing a potent loving presence. I also recognized that his teaching offered real help, perhaps with enough power to blast through the six feet of cement I had built around my wounded heart.

Several months into that work I came upon my next big *aha!* That rainy Tuesday morning, sitting in the refuge of a private session, my teacher pointed something out to me that took me by surprise. He said, "It seems, Peggy, you are totally invested in a fantasy. A fantasy that one day you will wake up, get out of bed, and stand five-and-a-half-feet tall. And of course then all your problems will be gone."

Compassionately, yet sternly, he continued, "I bet your success level would be much higher if—instead of trying to change what you *cannot* change: your body size—you focus on changing what you *can* change, things like your identity, beliefs, attitude, choices and connection to spirit."

It startled me to see I still held onto that early childhood hope.

Like the serenity prayer, I had to accept what I could NOT change. That was my first step.

Appreciate what IS—period.

The next big moment of awakening came a few years later with the Fischer Hoffman process, which focuses on healing the wounds of childhood.

One significant Friday night I was presented with a stack of pillows, a bat, and an invitation to "let 'er rip!" and allow myself to feel and authentically express my pent-up anger, rage, hurt, and frustration.

I can't tell you how utterly stupid that seemed.

But after testing it out, it surprised me that it was actually liberating and exhilarating. My focus that evening: the "hurt" from not being treated as a whole human being. After about 45 minutes of hitting and yelling I got tired.

So I lay back on my pillows to rest.

When I closed my eyes I saw something inside my heart that changed my life.

I saw a diamond.

This was no ordinary diamond like the one you'd wear on your finger.

This diamond was huge.

Bigger than my entire body.

Brilliant, golden light streamed out in every direction from its center like the sun itself. Every facet glistened in rainbow colors.

Oh my! I see now, my inner voice exclaimed. *I really am this stellar beauty.*

I could barely contain the magnificence of my True Self.

My seams were bursting.

Wise people say *the truth will set you free.* Well this was my moment. The truth of my divine splendor blew the barn doors off my previously coveted conviction that I was broken, flawed, and somehow less than others.

In that moment I was free.

Yippee!

From that extraordinary awakening, I recognized what can come from simply appreciating what is, appreciating what's really going on inside (or outside) me—whether I like it or not.

I began to trust my feelings more and more—even the difficult ones—and made time to sit and just be present with them. As I practiced this, without fail my ugly emotions and dramas transformed into things of beauty and value. Hurt transfixed into compassion; hopelessness turned into strength; and confusion swirled into clarity.

And my fears?

When I've really been able to walk through the place of dread and terror inside—many times with the help of another who's been there before—invariably I come to a sense of deep unbounded inner peace and connection to everything and everyone.

My favorite inner journey, however, is when I muster enough courage to face my deep loneliness.

Somehow, miraculously, that awful place morphs, and who I am is clearly no longer an empty, painful shell, but a giant wave in the Ocean of Love. In each of these holy glimpses of my true, divine nature, I get a bit more clarity on what Wayne Dyer might be talking about: "We are not human beings having a spiritual experience. We are spiritual beings having a human experience."

My journey of healing and growth has continued.

Now—things are different.

In the morning when I awaken I'm thrilled. Thrilled that my beloved, my sweet, kind, devoted, and handsome husband lies there next to me. Thrilled that each day brings ample opportunities to contribute significantly to others through my work as a speaker, author, and coach. Thrilled that it only takes a breath to bring me home—to center, to inner peace, to my connection with God and all that is.

It turns out that being a little person has not been such a bad "gig" after all.

Imagine that!

Once tormented by the story I told myself—that it shouldn't be happening—I now find my perspective significantly shifted.

Now all I see is a life of countless blessings.

Along the way, appreciation has been the key. Appreciation of what is; appreciation of what I like; and appreciation of what I may *not* like—my body size, limitations, uncomfortable emotions, difficult relationships, injustice, cruelty, and war.

There's a lot I do *not* like.

But now I recognize that from deepening appreciation blossoms expanding inner peace and gratitude. Now I'm grateful for the opportunity to have grappled with my identity, as it opened to me the truth about who I am—not a body, personality, or biography—but something so awesome that words can't begin to touch it. I'm grateful for struggling with *not* getting what I wanted, as *my resultant surrender has brought inner peace and healing* to my heart, health, relationships, and connection to God.

I'm deeply grateful for my teachers.

Most of all I'm grateful for the grace and richness in each moment—which is my greatest wealth.

All I can I say now is, "Thank God. Thank God . . . I am a *little* person."

❤   ❤   ❤

Peggy O'Neill has been on the front lines of self-transformation. Peggy helps others transform through her work as a psychotherapist; an expert who speaks; an author; and a featured teacher in the movie, *The Opus*. She talks to kids in schools about honoring differences in others and celebrating their own uniqueness. She trains people in business to open their hearts and minds to one another, to contribute from their innate greatness, and to communicate in a way that generates harmony and genuine connection. She coaches people individually to break free from whatever holds them back, and facilitates healing from deep emotional wounds. Peggy also inspires people with disabilities—in fact, people of all ages and from all walks of life—to triumph over whatever challenges they might encounter, to unveil their inherent magnificence, and to walk tall. To get more support from Peggy's books, learning resources, and speaking services—visit: www.yopeggy.com or call toll free 1-877-Yo-Peggy.

Thank God
I Had a Liver Transplant

LONI MAYE ORTH

The Prophecy of Daniel

My mind swirled.

An unknown man by the name of Daniel saved my life.

*Are we destined to live our lives by our own free will as we
    choose?*
*Are we the tree that stands mighty against the forces, firmly
    rooted by the choices we make?*
*Or rather are we the leaf tugged off, carried along here and
    there at the wind's discretion?*
Is free will really free will?
*Or is free will something made up and passed along to
    generation after generation?*
*Is religion made up, spoken of in story after story to soothe
    our fear of death?*
Can we choose God—and with God have everlasting life?

These are some of the thoughts that ran through my mind.

What's in a name?
Do parents exercise free will when choosing their baby's
name—or is it simply an inspiration softly whispered into
the heart?

My mother named me after a woman at church—Loni—which is from the Hawaiian "Sweet Le 'Lani, heavenly flower."

"Loni" was a tricky name for me.

As a young child I often spelled Loni—Lion.

Lion. *Courage.*

Daniel—a man of courage—thrown into the lion's pit.

Daniel—a prophet.

Along came a Daniel to save my life. Was he prophetic? Had he seen the writing on the wall when inspired to designate on his driver's license—*organ donor?*

I didn't meet this modern-day Daniel, and I didn't know his last name. Was he married? How did he die? I didn't go to Daniel's funeral to pay my respects, yet we became inseparable—two peas in a pod. I would have seen Daniel off—this man of courage, thrown into the proverbial lion's pit, a prophet—but the day my Daniel died is the night I had life-saving surgery.

A liver transplant.

Daniel's liver.

I Thank God for my modern-day man-of-courage Daniel.

Resurrection

I can best describe Tuesday, January 7, 2003—as unreal.

It was 10:45 PM and I sat with my husband, Jeff, watching *The Tonight Show*—when the phone rang. Our 17-year-old son, Joe, stuck his head in the doorway and grabbed the phone.

"Sorry, Mom," he apologized, thinking it was for him. We had rules about incoming calls after 10:00 PM.

"Hello," he answered. "Who may I say is calling?"

"Mom, it's for you. It's Froedtert," he said nervously, stepping back into the room, followed by our 15-year-old daughter, Erika. He handed me the phone.

"Hello," I said.

"This is Sherrie at Froedtert Hospital. We have a liver available."

"All right," I said. I listened quietly as she told me to pack light—and told me which hospital entrance to use.

"Wow. That was fast," said Jeff. "I was under the impression it would take months—not weeks. That's great, Sweetie. Good for you."

I wasn't feeling "good for me"—and told him so.

I fell silent while I packed this and that, and chewed the inside of my cheek. I suppressed tears that threatened to fill my eyes.

"You'll be fine," he assured me, knowing I was afraid. "Are you ready? I'll pull up the car."

I hugged and kissed the kids good-bye, and patted Korn Dog on the head. *Would this be the last time I saw them—Jeff and Joe, Erika and Korn Dog?* This was my thought as I stepped out into the cold and silent January night.

Jeff opened the car door for me. I sat down. It was warm inside. I clicked my seat belt. I looked toward the house.

Another last time?

The moon was bright; the dark sky clear, and our cream stone ranch was visibly illuminated.

A chill ran through my body and I shivered.

"You have nothing to worry about," Jeff reassured. "You'll come out the other end just fine."

I nodded and smiled and as we pulled away . . . finally letting go.

Tears streaked down my face.

I cried for myself.

I cried for Daniel.

Jubilee

There are times in life for a celebration—a birthday, an anniversary, a promotion, or a second chance at life.

My specialist, the surgeon, and the transplant post-op staff were all impressed with my initial progress. Eight days and one organ rejection episode later, they released me from the hospital.

My husband pushed my wheelchair past the room of another liver transplant patient who had surgery a few days before me. She had contracted a bacterial infection and was not responding to intervention medication. Posted on her closed door was a sign that read, QUARANTINE.

Were her goodbyes her last? I wondered as the wheels of my chair rolled smoothly forward.

I was fortunate.

Thank God I was going home.

A Cross to Bear

My recovery was long and littered with complications.

But in time—and with a heavy price to pay—I came through the other side grateful to be alive.

I was alive to see Joe and Erika graduate from high school. I was alive to say farewell to my aunt and best friend, Jean, who died of cancer. And I was alive to provide refuge for my granddaughter, Alyssa, when her mother, Tina, was unable to care for her.

I experienced all these meaningful events and more. And yet having a liver transplant became a heavy burden many times over. I found the struggle with "self" far more challenging—a cross to bear.

The magnitude of a second chance—and the sense of obligation that came with it—propelled me down a path of desiring to make a real difference in the world, for Daniel and for God.

I expected a soulful and spiritual transformation in addition to my physical transformation—and was disappointed when those "disliked" qualities of myself "lived on." I battled with this acceptance.

Expectantly I prayed to God and asked, *What can I do to repay my gift?*

But I could hear no answer.

I meditated and kept a journal.

I read the Holy Bible, quieting my mind and searching my heart for guidance, and again asked, *What can I do to repay my gift?*

Still I heard nothing.

Determined to make it happen I went forth. I set goals, planned this and that, and visualized other things—all with gratitude and inspiration in my heart, and with expectations of fulfillment—and still nothing.

Without clear directions, road signs and guidance, the paths lead nowhere, and attempted projects and business ventures ended in futility. I reached out to others—and felt alone and rejected by the lack of freely given reciprocation.

As frustration and discouragement replaced the inspiration in my heart, gratitude faded away. Again I pleaded—loudly this time—*Please God, what must I do?*

I strained my ears and listened. And just as loudly—heard nothing. Nothing. Nothing.

Nothing.

Anger replaced discouragement, and a void entered my soul as I realized I had no purpose. It had all been for nothing.

All of it.

I no longer sensed "gratitude" and "thankfulness" in my heart, and so—like the little child with no one to play with—I picked up my marbles and went home.

I became withdrawn and depressed.

I was ungrateful for the liver transplant.

The Holy Grail

Milwaukee has one of the most beautiful and diverse park systems in the United States. The Mitchell Park Domes are a horticulture wonder visibly seen from the interstate. After many years, I had the opportunity to visit it to attend a self-growth meeting.

This particular visit offered a unique experience—as the domes are not open to the general public during the evening. It was dark and chilly inside the large glassed enclosures and the outdated attached atrium stood empty.

Initially I resisted the assignment of being led blindfolded through one of the large horticulture domes, but eventually I relented. I started out warily with small stiff steps—hands held out directly in front of me—completely uncomfortable with the experience.

Not having control triggered fear in me.

A third of the way through the tropical dome I relaxed. I noticed how my other senses heightened and compensated for my loss of vision. I found the soft, bubbly, pleasant sounds of the waterfalls—and the fragrant aroma and warm humidity—a welcome experience on this cold winter evening. The uneven path crunched beneath my feet, but my guide kept me safe, walking quietly and slowly at my side.

The next morning as I waited for water to boil for tea, I thought about the night before at the Domes.

I searched for its meaning in this once-in-a-lifetime experience. *Whys* had become my Holy Grail. I acknowledged the similarities between the Domes assignment and my life. I felt blindfolded as I walked through life—the road bumpy and uneven with my hands out in front of me. I was fearful, resisting moving forward, unsure of where I was going, my path uneven.

Did God walk quietly and slowly at my side keeping me safe?

There was something more.

What?

I closed my eyes. The ceramic floor was cool beneath my bare feet, and the ceramic mug was smooth and hard in my hand. Korn Dog's faithful presence was beside me.

I opened my eyes and saw a small inexpensive picture I picked up at the drug store. I got it not so much for what it said but rather for the dark, handsome, wooden frame underneath the parchment matting that was dotted with hues of green and purple. It matched my décor.

More . . .

I closed my eyes, again, and listened for the sounds of steam rising from the kettle.

Nothing.

Then it came loud and clear. I opened my eyes. This time I read the words—for the *first* time. "Every new day is a gift—that's why it's called *the present*."

It was the handwriting on the wall. I immediately felt my cross lift as tears burned my eyes. I finally understood. God wanted *nothing* in return. It was a *gift*.

It was a present.

And then the soft whistle blew and white steam escaped from the kettle's spout. I poured a cup of tea and quickly wiped down the counter. I tossed Korn Dog a treat. And with a grin on my face, I joined Jeff on the sofa. It was our morning ritual—Jeff with his cup of coffee, and me with my cup of tea.

"What's so funny?" he asked, seeing a smile on my face.

"Life's good, that's all."

"Yes, life's good," and he smiled, too.

In life we all have our "crosses" to bear. While felt as "burdens," they are actually "blessings" because they are the instruments used to bring us closer to God. After all, God just wants to walk quietly and slowly beside us, keeping us on the uneven paths that crunch beneath our feet, safe from harms way.

Thank God I had a Liver Transplant.

❤   ❤   ❤

Loni Maye Orth, a five-year liver transplant survivor, is a certified bio-feedback specialist/practitioner (CBS), and a *Thank God I . . .* ™ Core Team member. Loni is the owner of Body Balance Wellness, specializing in stress reduction and gratitude coaching. She focuses on the body, mind, emotional and spiritual aspects of health and wellness. Her compassion, motivation, and desire lead her to help others find "The Secret to Health." She currently presents educational webinars on Organ Transplant Integrative and Alternative Wellness. For more information, e-mail Loni Maye at BodyBalanceWellness@yahoo.com.

Thank God
I Went Out of My Mind

DEBRA PONEMAN

I had prided myself on *only* doing work that I loved.

The truth is I didn't have a "real" job until I was almost 30—except when as a teen I worked as a cashier at my dad's corner drugstore and as a summer camp counselor for special-needs kids. But once I graduated from high school in 1970—as was the next predictable step for any self-respecting member of the Woodstock generation—I learned meditation and, after experiencing its life-changing benefits, became a teacher of TM (Transcendental Meditation). For the rest of the 70s—when I wasn't in Europe studying with the organization's founder, Maharishi Mahesh Yogi—I taught TM full-time and worked as an administrator at Maharishi International University in Fairfield, Iowa.

Being part of the non-profit sector for almost a decade—and living on not much more than $500 a month—took its toll. In 1981 I moved to the West Coast to work as an account executive for an LA-based financial company—which is a fancy way of saying I sold "investments." My decision to venture into the world of finance (which was about as un-natural for me as roping a longhorn—and I'm not even sure one ropes longhorns) was solely to make money fast so that I could get back to Iowa and do what I loved to do.

One December evening a colleague asked if I would like to join her at a "money" seminar. Knowing I would get points with my boss, and hoping to pick up a tip or two, I figured I could sacrifice a night to sit through another "boring" financial tutorial. Yet the minute I walked in the room I knew there was something different about this one. This room wasn't filled with the usual "suits," but with people who looked more like the Learning Annex crowd. The air was lively with anticipation. The seminar leader's name was Chris and, although I wouldn't see him again, from the moment he began to speak I knew what I was going to do with the rest of my life.

I sat transfixed as he shared radical ideas about how "prosperity" is really created—ideas that had nothing to do with working hard, opening a 401K, or investing wisely. He talked about how your dominant thought— whether it is of lack and limitation, or affluence and abundance—would manifest in your life. He said that the quickest way to become wealthy and successful was to help others become wealthy and successful. He told us to put a $100 bill in our wallets, so that every time we reached for some cash we would receive the message, "I am affluent."

I could hardly contain the energy in my body. I felt as if every fiber was humming with Chris' words. I had no doubt as I walked out of that room that my life's work was to plunge headlong into studying this knowledge and sharing its message with the rest of the world.

The next morning I quit my job and spent months immersed in the teachings of the great masters of success and prosperity, including Napoleon Hill, Wallace Wattles, Earl Nightingale, and Florence Shin. In early 1982 I founded my company, Yes to Success, Inc.

My personal mission statement:

I give seminars and write books that uplift,
inspire, and provide people with the tools they need
to transform their lives in the direction of greater success,
true prosperity, and deep and lasting happiness and fulfillment.

Within one year from the night I sat at Chris's feet I had established my Yes to Success seminar in over a dozen major US cities, and one year after that it had been taught in seven countries worldwide.

I soon became a favorite talk show guest, and appeared on radio and TV from coast to coast. Articles about my company and the radical concepts of manifestation which I taught—now popularly called "The Law of Attraction"—appeared in papers from the *LA Times* to the *Boston Globe* to numerous farmland papers in between. As a corporate trainer, my client list included Mattel Toys, McDonnell Douglas, the Xerox Management Group, and International Trade Management. As a keynote speaker I presented to Women in Management, Women in Business, Business and Professional Women, and many other top national organizations.

I developed a tape cassette series and, in 1984, I had one of the first infomercials in the US. The infomercial was broadcast in 22 markets and thousands of tape series were sold.

Perhaps most significantly my seminar was the launching pad for the careers of many now-renowned transformational leaders. The list includes Marci Shimoff, featured teacher in *The Secret* and *NY Times* best-selling author of *Happy for No Reason,* who was actually one of my very first employees; Janet Attwood, *New York Times* best-selling author of *The Passion Test: The Effortless Path to Discovering Your Destiny,* who followed me from city to city and took my seminar almost 20 times before I hired her to be one of my original trainers; and even Dr. Deepak Chopra, who attended my seminar three times in 1982 and 1983, and was so inspired by this knowledge that he left his practice to write his first book, and invited me to come to his home and present a private seminar for his family and friends.

My company continued to experience tremendous growth, and by 1987 I was being represented by a top literary agent who was in conversation with major publishers to put the Yes to Success principles in book form. I was also in the middle of negotiations for my own daytime TV talk show, where I would be interviewing people who had made contributions to society and could share inspirational and uplifting stories with the viewers.

Every goal I set when I wrote my mission statement in 1981 had been realized more spectacularly than I had envisioned.

And in July of 1988—I gave it all up.

Every bit of it—the seminar company, the book, the show, the speaking.

Done.

I didn't return to the industry for almost 20 years.

No—a "tragedy" hadn't befallen me.

There was no accident or death.

I didn't uncover a suppressed childhood trauma or realize I was an imposter.

Actually—quite the opposite.

On July 5, 1988, I gave birth to a baby girl.

And the moment the midwife handed me my daughter and I looked into her eyes and touched her little fingers, I experienced a feeling of love beyond anything I had ever felt before. And as the time approached when I was scheduled to fly to the West Coast for my post-baby business planning meeting, I knew that if I was going to be true to my own teaching—the cornerstone of which was to follow your heart—I knew that my career had to come to a screeching halt.

If I didn't walk my own talk, how could I expect anyone else to trust my words? I believe that people have built-in authenticity meters, and my meter reading would have been way over in different territory if I kept traveling around the world when my heart was home with my daughter—and three years later my son.

I had a line of people who had been waiting for me to have the baby—and get back to work. The agent was waiting, the publisher was waiting, the producer was waiting, and my clients were waiting.

"Sorry. Call me in 18 years."

Everyone thought I had gone completely out of my mind.

And they were exactly right.

It's precisely what had happened, and I thank God for it every day: I had gone completely out of my mind, and right into my heart—and didn't turn back.

It wasn't that I sat home and hand sewed my kids' clothes and churned my own butter, but I lived each day doing what I loved to do—which meant I was the "room mom" and the "team mom" and the "field-trip mom" and the "stage mom" and all the other kinds of "mom" you could possibly be.

I did fit in a few keynotes and co-authored a book on how to cook for your vegetarian kids. I ran a home-based business that helped educate people on the importance of creating non-toxic homes and schools for the health of our children and the future of our planet.

But I only did kid-centered work—and only when there were no basketball games to cheer at, music and dance recitals to burst with pride through (and it didn't matter to me if my daughter went right—when all the other little girls went left), or birthday parties to bake for.

And there were very few nights when I wasn't home to tuck my children in bed and kiss them goodnight.

Was I grateful that I'd listened to my heart and took almost 20 years away from my career? There were certainly moments when the answer was "no"—like during the teenage years when I started to believe that everything I thought I had done right, had in fact been done terribly wrong. But deep inside I knew that what I taught in my seminars was true—and that is that each of us was put on earth to fulfill a God-given purpose, a calling, and if you follow your heart and take what appears to be a detour, your God-given purpose is not going to go away.

If you follow your heart—whether it's to take time away from your career to be with your kids *or* to leave your practice to become an actor *or* to quit your job to do work with AIDS patients in Uganda—you'll be in tune with your life's purpose, as long as you're listening to your "inner" guidance—even if it appears you've gone out of your mind.

The impulses of your heart are nothing less than your destiny calling you.

Fast forward to 2008.

With my beautiful baby girl off to college and my 16-year-old son the president of his own flourishing company—and about to graduate from high school—my mission is still there waiting for me, and the principles I began teaching over 26 years ago are as vital today as when I founded Yes to Success in 1982. But the priceless wisdom and insight into the human spirit I gained from being a "mother" have enriched the knowledge I now share—more than I could have ever imagined.

I thank God I went out of my mind and followed my heart—and 20 years have gone by in the wink of an eye.

❤   ❤   ❤

Besides being a wife and mother, Debra Poneman is an award-winning keynote speaker, seminar leader, business owner, and author. As founder and president of Yes to Success Seminars, Inc., her breakthrough methods for creating true success and prosperity have been instrumental in transforming the lives of hundreds of thousands of people around the world. In her Amazon.com best seller, *Chicken Soup for the American Idol Soul*, which is filled with stories of how the American Idols overcame great obstacles to create their mega-success, we hear Debra's message inspiring us to create our own. Please visit Debra's website at www.yestosuccess.com.

Thank God
My Divorce Almost Killed Me

MOREAH RAGUSA

It was 6:00 PM and I sat in my car at the intersection.

The light was green.

I snapped—I literally lost my mind, my memory, use of my nervous system, and my ability to function.

Somehow—after a while—I managed to get to a pay phone.

I dialed my dad's number and the recording of the operator's voice came on.

"You are dialing a long-distance number. Please check the number and try your call again—or call the operator for assistance."

I tried again—and got the recording.

I was crying, confused and afraid.

I called the operator and explained that I *needed* to talk to my dad. I gave her the number, and she said that I was calling from a pay phone in Edmonton, and the number I was calling was in Lethbridge—a city 513 km away.

I didn't understand; she repeated herself.

175

I sobbed uncontrollably.

She patched me through—and my dad answered the phone.

I started rambling to him; my mind had unhinged; I couldn't put the pieces of my recent past together—I was terrified.

Who was I?

Where was I?

Where were my girls?

Dad told me he'd been very worried about me—ever since I discovered the affair Adam was having.

The separation from Adam after the pregnancy, and the birth of my third daughter was becoming more than I could bear. I was just 20 years old. Dad shared that I had not been myself for months; I believed that I had been through so much loss. He said I was about to discover that divorce is a time of endings and beginnings—for me it felt like a time of crucifixion—a long-suffering death with no resurrection in sight.

The following day I went to see a doctor who diagnosed me with nervous exhaustion. I weighed 96 pounds. The doctor explained that all my nerve endings were damaged. My condition was due to high levels of stress, poor nutrition (I was anorexic), and lack of sleep. The doctor explained that the symptoms of this illness would leave my body unable to receive the messages that my brain was sending through my nervous system.

I felt drunk without drinking.

It took me an enormous effort to pick up a cup or walk; my speech was slurred and drawn out—I was a mess. The doctor said it would take six months to a year to recover. In some ways it would take much longer than that—and in another way the healing was instant.

Five months after my third daughter Sara's birth, and following an enormous struggle to regain some of my self-esteem—lost because of the infidelity in our marriage—Adam made a suggestion that forever changed the direction in which our lives went. He suggested that he and his girlfriend take the girls to live with *them.* I was outraged.

Protective maternal instincts pulsed through my tiny exhausted body—and I refused.

A week later he repeated the request and told me that *if* I really loved the girls, I would do what was best for *them*—not *me*. His truthful words exploded inside me. Something in me knew this was a prophecy, and it felt like shrapnel piercing my heart.

I was speechless.

Time stood still.

My future—now proclaimed.

As I reflect upon it now, I see this was one of those life-defining moments.

My withered sense of "self" was so crippled that I began to consider his words. It was true that I was struggling in every area in my life, emotionally, psychologically, and financially. I was working long hours at multiple jobs and could no longer find the resources to give more than I was giving—but *he* could. He reminded me weekly that I was not being a good mom thinking only of myself. My heart and head felt torn apart, moving me in opposing directions.

I asked God, "What would *love* have me do? What is truly best for our children?"

Another week passed—and again the request came. I felt destiny taking over. My will collapsed. I surrendered and agreed the girls could live with them. Just weeks later, Adam and his girlfriend took off early one September morning to a city 300 miles away. They escaped in the night—stealing my children from me.

My babies were gone.

My nervous system crashed.

The following 14 years of being alienated from my daughters became the greatest teacher I would have. This life lesson would turn whatever was brass within me into gold. The process involved red-hot irons that punctured my armor, illusions, and my beliefs about my self and the world around me. The flames of purification came in the form of not knowing where my children were, repeated court visits, countless hours with lawyers, psychological evaluations, hearing my children say, "Mom, you left me. I hate you!"

I tortured myself listening to my inner critical voice that whispered, *You deserve this pain.* Words like dishonesty, shame, guilt, fear, and rage filled my thoughts.

I needed to own my part of the "dance." Yes, if I were truly to heal I needed to look deep within myself and ask what part in all this was my fault—and then face it. Only then could I honor myself and begin a new life. I realized that I could only save myself if I became wise enough to ask questions that would help me overcome three decades of hurt. Wisdom would come from deeper questions that would help me help others, and clarify how divorce is used by God to reveal who we authentically are.

When you are faced with the completion of a marriage—one that you hoped could survive all the soul growth your life is aiming to allow—you begin to take serious stock of the beliefs you once held. You re-examine what is important to you. You revisit how you have used your moments, and how you may have wasted them. You look at your kids through new eyes. You look at potential new mates differently.

And if you stay present, *you begin to see that everyone is reflecting you.*

As I write to you in this moment I say, *Thank God I got divorced because in completing my "dance" with this experience, I learned what love really means.*

I learned not to cling to things in search of security or relationships in order to define myself. I learned that unions are sacred, and that they sometimes have a "season" rather than a lifetime to unfold. I learned to love who I am. I learned to accept and appreciate both the "shadow" and "light" in another—and therefore in myself. I learned that love does not possess, and that true love allows us to remain interconnected with everyone regardless of what appears as separate.

I learned the fact that we live in a world of inseparable opposites— *up* comes with *down, hot* with *cold,* and *loss* with *gain.*

I discovered that all events have two sides if we look honestly into them. I learned that the ego is NOT interested in love—but is addicted to using people for its gain. Most of all—through leading a life blessed by divorce—I learned that when we take personal responsibility for our part in the relationships we enter, we can use the transitions as a catalyst to a new life.

The blessings in my life are many as a result of divorce. I cherish my children and remain focused on the importance of feeding the relationships with them, knowing it also feeds me. I now understand that my lifelong journey—that was paralleled by the experience of divorce—made me an expert in this field. It gave me the wisdom and confidence to guide others through this journey.

In these past 22 years, I've learned the importance of emotional and spiritual excavation in order to honor heartache, self-doubt, and money.

Thank God I got divorced because now I am on a lifelong path, awakening people to the opportunity to experience divorce as a gift in their life.

Moreah Ragusa impacts people worldwide. She wakes people up to identify and then access their personal power. Her get-real style, humor, and honesty mesmerize audiences. For 25 years, Moreah has spoken, taught, written, and coached her audiences to unleash their potential. She is a visionary leader with an innovative approach. She's authored six books on relationship success. Moreah is a practicing psychotherapist, a registered family mediator, mentor, and life and relationship specialist. Moreah has tenaciously made her mark in the divorce industry by pioneering the *New Divorce Paradigm*®. She is a frequent guest on nationally syndicated TV and radio shows, discussing the importance of reclaiming personal power in one's life and relationships. In high demand, Moreah is a dynamic keynote speaker and seminar leader, addressing audiences around the globe, leaving them feeling powerful, confident, courageous . . . and unstoppable. www.moreahragusa.com.

Thank God
... for Christopher

EMBRACING AND RELEASING

JAMIE SANDERS

Isn't it amazing how people come and go in our lives, and often we don't really notice the roles they've played in helping to create who we are?

It has taken me several years to come to the understanding that—as spiritual beings—we are given gifts in many forms to move us along our path. People touch our hearts; they reach the depths of our soul and can change us on a cellular level when we truly see them for who they are. When I sit and reflect on the faces of those who have taught me many of my most treasured and even "painful" lessons, it reassures me that I am truly blessed. Many of these individuals have moved on, crossed over, or still remain a part of my life.

Recording artist and motivational speaker Naomi Judd once said, "Life is about embracing and releasing." She explained how people come into our lives, and we embrace and love them.

We learn from them all that is needed.

Then the time comes when we must be willing to let them go.

I remember the first time I read that statement and just how powerful those words were to me. In that instant I somehow understood her words completely. How many times had I found someone my heart reached out to or believed that I had found a connection with—a bond—just to find several years later that they were no longer there?

Release can be a painful lesson—or a gracious friend that strengthens us. Whether through the ending of a particular relationship or through death, emotional release will move us to another level of growth and understanding.

On December 6, 2000, life presented me with a lesson on loving completely. Christopher James Sanders, my brother's 18-year-old son, died peacefully in a hospital room, while family and friends stood silently in the quiet halls waiting, watching, and praying.

Chris was not your typical teenager by any means.

He was thoughtful and loving to most everyone; he told those he loved that indeed he *did*. He literally brought life, laughter, and joy wherever he was. He was that one unique ray of sunshine that each family possesses and considers their touchstone and center.

He and I were more than just uncle and nephew; when he was a small boy we became more like the best of friends. I knew there was something special about him by the way he reached out to others. He was genuine in his spirit.

He was a light for *me*.

Actually, he was a light to the *entire family*—and we all knew it. I could become a kid again with Chris and not worry about how foolish I looked or sounded when we laughed at something in which no one else would find the humor.

He was in many ways my own son—or the younger brother I had wanted. I enjoyed giving him money, rides, and gifts; they came from my heart because I truly loved him. He didn't ask anything of me, really; he just wanted to talk or laugh and be himself. His company was not a bother for me, but rather a wonderful distraction from my usual daily activities. No matter how bad a day was or how upset I may have been about some trivial event in my life, Chris found a way to reach that place in me that made me laugh and forget.

When we first found out that he was seriously sick, the family panicked. What family wouldn't?

Not Chris. Dear God, please not Christopher.

My spirituality—my faith—has not been something I casually turned to or practiced. It is something so much a part of all that I am that I had to find that presence within, if I were going to face this situation and emotionally survive it. I knew that no matter what the outcome would be—I had to totally trust Spirit. I had to *believe.* I had to cling to the truth that God was in charge, that this experience was part of Chris's journey. I had to find inner peace in learning how to honor what his soul was choosing to do.

I watched my family go through torment as they prayed and cried their way through each passing day. Test after test, chemo treatment after chemo treatment, the days passed slowly. The once lively spirited young man we knew and loved became a thin, weak, and quiet person who wanted to sit in the hospital room with the shades pulled and the lights off. He didn't talk much, anymore; that once blazing spark of life he displayed was dimming. We tried to keep our smiles painted on as we'd visit, holding back the tears, trying desperately to be strong. We would urge him to eat just a little something so he'd feel stronger—but to no avail.

Chris and I talked several times about God, death, and why this was happening. I remember telling him that as long as I lived, I may not be able to explain fully the reasons why . . . but I wanted him to understand above all else that he was not being punished. God was *not* making him sick. I searched earnestly for the right words. I talked to him about how we make choices in life, and how we stuff our feelings for fear that *if* we said what we felt or thought, we wouldn't be loved or someone would be hurt. Feelings of hurt and resentment held within— that go unspoken and unhealed—begin to make us toxic. I wanted him to burst forth and spew out his feelings, to purge his emotions, and to make this cancer stop.

He sat watching me—just listening.

At other times he cried.

I hugged him and cried as well. I couldn't imagine a life—my life—without him in it.

Those moments mean so much to me now. They were real, gut-wrenching moments of the heart. At times, overwhelming feelings of anxiety and fear suddenly swept over me, and I would just want to start running. I wanted to run from all of it—his pain, my pain, everyone's pain. I had released many people in my life who I had loved through their dying—and had handled it well—but this one I knew would bring me to my knees.

I kept affirming, *All is well; God is in control;* and *There is nothing to be healed—only God to be revealed.*

But somewhere inside, I knew that this was Chris's way of leaving this life.

So much went unspoken.

So many unresolved "hurts" in the family could have been addressed and healed.

And yet the silence grew only louder.

Chris would get upset with me for being so outspoken at times, but I learned from a friend of mine—who spent time with him—that it was actually one of the things he admired most about me. I smile about that now because I used to urge him to do the same—but he rarely did. I see the pain in the eyes of my mother, his grandmother, who loved him with every piece of who she is. She stayed by his side through most of his hospital stays and didn't begrudge a minute of it.

For her, it was an honor to share the times of silence, the tears, and conversations known just between the two of them.

I know without a doubt that our lives were touched by having had him for the short 18 years that we did. I know that his life force—his spirit—touched my heart and soul on a level of love I hadn't known before. He taught me many things about what life *is*—and so much more about what life *is not.*

I live in gratitude now for every day that God gifted me with the very essence of love that is Chris. I say *is* because I know that the power of love is eternal. It lives on forever. It goes onward with the spirit of the one who has passed.

I find moments in my day remembering him coming through the door smiling at me or calling. I have moments where I give thanks for having had him in my experience. I have moments of tears that come unexpectedly.

There was a song that I heard several years ago by Regina Bell that made me think of Chris. It's called, *If I Could.* I found that song the other day and thought twice about putting it on. I finally did—and then I cried as I hadn't cried since the morning he died.

> *If I could*
> *I'd protect you from the sadness in your eyes.*
> *Give you courage in a world of compromise.*
> *Yes, I would.*
> *If I could.*
> *I would help you make it through the hungry years,*
> *but I know that I could never cry your tears,*
> *but I would*
> *if I could.*

I listened to those words as I sat on the end of the bed. I let the tears that I'd held back for months burst forth. When the song ended, I felt an inner peace sitting there staring at his picture. "Embracing and releasing." I heard those words once again. I know that no matter how many years pass, how much joy I find in my life in the days ahead, I will have the memory of my years with Chris.

We will remember his laughter and the kindness that he so willing shared with us all. I know he is fully aware of the love that we feel for him. Life offers us such great gifts when we take the time to notice that they are standing before us.

Embrace what is there in the moment.

Love the people who bring you fulfillment.

And when the time comes to release them . . . you can do so with a full heart and grateful spirit.

♥   ♥   ♥

Jamie Sanders is a New Thought Minister ordained through both The Barbara King School of Ministry in Atlanta, Georgia and The World Federation of Practical Christianity. He has been the producer and host of his own weekly television program, *Positive Living*, and is an active speaker, workshop facilitator, and performer for Unity Churches, retreats, and other New Thought organizations. He is a featured columnist for *The Light*, *Kaleidoscope*, and *Alternatives* magazines—as well as other spiritual publications. Jamie holds a BA in Metaphysical Studies, is a certified pastoral counselor, and is now serving as the minister at Unity Church of Christianity in beautiful Pensacola, Florida. You can visit his website at www.jamiesanders.com and join his online mailing list or e-mail him at Jamie1118@aol.com.

Thank God
I Found My Life's Purpose

SCOTT SCHILLING

Have you ever had a friend—or known someone who "had it going on"—who didn't seem to be fulfilled? They had a great life surrounded by so many blessings and still something seemed to be missing? For the most part they did the right things, said the "right" things, and had fun along the way. In essence they did the best they could with what they knew at the time. Nothing really "bad" happened; it was just what it was. Could there be more?

Yes—a whole lot more.

My beautiful wife, Peggy, and I had been married for about seven years at the time. I was eight years into a corporate Vice President of Sales and Marketing, and while we were doing just fine—we were only doing "just fine." I was frustrated professionally and personally. Life was comfortable but not yet exceptional. We knew God had bigger plans for us personally, professionally, and most importantly spiritually. We were seeking how to live a more fulfilled life and contribute more to humanity.

It started on Easter Sunday in 2003. Peggy and I went to the Easter service at the Fellowship Church lead by Ed Young in Grapevine, Texas. There was something different about this Easter morning—we couldn't identify it when we got there, but boy we sure could as we left.

The Fellowship Church is known for its progressive delivery of God's word through its music, dramas, and presentation. This Easter Sunday was about to be even more exceptional. After some initial praise songs and messages, the lights dimmed, the music wound down, and the curtains opened.

As the praise team and band started pounding out the Evanescence hard-rocking song, *Bring Me to Life,* Roman guards escorted Jesus to the cross positioned mid-stage. As the song continued, the guards calmly placed Jesus on the cross, mimicking the driving of the nails through his hands, and attaching the crown of thorns around his head. They pulled the cross forward, leaving Jesus to "die upon the cross for our sins."

During this visual sensation, the praise team played and sang in a way that even Evanescence had not performed this song. The lyrics rang through loud and clear, "Wake me up inside," "Save Me," "Call my name and wake me from the dark," "Save me from the nothing I've become." And then it happened—*Bang!*

There was a physical *bang* that touched both of our hearts in a deep way. There was a new awakening, a new awareness, a new feeling, a new compassion, and a new desire to help others feel what we had felt. It truly was a "Bring Me Back to Life" moment. The Spirit had landed. That was the start of working to seek more, study more, and ultimately share what had touched our hearts at such a profound level. I realized that I needed to move from my humdrum corporate existence to a life committed to empowering others through professional speaking and writing.

Within weeks after this Easter Sunday revelation, I met Jack Canfield for the first time. Being a student of Jack's for many years through his cassette series (yes, I became a student a long time ago), now CDs, DVDs and books, it was an honor to meet him in person. In our time together, Jack's encouragement was amazing. He definitely had more confidence in me than I had in myself at the time. He encouraged me to continue to increase my awareness of new things around me, and then take the appropriate risks to act on them. He said that it's only through greater awareness and risk-taking that we ultimately grow. I stayed the course—ever seeking, ever questioning, and working to learn more.

Then a number of years ago, as I searched for still greater fulfillment and enlightenment in my life, my mentor—Mr. Jack Canfield—took me aside and said, "We are all far more talented and capable than we experience here on earth. In fact we have only been put on this earth for two reasons: to have a fabulous life, and to help as many other people as we possibly can." He continued, "And if you're not having a fabulous life, the chances are you are not helping anyone else. And if you're not having a fabulous life—and you are not helping anyone else—you're robbing humanity. You're cheating humanity. You're being selfish."

I went back to my room and thought about what Jack had said. It really lay on my heart and made me search internally. Was it truly possible to have greater fulfillment in my life by maximizing my ability to put others first? I had worked toward coming from a place of service to others, but what if I intensified that concept in all I did? Something immediately tugged at my heart. It felt right.

That single piece of awareness has taken me on an ever-increasing path to greater personal fulfillment. More importantly, it became the rallying cry to drive me to greater heights professionally in my speaking and writing career. Not long after that conversation, I put to use some of the tools Jack created for developing a life purpose statement. By thinking about it, working at it, focusing on it—it's amazing what surfaces. As clear as day it appeared. My life's purpose is to "inspire and empower others to achieve their optimum life purpose to serve humanity with love and joy."

This life purpose statement brought a greater focus to my actions and to what I was seeking. Amazingly enough, what I'd searched for started showing up in virtually everything I did. The power in knowing what you want is recognizing bits and pieces that consistently show up.

Things started to become increasingly clear.

Be a change agent for all things.

This is first a mindset and then, by adapting it, all things follow.

Soon after at Mark Victor Hansen's MEGA Speaking event in Los Angeles, Cynthia Kersey made an impassioned plea to support Habitat for Humanity. Wow. Talk about tugging at your heart. I wanted to support her. I needed to support her. But, I didn't have the funds to support her.

Oh no. Not this time. God gave you unique talents. Use them!

How?

Stop focusing on the how.

Understand the what and the why.

On the flight home that night it came to me—the title of the book that could be sold to raise money to help Habitat. The title popped into my head, *Talking with Giants! Powerful Leaders Share Life Lessons.* We could support Habitat and the 20 other charities represented in the book by the various Giants interviewed. Not only could this book be written, there could be additional titles like *Talking with Giants in Health & Wellness, Talking with Giants in Spiritual Development, Talking with Giants in Transformational Leadership*, and many more. We could do radio shows, websites, seminars, trainings, you name it, all with one single intention: to help others and ourselves maximize our ability to contribute to humanity as a whole.

Awesome.

The life-changing events put into action by the various stories in the books have been phenomenal. People gained courage by being empowered and inspired to seek their highest visions. Readers found their hearts contributing and giving back—paying it forward.

The revelations flew fast and furious. From Easter Sunday to meeting Jack Canfield for the first time was less than two weeks. The fateful meeting with Cynthia Kersey was just four months later. God works plenty fast in your life when you open yourself up to the plan.

The impact of being touched by Cynthia's message resulted in my touching those around me—and many others worldwide. The $100 million dollars in charitable giving I asked the Universe to attract into my life is a daily reality. We are raising money for causes around the world, touching lives one at a time, speaking to groups of thousands at events, producing books, radio shows, DVDs and CDs of encouragement. Generosity truly does build prosperity.

The original idea of the book itself was only the beginning. Once that first decision was made, additional ideas popped up. You start looking at the world in a totally different way. What a transformation takes place when you move to a state of gratitude and truly appreciate everyone you meet! Living the life of your dreams is within reach; sometimes you simply have to stretch out your hands and take hold. Do your part. You have it in you. And when you let it out, you'll be amazed at how you feel.

The lesson is simple.

God has made each one of us unique with our own talents, our own gifts, and our own capabilities to impact this world creatively. Whether we come together as great people or we choose to work individually, you can and *are* making a difference in our world daily. God is the master craftsman and does not make mistakes.

We all play a valuable part in this thing we call *life*.

Are you doing what *you* want to be doing?

Are you living the life of *your* dreams?

Most importantly the question becomes, *Are you fulfilling your life's purpose?*

❤   ❤   ❤

Scott Schilling brings over 30 years of experience in sales, marketing, speaking, and training to the financial and service industries, business owners, corporations, and entrepreneurs. Through his affiliations with Fortune 500 companies, innovative start-up companies, and high-paced individuals, Scott brings a wealth of knowledge, sales, marketing, implementation strategies, education, and expertise to the podium and to print. Scott's books to date include, *Talking with Giants! Extreme Excellence, Conversations on Success,* and *Wake Up . . . Live the Life*

You Love. As an accomplished and entertaining presenter, Scott has spoken to thousands of attendees across a range of industries. Scott's goal is to maximize the potential and God-given talents of the individuals and the organizations he encounters. Delivering content in an "easy-to-understand-and-digest style" make his presentations practical and extremely valuable. You can contact Scott toll free at (877) 305-6565, via e-mail at scott@scottschilling.com, or by visiting his websites at www.scottschilling.com or www.TalkingWithGiants.com.

Thank God
I Was a Single Teenage Mother

YESENIA SORIANO

Alone, frightened, nervous, and unbearably overwhelmed, I found myself in the situation I swore would not happen to me. I was 18 years old in the delivery room at General Hospital in Los Angeles.

How did this happen?

I wasn't affected by peer pressure—but I did give in to *peer expectation.*

Then I discovered I was *pregnant,* and I dreaded telling my parents. I knew the financial burden this would have on our family's already troubled situation. When they learned about the pregnancy, they asked questions that I couldn't answer—partly due to my own denial and partly because I just didn't know what to do. They lectured me for what seemed like hours. I silently chastised myself, thinking of all the sacrifices they had made to save my life by taking me away from the raging civil war in El Salvador.

And this is how I show my gratitude.

My eyes focused on the floor and my face showed no emotion. I blocked out their words as thoughts raced through my mind.

This wasn't supposed to happen to me.

Frozen with fear and numbed with gut-wrenching guilt, I realized the impact this would have in my life. I wanted to disappear from the face of the earth.

Then their words flooded in, causing anger to rise within me. I stood proud, refusing to allow them to treat me like this. I took my stance and argued back.

My father threw me out of the house.

I had nowhere to go, but I felt anything was better than putting myself through this humiliating experience. My back was against the wall, and I wanted to run away from my new reality. Adding to the pain, I discovered that my boyfriend's ex-girlfriend, with whom he had a previous child, was *again* pregnant by him. But I felt I didn't have any other options; I decided to go live with him.

That first night—and many more to come—I cried myself to sleep.

I felt alone, stupid, and ashamed.

I briefly considered giving up my baby, but I wanted to know how her life would turn out, and knew such a decision would bring me a lifetime of guilt. My boyfriend promised he would be there to help me. I believed him.

We lived in a decrepit Hollywood neighborhood that was infested with drugs, gangs, and prostitution. Drive-by shootings and fights between neighboring gangs were commonplace. As a child, I'd witnessed death back in El Salvador and these senseless killings brought flashbacks and graphic memories. I didn't want to raise my child in such horrible conditions. I felt like a fool for choosing to leave the comfort and support of my parents, and I realized "freedom" was not all it was cracked up to be. Neither of us had a job—we couldn't even buy food. Sometimes when I couldn't bear the hunger, I went to the local supermarket and, humiliated, ate whatever I could without getting caught.

It dawned on me that this baby would need food and clothing. I couldn't even provide for myself. My boyfriend—a teenager himself—didn't take this situation seriously. He continued with his partying and gangbanging lifestyle. And to top it off—I caught him cheating on me, again.

I realized that I would be the only one responsible for raising this child, so I decided to stay in school, graduate, and do something with my life for the sake of my baby.

One morning, my boyfriend and some of his gangster friends were driving me to school when the police stopped us. In a panic, my boyfriend put his gun in my purse. The police found the gun when they searched our personal belongings and arrested us.

Because I was a minor, they released me to my father. I couldn't look him in the eyes, but I could feel his disappointment and frustration. We left. Then with my tail between my legs, my heart racing, and a knot in my stomach—I ran away from my father without saying a word.

After this incident, afraid for my life in that neighborhood, I swallowed my pride and returned to my parents' house.

I was ashamed and humbled when they took me back.

Guilt filled me for putting them in this whole mess. I wanted to apologize but didn't know how, and I felt like an unwelcome stranger in my own house.

Our relationship became so strained that when the time came for me to deliver, my mother told me to have my boyfriend drive me to the hospital—as she had to work. He did drive me, walked me into the emergency room, and then LEFT ME there. I was alone in this living nightmare. The contractions brought such intense pain that I wondered how I'd make it through. Fear of this very real new responsibility enveloped me at the moment of my baby's birth.

The doctor asked if I wanted to see her.

With a sinking feeling in my stomach and wanting to run away from the hospital, I took a deep breath and hesitantly said, "Okay."

They placed her in my arms—and I didn't know what to do.

She looked at me with her big, beautiful, brown eyes.

I started to talk to her—and she started to cry. I felt she cried out of resentment towards me for all my thoughts of not wanting her and thinking of giving her up. I was drowning in guilt and burst into uncontrollable tears.

A nurse offered to page my family, but I knew I was in this all alone.

Then I resolved to be "tough."

I stopped crying, wiped my tears, and told myself everything would be all right. I decided this would be the last time my daughter would see me cry. I was going to take on this challenge, and I would be strong.

As the years went by I can't say that things were easy. I worked a full-time day job and attended full-time night school, leaving me with little time to learn how to be a mother. Fortunately, my parents and family offered their support. I wouldn't have made it those first few years without their help. However, I kept all my fears, questions, guilt, and emotions inside me. The anger and frustration that caused my teen years to end like this quickly forced me to change my priorities.

I focused on finding a father for my daughter and, in the process, lost myself. I believed no one would love me because I was "damaged goods." I had an affair with a married man, who I allowed to brainwash me into believing that I wanted this kind of relationship. I lost my self-worth and power—and even continued a relationship with a man who raped me. I became pregnant by him—and had an abortion for obvious reasons. Then there was a third pregnancy from a different boyfriend, resulting in yet another abortion.

I feared what my parents would think and say about me, and that they might throw me out of the house again. I couldn't afford to have my daughter out on the streets with me.

Then I entered a nine-year relationship and, even though I wasn't fulfilled, I thought I was giving my daughter a much needed "stable home." All I knew was that I had to provide for my daughter—even if it meant sacrificing my own fulfillment. I hoped with each relationship that maybe this time *he* would be the perfect father. Instead, I put my daughter through an emotional whirlwind.

And then it hit me.

How could I dare hope that my beautiful little girl would grow up emotionally healthy if she didn't see those qualities in me first? How would she learn what loving relationships are—and how to create them—if I didn't model one for her? How could I hope that she would learn to love herself—and be able to teach others how to love her—if I couldn't do that for myself?

But how could I become the example I wanted to be? Who would teach *me?*

As I paid more attention to my daughter, I noticed how easy it was for her to embrace me no matter my mood. It was easy for her to hug me, tell me she loved me—and she was quick to appreciate. This realization pushed me to be more like her. As I learned to love her in this light, I learned to love myself. Through her actions of unconditional love and respect for me, I learned to be more appreciative. This child was more patient and tolerant with me than I was with her.

It took me about 14 years of seeking with the support of mentors along my journey of self-love, but gratitude now fills my heart and soul with a kind of joy I'm just now experiencing for the first time. I discovered that everything that happened in my life helped me become the person I wanted to be. I recognized that I have the capacity to love and care for others.

We all do.

But my fear of opening up my heart—and being hurt—prevented me from loving my daughter, people around me, and myself. I now know my fulfillment is not dependent upon my circumstances or the people around me. I create my own reality with my daily and momentary choices to love and let people into my heart.

I'm also a work in progress.

My daughter, now 18 years old, has taught me so much. God sent me this little angel to teach me the lesson of my life. I'm thankful I now have the wisdom to see, hear, and feel God's message of compassion, unconditional love, and appreciation. I'm grateful for my daughter and the experience of being a teenage single mother. I wouldn't change a thing because I wouldn't be the mother, daughter, friend, sister, aunt, and girlfriend that I'm learning to be.

Thank God I was a single teen mother, and thank God for the opportunity to share my story with those who might learn from my experiences. Many blessings to you, and may you feel unconditional love and compassion through *your* journey.

*"The journey is what brings us happiness,
not the destination."*

~ DAN MILLMAN ~

❤   ❤   ❤

Yesenia Soriano survived a devastating war in her native country, El Salvador. At age 14 she immigrated to the United States. Now at 36, she enjoys a life dedicated to her spiritual unfolding and empowerment. She currently works with Lisa Nichols, from *The Secret,* on her "Motivating the Teen Spirit" program. Yesenia dedicates her life to empowering teens and adults alike to recapture their true spirit of love, gratitude, and appreciation through speaking engagements and workshops all around the country. You can e-mail Yesenia at yeseniasoriano@yahoo.com or find her at My Space. For more information on Teen Empowerment workshops, please go to www.motivatingtheteenspirit.com.

Thank God
I Chose to Live

SHEILA Z. STIRLING

"Don't go too far" was a phrase I heard almost on a daily basis.

I was one of the wild ones—the "flower children" as we were called.

I was a teenager living in Southern California in the 60s, the youngest daughter of an artist and a champion swimmer. I attended high school during the day, and then I sneaked out by 10:00 PM to dance all night in Hollywood. By the time I was 15 I had danced for Frank Zappa. I lived life to the fullest, experienced the excitement of the peace movement, stood up for social injustice, and pushed the envelope in every way.

My friends and I were rebels. The world was at unrest and so were we.

At the core of my being I "knew" that I was part of something vastly larger than myself.

I was mature for my age of 15—already five-foot seven-inches tall. I had long blond hair and a rather developed chest. Personally, I knew that I could and would change the world.

My mom was a wonderful mother and artist. Each year she took my sister and me to the Laguna Art Festival. We'd walk up and down the decorated streets all day going from gallery to gallery. Mom was at her happiest then; her eyes sparkled as she shared her thoughts on the day. Her true artist soul shined all the way out into the world. I loved all the beauty and the creations that I saw.

By early afternoon, my sister and I would start to complain about being hungry, knowing mom would take us for a long and relaxing lunch. Then we'd talk about all the art and beauty we'd seen.

The summer of '65 I wasn't content just to walk around. I felt restless and distant. The blue sky and sea breeze called to me. *Here is the real painting: the true beauty of the day,* I thought.

"Sheila?" My mom woke me from my daydream.

"Mom, I just want to go to the water. Please, can I go and get in the water?"

Reluctantly she agreed to let me go on my own. "Be back here in two hours—and don't go too far" were her instructions.

I jumped for joy, bewildered that she actually said I could go.

I ran down to the beach.

The sand was hot.

I hurried down to the edge of the water trying to keep my feet from burning.

The cold water felt great.

Although I was 15, my wildness had taken me through many expanding experiences, including what I believed to be an encounter with angels just the year before. Standing at the shoreline brought all that back to me.

It was like magic.

I jumped in, diving under the rolling waves. As I swam beyond the waves, the water became a bit colder, but since there were other swimmers, I thought everything was fine . . .

I began to swim back to shore—but with every stroke forward I seemed to be *getting farther away*.

For a moment I panicked—*what was happening?*

I was being dragged farther out to sea . . .

I saw about six other people, all treading water, looking at the shore growing smaller.

One man yelled, "The flag is red!" It meant everyone out of the water because the rip tide was in. A rip tide is a strong surface current of water returning seaward from the shore. The words of my father, who was a world-class swimmer, echoed in my mind. *Sheila, don't ever try to fight the current.* I kept saying it over and over to myself.

The current pulled us farther from the beach. What was I to do? My mother's words joined my father's—*Don't go too far.*

Don't go too far.

I worried about how much trouble I was going to be in when I did get back to shore. My panic intensified.

What if I don't get back to shore?

How am I going to get back?

I looked at the other people, who by now had formed a small group as we bobbed up and down on the swells, about 20 feet apart from each other.

At that point, I was thanking God for Dad teaching me how to tread water. The sea seemed colder and rougher, and the shoreline seemed farther away. I wanted to cry out in sheer desperation, but I knew somehow not to allow that emotion to come forward.

One of the men told me to pray it didn't last long because then a lifeguard could come to our rescue. I felt better for a few minutes—until I realized how tired I was. Fear took hold of my thoughts. Sharks, jellyfish, and large swells made it difficult to stay afloat.

I closed my eyes and prayed.

I thought of my mom and dad, who I knew loved me so much. I thought of my cat and my dog, Mimi. I thought of all the experiences in my young life. Maybe I wasn't so indestructible; maybe this is how it ends. Maybe my life could be gone in an instant. I felt very isolated.

I put my head back and closed my eyes for just a moment to rest, making long, slow, circular motions to stay afloat.

I realized I might not see or be with my friends or family again.

Just then a swell rushed over me and I got some water in my mouth.

I coughed and began to shake.

Okay! Pull yourself together! Just keep kicking!

I was tired and cold; my entire body was numb; my fingers were white and wrinkled. It had been well over an hour and fatigue was taking its toll, so I switched from treading water to using *only* my arms—then my legs.

As I closed my eyes again to rest, calmness came over me . . .

The water turned into a shimmering field . . .

I could no longer feel my body . . .

No pain; no panic; I felt calm . . . and blissful . . .

I wanted to stay here in this place . . .

Rest . . .

Calm rest . . .

"HEY!"

I jerked my eyes open and realized I was slipping away to a place from which I would not return. Exhausted, I felt a pull from beneath and beyond. I knew this was a moment of choice.

Doubt and confusion.

Swells of icy water reached my mouth with every wave.

My eyes burned from the salt.

Oh, God—can this really be happening?

The group remained around me and I looked at them without saying a word. Inside I wept and shook. One of the others yelled to me, "You're doing great. How old are you?" I feared that if I opened my mouth to answer, the sea would finally take me.

So I just smiled and nodded.

I could see everyone was just as tired.

But I thought maybe I could make it—if I just kept praying.

I thought about my mom saying, "Don't go too far," and it almost seemed funny. *Boy if she could see me now.* I wanted to fight to keep my place on earth. After all, I was going to change the world.

My time can't be over yet.
Can it?
No—I will not give up . . .

I fought now for every breath and every movement of my body, and would not allow myself to slip into the depths of the water.

I silently thanked God for everything. With every breath I'd think of one more thing for which to be thankful. I had great clarity about pulling myself through this—no matter what it took. When feelings of giving up came upon me, I just shook them off and went on thinking and dreaming about my future.

I was so wrapped up in thought that I barely heard the voices calling in the distance.

"Hold on! We're coming to get you!"

I looked up to see three lifeguards.

I wept with relief. My body shook from sheer exhaustion; I gasped for breath. Gratitude flowed through every cell in my body. I looked at the others, and they all seemed to be exhausted, too—but fine.

I learned that we'd been carried out to sea and had tread water in those dark blue swells for nearly two hours.

Thank God we all made it.

Thank God for the brave lifeguards who risked their lives to save ours. I now felt how miraculous and precious each moment was. Nothing seemed the same after that. I viewed life from a far different perspective.

Yes, I could still change the world.

I believe the inspiration and light of the healer within was ignited that day in the deep blue of the Pacific Ocean.

I know that we all have an incredible story to tell. Our life experiences and challenges act as our catalyst for opening to a greater understanding of our own potential, a greater connection with the divine presence that lives within us. We grow into being grateful for every moment because we *do* have a choice every moment.

The experiences in my life have pushed me far beyond the envelope of what most people would call the norm. You think your heart is open—and yet each experience pushes you further.

At 15, I considered letting go because I had doubts about my life to come. But at that moment of choice I saw it was my ego, my outer shell that wanted to go into the deep.

I could die by giving in—or live by fighting.

Hope gave me the strength. Hope was the future. Hope was the possibility of a glorious life . . . and I wanted to be a part of it.

Remember *hope*—it lives deep inside of you.

You are a magnificent being who can change the world.

You are the hope for the future.

❤   ❤   ❤

Besides being a mother, grandmother, and a teacher dedicated to raising the frequency and consciousness of all humanity, Sheila Z. Stirling is a sound and vibrational healer who lives in the "energy of gratitude." She shares her channeled information in a breakthrough workshop that assists people in raising their frequency and releasing trauma from all 100 trillion of the body's cells, bringing joy and fulfillment into one's life. An international inspirational speaker, Sheila's *Intentional Wellness* workshop seeds the shift we are all seeking. Titles include: *Embrace your Evolution*, and *Gratitude is the Seed of Change*. You can visit Sheila at: OpenWisdomInstitute.com, Intentional-Wellness.com, or you can e-mail her at openwisdom@cox.net.

Thank God I Burned Out

ANTONIO VALLADARES

The summer of 2005 was quite similar to most every other one in New York City—running around the city with friends, dating beautiful women, going to concerts, and spending the weekends at the beach.

As the summer came to a close I didn't want the fun to end.

So I kept it going.

I believed that having fun was an integral part of a healthy and inspired life. However, I didn't respect limitations in my work *or* in my life. I engaged in too much fun—and worked too hard. This distracted me from my *self* and, as a result, I didn't pay attention to my own health. Even though my intuition told me to refocus, I didn't honor my own instinct.

I should've known that the fun was about to come to a screeching halt.

In autumn as the weather cools, New York City becomes quite beautiful, and the change in weather turns the trees in Central Park different shades of yellow, orange, and brown. I also experienced change—each week I became more irritable, and began to feel fatigue throughout the day. I found this change foreign because my whole life centered on athletics, which led me to my 15-year career as one of New York City's leading fitness and nutrition experts.

After a few weeks I had trouble falling asleep at night. Then, finally managing a restless sleep, I awakened at every little thing. Things worsened. I couldn't fall asleep until almost time to get up just before sunrise, which gave me only about an hour of sleep per night. I struggled to get up in the morning. I behaved in a surly manner and often arrived late for my appointments. I continued this way for two months before I even cared enough to pay attention and ask for help.

My exhaustion and my weight gain showed. Because I'm normally a lean, energetic person, my decline became obvious to me and everyone else. Dark circles developed under my eyes. I now routinely arrived late for my appointments and canceled others due to my overwhelming sense of disinterest for life. I'm the type of person who has a great appreciation for health and the human body—so not feeling and looking my best took a huge toll on my self-esteem. I was frequently bloated and suffered dizzy spells while working with clients.

Why I felt so poorly confused me.

More and more, my clients cancelled their appointments and didn't return my calls and e-mails. Frustration added to my depression and confusion. With no idea as to why this occurred—I felt powerless. My debt mounted, as did my fear for my future. I couldn't focus on a solution—and it sucked.

My health progressively declined along with my client base and bank account. The day came when I owed more money than I earned. I couldn't see any light in my dark tunnel—and I cried through the night. My teary eyes and snotty nose made it difficult to breathe, causing me to toss and turn all night. I hadn't cried in over 20 years. I'd experienced health my whole life and enjoyed a successful career. Now I was broke and lived in fear—as I continued to gain weight.

A dominant thought ran through my head all day long, *What the hell is wrong with me?*

I spent Christmas and New Year's Eve alone, too embarrassed to ask my family for help. I didn't approach any of my colleagues for help—out of humiliation and a fear that they might see me as a hypocrite. Living in my small East Village studio apartment felt like solitary confinement. I didn't know what to do, which frightened me.

I found the one sliver of hope in some books that collected dust on my shelf. My interest leaned toward personal growth, spiritual development, and success psychology, so I had a few books by Bob Proctor, James Ray, Paul Chek, Dr. John Demartini, and Tony Robbins. The one consistent element shared in the books by all these teachers gave me hope—along their journey to becoming who they are now, each had a great "breakdown" just before their great "breakthrough." It seemed almost like some sort of universal requirement.

It gave me hope that no matter what happened in my life, I knew I would come out a winner.

When the dizzy spells started, I felt that enough was enough. I came to the realization that apart from what was happening with my business and my health, I had mentally become my own worst enemy. I felt sorry for myself—which I knew wasn't helpful—so I decided to turn it around. I had healthy and successful friends in my industry, so I decided to reach out.

This was my *first* turning point.

I asked three friends on separate occasions which books they read for business success. They all said that they didn't read anything on career development; they felt their business success was a reflection of their own consciousness.

As a teenager I lived in India and Israel, and studied Eastern philosophy and metaphysics for years. I knew deep down inside that if anything were going to change, it would have to be me. The *Bhagavad-Gita* is India's legendary scripture of a soldier on a battlefield who gets cold feet just before going to war. I determined that from now on when my intuition spoke, I would listen. I started my own hero's journey, and mind-mastery was the war I knew I had to—and could—win.

I devoured the books, finding the work of Dr. John Demartini to be the most impacting and inspiring. In his "Business Mastery" program, Demartini teaches that your business is a reflection of your inspiration.

I looked back at the darkness, fear, pain, and confusion that dominated me for almost eight months—and used it as a catalyst to take action. I didn't like my current situation, so I did everything and anything I could to find that inspiration.

I worked with colleagues, friends and mentors—physicians who practice Functional & Integrated Medicine, chiropractors, nutritionists, Qigong masters, healers, and acupuncturists. Functional Medicine is a modern and more holistic approach to managing health, and preventing disease and dysfunction than our current model of medicine. I ordered functional lab tests to determine if I had any hidden sources of stress and fatigue.

The lab results immediately brought enlightenment. I was suffering from a deep state of adrenal fatigue, which explained the sleeplessness, fatigue, decreased sex drive, and irritability. Adrenal fatigue is the physiological term for hormonal "burn out." Some experts consider it to be the number one source of depression. Not only did my results come back with a positive answer and a recovery protocol, they also indicated that I might have some type of digestive dysfunction, including food sensitivities and parasite infections. After a few more tests, sure enough, we discovered a gnarly parasite infection along with food intolerance, which explained the bloating, cravings, and mood swings.

I reached out to another friend who suggested I dive head first into energy healing and study the chakra system in greater depth.

The pain from my eight months of darkness was my incentive to continue the search. I read every book, article, and website I could find on personal, professional, and spiritual development. I threw out my TV and spent every available moment doing whatever I could to find inspiration and improve my health. I practiced Qigong on the rooftop daily, and received acupuncture weekly.

The most profound change I made was in my mind.

Instead of focusing on my lack of finances or getting angry because I didn't have any clients, I instead concentrated on what I could do to attract more clients, and how to manage my money better.

Another consistent message in the books I read and classes I took was that gratitude is a powerful healing force. I found it difficult to be grateful for my situation at first, but I was committed to healing and rebuilding my life. I worked hard to develop genuine appreciation for whatever I could find.

In late spring, I went snowboarding on what turned out to be an epic day. While riding the chairlift up in the brilliant sun and crisp air, I did my Qigong. Energy filled my body, my heart opened, and I felt gratitude to be an integral part of such natural beauty. For the first time in almost a year, I felt a genuine sense of calm, and all I could say was, "Thank you for your magnificence."

A few days later I attracted new, highly qualified, and wonderful clients. These clients were very much interested in my new work, as well as the lessons I shared from my experiences. I slowly rebuilt my business without any marketing. This increased my understanding and faith in everything, and I began to live with more gratitude and less judgment.

I started asking empowering questions like, "What is the lesson here?" I rebuilt my business and my faith in myself. It took me one year to recover from adrenal fatigue, and even longer to heal from the parasite infection, but this experience enriched my life's journey like no other.

I created my own mind-body exercise routine that reduces stress and increases energy, which I now teach to all my clients. They appreciate and "need" it in this concrete jungle known as New York City. I studied business and financial mastery, and learned about client management. I developed new skills and a deeper understanding of my craft, which allowed me to offer even more value to my clients. My experience brought me to the cutting edge of a new model of medicine, one that is much more effective at helping people get healthy by addressing the hidden causes of stress and dysfunction. Because of the focus on prevention—rather than emergency intervention—it aligns with my core beliefs.

I now also have relationships with other experts around the world who I refer to often. I've started making new friends who are going through similar healing experiences, and I have a lot to offer them in their journey.

It took some time to heal and get healthy, but I would not change a thing. Deep down, my experience taught me lessons that I desired to embrace. It brought me closer to my true self, enhanced my career and my understanding of the universe. It is clearly the most important experience in my life, and I can honestly say, "Thank God I burned out."

❤   ❤   ❤

Antonio Valladares is a certified Holistic Nutrition and Lifestyle Coach, Corrective Exercise Kinesiologist, and has been a certified Personal Trainer and a licensed Massage Therapist for more than a decade. He has practiced yoga and martial arts since he was a child, and brings a whole-person approach to eating, exercise, and living a healthy and inspired life. He is founder and president of Burn Sports (www.burnsports.com), a holistic fitness, nutrition, and stress management company based in New York City. Antonio can be reached at Antonio@burnsports.com.

Thank God
My Father Died When I Was Four

MARY FOSTER

I asked my husband, "How can a blessing be in disguise if it becomes apparent that a disaster has served you throughout your life?" The disguise was hidden in plain sight in everyday life.

She was lying on her belly in the grass with bent knees, legs waving in the air, smelling the lingering fresh aroma of newly cut grass, thanks to the old gas mower that had chugged and chomped off the expansive lawn only hours before—also shredding the newly fallen leaves, which added to the wonderful smell. Mary was making little piles of cut grass and leaves, constructing homes for the bugs. The almost sweet smell of the burned gasoline and oil from the mower still clung in her nostrils and in the back of her throat, as she looked up with large green eyes, squinting into the setting sun, where clouds folded over it like a cuddly blanket, tucking it in for the evening.

A big black car came bobbling down the long, straight, rutted dirt driveway, kicking up billows of fine dust that settled on the rows of crunchy corn stalks lining both sides of the path, drying and ready to be harvested soon.

Dressed in a navy blue suit and a felt brimmed hat with a tiny red feather stuck in the band, a very tall man got out of the car and rushed up to the spanning front porch of the large, white, friendly farmhouse. Lace curtains fluttered in the open windows letting the last of the warmed air in for the day, before sunset gave way to the moist chill rising in the autumn air.

Mary was curious about the man. She had not seen him before. There weren't too many visitors that this little one didn't know, but since Mary was only three, her repertoire of people was very limited.

This little toddler with waist length, gently curling blonde hair— long for her young age—understood the language spoken by all those around her, but still was not able to articulate well. She was often frustrated by this inability, which made her appear shy and introverted. She had the language fully developed in her mind, but was not quite able to compose her thoughts into coherent communication—and she knew it.

This little nature lover got up from where her small and lithe body had made an impression in the grass. After she rose to head into the house, she could hear some of the grass as it flicked and popped back upright. Walking through the prickly grass with tender bare feet was not very comfortable—but with quicker, lighter steps it wasn't so bad.

As she got closer to the rusty, bulging, mended screen door that led from the porch into the house, she noticed a sound she didn't recognize. Mary hit her shin on one of the rocking horse runners—her mother had put the rocker on the porch deck so she could ride in the warmth of the afternoon sun. Putting the pain on hold, Mary's little fingers wrapped under the bottom edge of the warped door. She opened it and went into the house, eyes wide and dilated in anticipation.

Mommy was in the soft yellow kitchen making a sound like crying, but she was talking and crying at the same time. Tiny Mary had not heard her mommy cry before, and this cry had something else in it for these tender ears to try to learn and figure out. The man was holding Mommy's shoulders, as Mommy dabbed her wet face with a hanky that Grandma had given her on her last visit—it was lovingly decorated with delicate tatted lace.

In the next months Mary was repeatedly ushered in and out of doctor offices and hospitals, hand in tow by her concerned mother, not quite knowing what was wrong with her daddy. What she did know was that he was hurt while taking Big Brother on a tickler ride. Daddy thought there was one more hill to make that funny feeling in the tummy when you go fast over hills on the dirt road that ran by the house. Instead of one more hill, Daddy skidded into the ditch where the road ended, and—while trying to keep Big Brother from hitting the hard dashboard of the cushy brown velvet, upholstered 1947 Packard—hit his head on the steering wheel.

Months had now passed, and they were taking Daddy away to heaven in a wheelchair bumping through the grass. This was the last time Mary saw her daddy before the funeral, where he lay in a flower-strewn casket.

Mommy was crying often, alone now with only her three children's presence for comfort.

In the big, airy, white farmhouse it was quiet for a long time.

Mary missed the hugs and snuggle time with her daddy, but even that memory faded as the years passed. Moving from the country house into a city far away helped to hasten the dwindling memories of him and the short time they had together.

But she didn't forget his voice—and she longed for him.

Growing up without a father had a hidden blessing for this little one. She did domestic chores alongside of her unflagging mother throughout childhood and adolescence. They planted and harvested vegetable gardens with flowers on either end. They replaced and puttied broken window glass, fixed holes in screens, built cement pathways out of pieces of old torn-up sidewalks the city left behind, built stone walls to keep earth from washing down a hill onto their driveway, painted and restored toys, repaired and tinkered with appliances, tended to the house and auto when necessary and possible. There was no job that was tackled without the "I think I can" attitude.

Her grandfather, a ship builder and carpenter, would give this little one a hand full of nails, a block of wood, and a hammer to "help" him when she followed him out of grandma's house into his workshop. As she got older, he included a small handsaw, and taught her how to use sawhorses, hand drills, and even how to carve an apple with a very sharp pocketknife, making fast work of it down to a very small core. Mary and her grandfather shared many apples and sometimes oranges this way.

But he, too, passed on before she was 12.

Mary spent lots of her summer time watching road crews build new neighborhood sidewalks, curbs, and streets. She even watched the junior high school go up little by little down the street. One day, she would attend it on the edges of town where she now lived.

To this day—like she has through the years—Mary still surprises many with her ability to wield a screwdriver, hammer, saw, shovel, axe, wrenches of all types, some power tools, and those tools usually reserved for men.

There was the time she saw a team of friends and relatives repairing an arbor in the courtyard of her adult home. Not too comfortable with ladder heights, she stayed on the ground, handing up boards to fasten onto the long, lavender, blooming wisteria-covered structure. The men took turns handing off and leaning on the power drill to put long screws into treated pine—a soft wood—one after another.

"Geez, this is hard wood," they all agreed.

She chuckled and finally said, "How about taking the drill off reverse?"

Everyone laughed and there was quiet jubilation and fast work to the finish—now that the job was much easier!

Tidbits of know-how have built a library of experience from which to draw to solve the fix-ups and repairs that pop up from time to time. *Ingenuity* could be used in lieu of her middle name, *Ellen*. And when something does function after a repair or reconfiguration, there is that "How about that!" wonder that follows with a single nod of the head.

Her applied knowledge of using tools and imagination to fix things—or her ability to figure out practical solutions for making something function better or more smoothly—is a notch in her belt. This is afforded to her by being raised without a father. She inherited the attitude of "Stick to it; I'm not finished until it works—or works better."

The resiliency, fortitude, and determination still serve her well in all aspects of life. Without Daddy, this gift will serve a lifetime—the gift he did not know he brought to her in his death.

When Mary's mother transitioned in 1991, some of her father's clothes were found hanging in her mom's bedroom closet—way in the back where no one ever went. Mary instinctually grabbed them up in her arms, pressed them to her face, and inhaled deeply through her nose, struggling to recognize if anything she smelled was of her father.

Thank you, God, for taking my daddy.
Mary

❤   ❤   ❤

Mary Foster is an artist and mother of three. After drawing, painting, and sculpting throughout her life, she now loves to write; her current projects include a children's series and books about spiritual enlightenment and gifts. She studied in Spain and Italy and has a BS in psychology with a minor in biology, and a BFA in art. Mary has been a spiritual teacher and lecturer since 1971. She lives in Iowa with her husband George, a book cover designer, assisting him as an art director at Foster Covers. Contact Mary at: mary@fostercovers.com.

Thank God ... for 9/11

FINDING MY RITE OF PASSAGE

TISH WILLIAMSON

February 14, 2001

A gallery in the East Village. I pass through a loud, smoke-filled bar at the entrance and slip into the crowd, making my way through the room. Two guys carrying guitar cases stop to ask if I'd like to smoke a joint, and sign a petition for the MRP.

"What's that?" I ask.

"The Marijuana Reform Party."

That's a flashback to my days in art school when all of my boy-friends looked like Jesus and smoked pot.

I thank them for the invitation but politely decline. I blow them a kiss and pony away through the crowd. They call out, reminding me that I can change my mind.

I spot a tall, handsome man standing with his back against the brick wall on the other side of the room, staring at me. We make our way across the room towards one another. As we inch through the maze of bodies gyrating to the pounding beat in the thick, blue smoke, oozing perspiration and patchouli oil, our eyes remain glued to one another. Finally we meet face-to-face. I suddenly feel like a teenager and giggle in spite of myself.

"Would you like a drink?" he asks. At the bar we talk and laugh our way through one glass of wine and three pitchers of ice water. Vinnie won't touch a drop of alcohol, but he loves to talk.

"So," I say three hours later, "in a nutshell . . . you're a non-drinking, non-smoking, non-swearing, guitar-playing, Philharmonic-loving fireman."

"I'm also a vegetarian."

I burst out laughing and almost fall of the barstool.

Now he's blushing. "I guess I'm pretty unique."

Vinnie leans towards me dreamily staring into my eyes. I can see he's totally smitten with me. We're both in heaven. We don't want this night to end. In this bizarre New York scene, I didn't expect to meet such a wholesome, upright guy—someone with manners, decent, and kind. We stay until closing then head out into the warm, misty rain. Vinnie walks me all the way home.

In the following months we became best friends and fell in love. We enjoyed a fairy tale romance of picnics and Shakespeare in the Park, Philharmonic concerts under the stars, and numerous afternoon delights. He told me of life growing up in Brooklyn, his travels through Europe, and made bashful inquiries about marriage and babies. Vinnie, the quintessential gentleman, called me his Goddess and thanked me for most everything.

Eight months later we had our first quarrel. Over the course of three or four weeks, we talked by phone and lovingly gave each other space to process the painful words we'd exchanged.

Vinnie told me he loved me.

I knew that we would come through; we just needed a little time.

He left a message on my answering machine, asking to see me on Tuesday night. My heart leapt for joy. Monday I left a message confirming that I could see him, not realizing that he would be working all night.

The next morning a delivery boy rang my doorbell. I opened the door and he cried, "Quick! Turn on the TV!"

"Okay," I said, running over to my little black-and-white portable. It was 9:50 AM, September 11, 2001.

Stunned, we stood side by side, watching the first Tower fall. He left and my phone rang off the hook—alarmed friends urgent to talk.

I telephoned Vinnie at home.

He wasn't there.

I tried the firehouse . . . no one answered. I called throughout the day and into the night. Finally at 2:30 in the morning someone answered. I asked to speak to Vinnie Kane.

"He's not here."

"What do you mean? Where could he be? Is anyone else there who might know?" After a piercing silence . . . he responded in a very shaky voice, "We don't know where *any* of them are. They're *all* missing. Sorry." Then he hung up.

I didn't see Vinnie again.

The firehouse received the alert that morning of a plane hitting One World Trade Center. Vinnie volunteered to go on the rescue mission and jumped on the red truck that sped downtown. Unwittingly, I witnessed his death on television that morning. Less than a month later, I attended his memorial service at Breezy Point and an Irish wake held in his sister's home. Vinnie's sister and I shared many beautiful memories of Vinnie. It moved me to know that he told her how deeply he loved me.

Two-and-a-half months later on Thanksgiving Day they found Vinnie's body at Ground Zero.

His family chose to have a private burial.

I was devastated that I would not be able to stand by in faith and devotion when they lowered Vinnie's body into the ground.

It took me five years to realize that this was a pivotal turning point in my life.

There were no self-help books or twelve-step programs to offer guidance on how to navigate the illusion of personal loss in the context of such an unprecedented act of global terrorism.

Everyone was in shock.

But while the world mourned in unison—I felt completely alone.

After they laid Vinnie to rest . . . time stood still. I moved forward with my arms held out in front of me, trying to fight my way out of the shadows. I knew I would have to create my own rite of passage out of the nightmare of the aftermath of 9/11; no one could do it for me.

The first couple of years I taught an arts program in New York City Public Schools, bringing together diverse groups of children ages eight through 11 and documenting their interaction. I gave them cameras to photograph images and stories that expressed their culture, and asked them to write about the photographs. A little girl from Red China took a picture of the sky. She said it represented "freedom."

This inspired me to start my photojournalism program called, "Children's Visions of Hope and Peace." I felt compelled to help give a voice and hope to these children. I watched as they discovered their similarities with one another. It was breathtaking to hear their deep desire for a peaceful world. I will forever be grateful to these children for their innocence and spontaneity, which kept me grounded in a world of joy.

When I started dating again, magical thinking ruled my judgment in relationships. I believed I could immediately trust every man who came into my life because, after such a horrible loss, surely Vinnie had sent these men to me. This led me down a gnarly path—until I woke up and realized what I was doing.

Spring 2006

I'm participating in a women's seminar, and unexpectedly stumble upon the root of my vicious cycle of suffering and inertia around Vinnie's death.

An Irish Catholic woman screams bloody murder.

"No! I'm a horrible person. I killed my baby! I don't care if I was 16. Abortions are wrong!"

The facilitator attempts to help her see the perfection in her choice as a teen. "Perhaps it was the best thing to do at the time."

"No!" she screams, "I don't deserve to be loved!"

My heart breaks for her.

Why is she punishing herself?

Why can't she honor herself?

Then it hits me.

Oh, my God—that's *me.*

My friend held me until I shed my last tear.

Silence.

A quiet calm filled every cell in my body.

For years after Vinnie's death I felt as though something was wrong with me. How could the man I loved have met such a ghastly end? I'd experienced a sense of stigma and shame, both from within myself and from the people around me. I unwittingly became a poster child for the disaster that was 9/11. My story was a reminder of the reality of what had happened. Because people wanted the whole thing to go away, it meant that sometimes they wanted me and my heartbreak to go away, too.

I suppressed my true emotions because the more I opened up to people, the more I felt pushed away. I had subconsciously punished myself over the timing of our quarrel, the missed connections, and the timing of his death. This, combined with the difficult exclusion from Vinnie's burial, meant that I had not begun to "grieve" until now—when I learned that rather than grieving I had found other ways to suffer.

I am now grateful for my heightened awareness.

It allows me to respond to my and others' pain with nonjudgmental presence, compassion, and love.

Ahhh, home again, I think to myself and start to laugh.

I must look like I've gone through a war. Well, I had gone through one—an inner war within myself. I imagine myself shouting from the top of Mt. Everest, "I'm free! I have climbed up out of the trenches. The war is over!" I'm free to rebuild my life joyfully.

I finally realize the exquisite and elegant perfection of my journey with Vinnie.

We were two people in love figuring things out.

We simply ran out of time.

The way in which one meets one's end doesn't define one's life or one's love. Vinnie died having known true love, and knowing this filled me with gratitude.

Vinnie, 9/11, and the beautiful children in my program gave me courage to go on and create value in this world as an artist and healer. They inspired me to create "Children's Visions of Hope and Peace," which became a part of a pro-peace exhibit at the United Nations, and is now an ongoing project.

The second step was to find gratitude for the tumultuous relationships that mirrored a deep, self-punishing belief I had tucked away from an emotionally abusive Catholic school upbringing. I now knew that I'd been dating the counterparts of the nun who instilled these false thoughts in me. I'd perfected the art of finding someone to punish me. Of course, I didn't know that I did this until after the fact, when I was finally able to release myself from the vicious cycle of suffering and inertia around Vinnie's death.

The truth is that Vinnie and I truly loved each other.

It's normal to miss him, but I know he doesn't want me to cry or suffer.

He wants me to LIVE, to have all that we had and so, so much more.

I will forever be grateful that we met, and that we shared so many beautiful moments together.

September 11, 2006

I'm standing at Ground Zero by invitation to participate in a Buddhist Memorial Ceremony to honor the victims of 9/11. World peace dignitaries and survivors of the deceased surround me. Standing in the morning light, I find myself talking to Vinnie.

Dead and gone.

Dead and gone.

Dead and gone? Hmm . . . it's been a little over five years. Seems like yesterday, Vinnie. Remember all of those nice people we used to chant with? They didn't forget you.

This is the first time I've been able to bring myself to the site.

I think I am surely going to faint from despair. No, truly. I think they're going to have to take me out on a stretcher—or I'll make a real scene and be on the evening news all over the world, black mascara and snot running down my face as I'm kicking and screaming, "Why God, why?"

No, Vinnie. Don't worry. I won't do that. It would be so embarrassing.

Actually, this is a beautiful celebration of life. The breathtaking light on the surrounding buildings is mesmerizing. Glistening light creates chasms of shadows that transform into magical shapes.

I feel the wind on my face and hear the resounding voice of people chanting in unison, a prayer for life filling the canyons of what was once a horrific gravesite. The gorgeous, pulsating sound, "Nam Myoho Renge Kyo," bounces off the buildings and through our bodies, lifting us higher and higher.

I can see forever, Vinnie. You wanted to see the world through my eyes. Now I see through yours. I feel you in my heart. You're standing by my side.

It's clear and crisp, the sun hot on our backs. Eerily like September 11, 2001. Instead of horror and despair, I feel 3,000 souls emerging from the earth, dancing and rejoicing, celebrating the human spirit and the preciousness of life.

I hear you playing your guitar, Vinnie, singing and cursing the Bush administration and the Spanish Inquisition.

I start to giggle and lower my head. I mustn't be irreverent at this sober memorial ceremony. Or mustn't I?

I feel like dancing. Do you want to dance, Vinnie? I've come through. I'm ready to LIVE. When the Twin Towers came down YOU rose up as a true hero. I was your angel lifting you up. You're free . . .

Fly, Vinnie!

Thank you for loving me and setting me free.

We left each other knowing love and knowing that there are wonderful people in the world. We were gate openers for each other.

❤   ❤   ❤

Tish Williamson, a professional performer, visual artist, and educator, resides in Greenwich Village in New York City. She's performed in lead roles with Broadway National Tours, Regional and Off-Broadway shows, and in numerous film, stage, and television productions. She founded Children's Visions of Hope and Peace, a project created to help children find their voices through media and writing. Passionate about storytelling, working with children, and inter-generational multicutural groups, Ms. Williamson facilitates healing transformations through the expressive arts. Her dream is to help foster a generation of expressive, capable young people who know they can make a difference in the world. Ms. Williamson is very proud to be a longstanding member of the SGI (Value Creation Society) and an author with *Thank God I . . .*™. She is the founder and CEO of Beauty Under Pressure, a whole beauty image consulting company designed for women on the go. For more information about The Children's Project and Beauty Under Pressure contact Tish at: twilli5478@aol.com and visit http://gallery.me.com/vision2008#gallery.

Thank God
I Am MAN-I-C

JEFF ZINN

*M*y wife and I sat nervously awaiting the psychiatrist to call us into her office.

I was anxious to see this doctor, as I'd been trying to get my wife to seek marriage counseling with me for months. The 15-minute wait seemed like hours as we sat glaring at each other. I was sure the psychiatrist would side with me, and tell my wife that she needs to *get her act together* and *do something* with her life.

Finally the doctor called us in.

I proceeded to sit by myself on the couch—20 feet away from both of them. That's when the doctor said to me, "Jeff, tell me what's going on."

I stood up to my full six-foot-four-inch height and in an extremely animated manner—all the while inching my way closer to them—blurted out in rapid fire, "I'll tell you what's going on. I'm a film producer, record producer, Plus Size Women's Clothing manufacturer. I know Thai Chi, and I'm now taking kick boxing"—which I proceeded to demonstrate with a double punch and kick through the air. "I do *all* these things, and *she,*" pointing my finger at my wife, "does *nothing!*"

I was ever so proud of my performance. I could hardly contain myself as I turned away to sit back on the couch, knowing full well I had to have won the doctor over. I stared with conviction at the doctor as she said, "Can you excuse me for a second?"

"Sure," I said, as I proceeded to pose on the couch with my legs crossed, arms stretched out, smirking at my wife, thinking, *Now what do you have to say for yourself?*

Minutes later a swift opening of the door harshly interrupted my egotistical gloating. Startled, I quickly glanced over to see two police officers and the psychiatrist walking towards me. One of the officers stretched out his hand as if to grab me, and said, "Mr. Zinn, could you please come with us?"

I was in shock.

Why were they here?

What had I done?

It was not until we made our way completely across the street that I realized we were headed towards the psychiatric hospital.

I stopped dead in my tracks, and asked the officers, "Why are we going here?" They responded by saying, "Mr. Zinn, it is the opinion of your doctor and wife that we admit you into the psychiatric ward."

I felt like a truck just hit me.

All the blood rushed out of my head into my gut.

This cannot be happening to me.

I went from feeling like I was on top of the world to wondering if I had any sense of reality. I blurted out in desperation, "It's my *wife*—not *me!*"

Hours later, after interviews with various medical people, they forcibly strapped me to a gurney, and injected me with various anti-psychotic drugs.

They then transported me to the hospital's psychiatric ward, where I was involuntarily committed for five days.

Thank God I was diagnosed with Bi-Polar 1 disorder.

Prior to the time of admittance to the psychiatric hospital, I had it made. I earned more than $350,000 a year, and was well respected in the most competitive business and industry in America—the fashion apparel business in midtown Manhattan, the garment industry capital of the world. I was living the American Dream. I had a beautiful wife, two sons, a million dollar home, three Mercedes, and more friends than I could ever dream of. In other words, *I was miserable.*

Beneath the surface, I lived an extremely stressful life. I spent three hours a day commuting back and forth to the city on a train. I worked more than 60 hours a week, and flew all over the country—up to two weeks out of every month. My physical health deteriorated rapidly. I was 40 pounds overweight and taking Maalox every day for acid reflux. I had high cholesterol, eczema, psoriasis, gout, sleep apnea, and—worst of all—a bad case of dandruff!

I was surely on the path to an early grave.

The five years following my diagnosis proved extremely difficult. I was given every combination of pharmaceutical drugs and creams known to mankind. I was taking 1,000 mg of Lithium for mood stabilization, tried seven or eight anti-depressants, Allopurinal for gout, Valium and Ambien to sleep, two different prescription creams for my eczema and shingles, and a Sam's supply of dandruff shampoo. I closed my business and proceeded to have four jobs in three years. The acute stress and body pain triggered frequent panic attacks, and I was falling into a deep depression. Just thinking about how to pay the $20,000 a month in overhead, plus the surge in medical co-pay costs, made me suicidal.

I was breaking down rapidly.

On March 5, 2005, thank God my psychiatrist told me to cease and desist my occupation immediately. Relieved, I sat and cried outside the doctor's office for what seemed like an hour.

I kept thinking, *All I have to do now is find a new career, downsize my lifestyle, sell my home, find a new identity (since I no longer was the successful garment center executive who everyone admired), and TELL MY WIFE.* Telling my wife I quit my $350,000 a year job was going to be as easy as walking in front of an 18-wheel truck carrying gasoline—with me holding a torch.

I thought that finding a new career was going to be a snap.

Heck, everyone called me the greatest salesman ever.

First, I determined to make some quick cash as a limo driver. Brilliant. I was a limo driver who was forever lost.

Second, I thought I could be the best surveillance camera anti-theft protection salesman ever. Instead, I became an anti-theft evangelist who gave away the cameras to protect the poor business owners from their employees and customers stealing from them.

My last attempt at employment was as a substitute high school teacher. I would have been the best ever if I could have stopped jumping out of my chair in panic every time the bell went off.

Thank God my psychiatrist told me that she was declaring me permanently disabled because of my acute stress and high anxiety, Bi-Polar I diagnosis, and DANDRUFF. I came up with a name for my condition—I called myself TRI-POLAR.

Thank God I listened to my wife years before and purchased disability insurance. Certainly, it was not even close to what I was making, but we could get by. We were lucky to sell the house before the crash in '06 and downsize our lifestyle accordingly. Now that we had downsized our life, I decided to do what I wanted to do—become the most famous stand-up comic in the world. I would show everyone once and for all I could come back and make it big. I took classes for four months and made my debut on Broadway in New York City.

I was so funny that my wife filed for divorce for mental cruelty.

Thank God I got divorced October 3, 2007. The divorce was both extremely expensive and emotionally crippling. During the divorce, I sank into a deep depression once again, and checked myself into a facility that treats individuals with depression, Bi-Polar disorder, and co-dependency.

It saved my life.

I also got to practice my comedy in the group sessions.

Thank God I met my astrological guide and New Best Friend in May 2006. At this point, most of my "friends" had deserted me, my wife had negotiated me out of my house, and I spent that summer working as a basketball coach at a sleep-away camp in the Catskills. At least I had a place to stay.

When I returned home after the summer of 2006, I began to talk more with my friend the astrologer. She opened up to me that she had been diagnosed six years before with Multiple Sclerosis. She explained that everything happens for a reason. I found out that she understood what it was like to live in fear of what each day might bring. My friend seriously studied psychological astrology, and as she delved more and more deeply into my natal chart, the answers to questions I'd asked myself began to fall into place.

Why did I focus on my grandfather, the honored philanthropist, Harry Zinn; and why did I yearn to be like him? Why did I want to protect the underdog, help those in need, and make the world a better place? Why, when I was manic, did I give away $100,000 to charity? The answers lay in the fact that when manic, my words reflected my true and deeply felt humanitarian desires—but my mania distorted my actions.

I began to study books on gratitude earnestly. I soaked in the knowledge that one needs to give to others to receive abundance. I learned to appreciate the gifts that God gave me, instead of focusing on the material losses that I had incurred. I began to surround myself with people who care about changing the world one person at a time. The more I followed a spiritual path, the more I experienced change—not only for myself but also for those closest to me.

So in review, I am now bankrupt, divorced, disabled, and I thank God I am the *most fulfilled* I've ever been.

It was because of everything I have shared with you that I finally connected with the people at *Thank God I . . .* ™. The process of writing this story—in the hopes that I might help others with similar challenges—has instilled in me the greatest satisfaction and personal accomplishment I have known to date. I am now fully aware of how the act of exchanging, of following a more spiritual path is far more important than all the wealth and material possessions I could ever acquire.

Although I know I have only just begun to downplay my ego and nurture my soul, I realize I must be on guard to monitor my mood swings—and stay in the moment. It's too easy to stray toward the illusions of false paths to fulfillment. I am so grateful for those people who have stayed with me during this process.

I plan to use this *Thank God I . . .* ™ Volume Two as a springboard to manifesting my dream of helping others like myself.

I am the kind of person who doesn't "get it" until the truck—that has already hit me once—turns around and is headed towards me again . . .

To that I now say, "Thank God I got it."

Thank God I got it!

❤   ❤   ❤

Jeff Zinn continues to spend a great deal of his time and energy raising his two sons, Jesse and Austin. Jeff and his friend host a live-streaming astrological show at www.KarmicEvolution.com. Jeff is currently editing 40 hours of video, chronicling his transformational journey from manufacturing women's plus-size clothing in 2000, to being diagnosed with Bipolar 1 disorder in 2001, becoming permanently disabled in 2005, performing standup comedy on Broadway in New York City, suffering a second manic episode in 2007, and his continual recovery. His intention is to use the documentary as a vehicle to help others diagnosed with similar disorders and their loved ones. You can check out his video clips on *Thank God I . . .* ™ and his websites www.MAN-ic.com, www.Tarzinn.com, and www.Zinnternet.com. Jeff's commitment to remain on his medication and continue his therapy is, indeed, his primary daily goal.

Thank God
I Love Being Me

CAROL GODDARD

Was simply being me enough?
The answer of "no" echoed within my mind.

I grew up fearing being me, feeling inadequate as a person. I often positioned myself in roles of pleasing everyone around me. As a result I felt empty, and I lost touch with who I was inside. Over time, my attempts to add to myself—in what seemed like an ongoing cycle—still didn't help me feel that I was enough of a person "just as I am."

I questioned, searched, hid, and overcompensated in an effort to feel adequate; however, the mask I used to greet the world still didn't fill those perceived gaps in myself.

My feelings of inadequacy built up through my teen years and into early adult life, and yet—perhaps as a way of searching for truth—the raw experiences in life drew me. Consequently, I developed a career in nursing and midwifery, where I experienced the spectrum of life in terms of birth and death.

These raw experiences allowed me to see that I am enough just as I am, and that I love being me.

Walking into the Birth Unit, I felt the buzz of a busy day, heard the sound of women at various stages of giving birth, and saw the activity of midwives moving around in response to the women. All the birth rooms were full. The hand-over between shifts was brief, as the night staff attended to the mound of paperwork they had to complete before they could go home.

I was asked to care for Susan, a 26-year-old woman in her first pregnancy, admitted in early labor at term. On examination the previous midwife could not hear the fetal heart. An urgent ultrasound confirmed Fetal Death In Utero (FDIU). FDIU has seemed such a cold term to me. Most pregnant women speak of their unborn baby, not their unborn fetus. Although "fetus" is the medical term, I much prefer to think and talk in terms of "the baby."

As I walked down the long corridor toward room seven, I shifted my focus from the busy unit to Susan, Peter, and their baby. I stood outside the door, and I heard the heartbreaking sobs of two adults grieving for the loss of their unborn child. I paused a moment and collected my thoughts. Part of me wanted to run and hide; part of me wanted to be strong; and a deeper part of me just wanted to be *me*. I knocked and then entered.

Susan and Peter, openly distraught, cradled each other. I introduced myself as their midwife. Peter looked up and tried to focus through his puffy tear-filled eyes. We looked at each other, and I could feel tears welling in my own eyes. For a moment, Susan and Peter became a blurred vision as I sensed the weight of their grief. I found my voice, "I'll be with you as your baby is born." Tears filled our eyes again.

We sat in silence for a while, not uncomfortably, just feeling the quiet. Then Susan's body followed nature's rhythms with another contraction. As the morning passed and Susan's labor intensified, she made a very conscious choice to continue without using any type of pain medication. "I want to feel the pain, not block it out and cover it up," she said with profound clarity.

Peter, keen to provide as much physical comfort as possible, supported Susan in her choice. My role became that of a resource, giving Peter ideas, and then stepping back and allowing him to provide much of the direct care. He lovingly massaged and stroked Susan, the effect obviously helpful. When Peter grew tired and needed a break, I flowed with Susan, massaging during a contraction, and gently stroking in between—the contractions providing a comforting rhythm. Susan sensed a change in the rhythm. Once again, gripped with overwhelming grief, she knew that her baby would soon be born. During her entire pregnancy, Susan focused on many birth rehearsals in her mind, anticipating a live, healthy baby, for whom they had so many hopes and dreams. Now, with her baby dead, there was no excitement, no anticipation, just loud, heart-wrenching sobs.

Susan gathered her strength and birthed her baby. The room grew silent—the quiet almost deafening—as we all longed to hear that first cry. Time seemed to stand still and the moment seemed to last forever. The silence continued until we could hold back no longer, and we cried for the loss of their baby.

The baby was a good size and looked perfect. We bathed Daniel together. Susan and Peter took their time, lovingly caring for their son. He looked beautiful; only his pale face and rosy lips revealed the "tragedy" and reality of the situation. Susan and Peter, aware that they had just this one day to spend with Daniel, took in a lifetime of memories. I took photos which, along with the hand and footprints, would be something for them to take home—something for them to keep.

I continued to look after Susan and Peter the following day. They had shared precious time with Daniel through the night. Each little thing meant so much. Susan and Peter openly talked about the life they had hoped for Daniel. They spoke of their love for him and their longing to nurture him. It all seemed so empty. After much talking, crying, and sharing together, Susan and Peter were ready to say their good-byes.

They cried as they cuddled Daniel for the last time, wanting to hang on, and knowing that he had already gone. We walked out of the hospital and towards the car in silence. Then Susan told Peter that she could feel Daniel still with them, the love still present.

With tears in the corner of her eyes, Susan took a deep breath and simply said, "Thank you."

Peter stood beside Susan as she spoke, and it was evident he was touched by the beauty and grace within his partner. In that moment, the pain and powerlessness that tensed his brow softened, and time stood still as love flowed from his open heart to hers. Peter looked into Susan's eyes, and tilted his head ever so slightly with a look of knowing and understanding beyond measure.

Susan and Peter could see and feel the love in each other, and they knew that they carried Daniel's love in their hearts. I could feel the love and the gratitude that Susan and Peter had for each other, for being with each other, and fully experiencing the rawness of life together.

As we hugged we could feel the intensity of this time together. We experienced the deep knowing of profound moments.

Two weeks later I received a lovely "thank you" card from Susan and Peter for helping them fully experience their time with Daniel. The thing that hit home most of all was the last sentence. They did not talk about my knowledge and skills. The thing that they had most appreciated was me simply *being* there with them.

I sat and re-read the last line, "The thing that we most appreciated— you simply being there with us." In that moment, I understood to the core of my being that I love being me. Being me just as I am is enough, and one of the most precious things of all is the ability to be myself. As tears filled my eyes, and my breath slowed, I felt my heart open to the flow of pure love and gratitude. The moment expanded and time stood still.

Now, I finally know that I am enough just as I am. And I can see that fear was an illusion, a block, a barrier in the way of Being Love. Seeing through the illusion led me to discover that I love being me. Thank you, Susan, Peter, and Daniel for giving me the greatest gift of all. You touched me in a way that allowed me to come home to myself, to the truth of who I am.

So now when I stand outside of a room, I pause a moment and sense my thoughts and feelings. The part of me that once wanted to run and hide, that wanted to compensate and be strong is no longer there, as a deeper knowing from the core of my being gracefully steps forward being me. I think of Susan, Peter, and Daniel, and I love being me.

Seeking my own truth led me on a journey to the richness that comes from fully experiencing life's rawest moments. I now know that when I awakened from the illusion of fear—from the dream that I thought my life was—I naturally became aware of who and what I am. I knew what I most love—and that is simply to be me. A sense of separation from Love is the only lack I needed to correct. Removing a block such as fear brought awareness of love's presence. By honoring myself I found inner peace. I now chose Love.

My experiences as a midwife helped prepare me for my current life work, which is to be with people as they open their hearts and to assist them to remove the blocks in the way of being Love. I offer my services through courses, presentations, and private sessions, helping others discover the truth of who they are. My experiences led me to co-author a book called, *A Life Like Yours*, written as a simple parable about finding love within your own heart.

It also led me to create a meditation CD, "Awaken to Stillness and Find an Ocean of Peace Within Your Heart." The words for this meditation came to me in a most amazing spiritual experience during the early hours one morning. The CD incorporates an inner body guided meditation with Tibetan Singing Bowls as the backing vibration, which gives wonderful resonance.

As our hearts open to Love and Gratitude, we begin to feel a deep remembering and re-connection with our true selves, and we are drawn to re-connect with others whose hearts are opening also. As more and more of us feel these heart connections, we experience the greater experience—Oneness.

From across the oceans and from countries all around the world, we are connecting and coming together as global neighbors. As our hearts open to Love and Gratitude, we are naturally drawn to connect to others whose hearts are also opening. I have expanded further by co-creating our "Love and Gratitude Community." This community is an ongoing global community experience, a gathering of hearts and minds worldwide. Seekers become finders coming home to Love and Gratitude.

Carol Goddard is an Australian author and presenter, an engaging speaker, and thought-provoking conversationalist. Carol is a reminder of who we are. She does what she loves most—being herself. Carol's experiences—from assisting people during the "raw" times of life—have equipped her with insights that she lovingly shares through her books, CDs, courses, presentations, and private sessions. Opening your heart and coming home to love allows resentment and fears to dissolve, as you now focus on what you truly love. Carol invites you to find what you truly love within. She is available to talk on a range of topics, including opening hearts, and coming home to Love and Gratitude. To deepen this experience for yourself, and to journey with Carol, join one of her courses, presentations, or private sessions, now. Please contact and connect with Carol at www.carolgoddard.net.

Thank God
I Had That Accident

STEPHEN LaFAY, DC

I was supposed to drive. But after another long, sweltering August day in the sun, repainting blacktop tennis courts up in cottage country north of Toronto, I was too tired to drive. So John, Peter, and I—three university students with no plans beyond a shower, let alone the end of summer—rode in the pickup truck along the two-lane highway lined with the Muskoka region's signature pines, lakes, and exposed rock.

As a diversion from the now boring commute, Peter and I took to bouncing a tennis ball at each other off the floor, which distracted John from the road just long enough . . .

"John!"

With barely time to yank the wheel back toward our own lane, we missed the oncoming car—but as we lurched and sucked in breath, John was losing control. We careened onto the gravel shoulder and—to the sound of splattering gravel—we slammed into an unforgiving wall of pink and black Canadian Shield granite.

I remember the rock face racing toward the windshield.

I know I had time to throw my hands against the dash and brace, but I woke up on the floor of the cab, stunned and blinking. Instinctively I moved my head, fingers, and toes—and immediately felt a bolt of pain pierce my lower back, take hold, and start to burn down the back of both my legs.

As I limped out of the hospital a couple hours later, by all appearances it looked like Peter and John had received the worst of it, with a bandaged chin and stitched brow. I mentioned the back and leg pain to the doctor, but he could only say that it could take a couple of days to see if it would be a problem.

Until this point I'd pretty much taken my health for granted. I was active, loved sports, and hadn't known physical constraints at all. I was taking a degree in psychology, but wasn't overly concerned with what direction, if any, it offered. But just as the genesis of the physical universe, and life as we know it, began with The Big Bang, that traumatic accident out on the highway—which I now call My Big Bang—was the beginning of events directing me to life as I now know it.

That was in 1990, and looking back on it, I can see that the crash was actually a resounding wake-up call, and the agonizing pain that refused to leave was my personal escort to a life of purpose and direction. Not that it was an obvious or direct route.

During the week after the accident, the pain in my back and legs progressed, just as the emergency room doctor predicted.

Soon I could barely walk.

After an examination with my family physician back home, he informed me that low back pain could become chronic and last a lifetime. Days turned to weeks; weeks became months, and I experienced a sinking feeling that my low back pain and bilateral sciatica would be with me for a long, long time.

As I completed my final year at university, eight months of physical therapy three times a week produced virtually no result—except increasing desperation. At wit's end, my physician could only conclude that I'd have to learn to live with the pain for the rest of my life, and referred me to an orthopedic surgeon.

The surgeon in turn said, "Son, you're only 20 years old, and far too young to have back surgery. Come back in 20 years if you're still sore, and I'll consider performing surgery on you, then."

The prospect of living in that state for the rest of my life devastated me. On my father's advice, I sought treatment with another physiotherapist, with the hope that taking a different approach might help. I was exasperated when the second physiotherapist gave up on my case after a few months of therapy, agreeing that I'd just have to learn to live with the pain.

Life with Disabling Pain

For that year-and-a-half, life was one long, intractable tailspin. Like many Canadian boys, I loved hockey, but going back to body checking or blasting a slap shot past a goalie was unthinkable. Swinging a baseball bat was definitely out. Over time the sciatica eased off, but the incessant back pain was a constant tormentor.

My outlook mirrored the suffering in my back. No longer feeling high-energy, confident and motivated, pessimism settled in. Self-pity drained away my vision. I drank more and paid little attention to what kind of food I ate. A lean, athletic build gave way to a soft and flabby body, obviously carrying excess pounds.

Each morning, hopes that the pain had spontaneously lifted overnight lost their luster. If anger and frustration could help, mine would have healed the entire world's woes, as I desperately appealed to God, *Why has this happened to me?*

While the answer tarried, I started to believe the pain wouldn't leave, and every aspect of my life spiraled downward.

My resentment spilled over into my relationships with my family, the woman I loved, and just about everyone else within reach. I nearly managed to push my girlfriend (now my wife, Michelle) right out of my life. Looking at myself in the mirror in a moment of sorrow and self-hatred, I seriously considered suicide. It was then that I heard the inner voice say, *You have something more to contribute to this world.*

But just what would that be?

After nearly two years of wincing and waiting for my body to correct itself, a friend of the family referred me to a local chiropractor. Chiropractor? I hardly knew the term. But it seemed like everyone else had given up on me—what was there to lose?

My Healing Experience

Dr. Brian Moore was the first person since the accident to physically lay a hand on me in any attempt to help me heal, and his certainty as he explained what he saw on my X-rays, gave me the sense that he could help. That was hope enough for a hope-starved man.

After the first startling *crack* as he adjusted my spine, the sense of relief was immediate and sweet. At last something happened! During the following weeks, the process of realigning my spine and rebalancing my nervous system also reflected in my mental state—I actually felt fine. In fact better than fine: I was regaining my health *and* my life. The downward spiral was reversing and my quality of life steadily returned.

The improvement was huge, so after six months I decided to continue regular care to see if a full recovery was possible, while knowing enough to accept that any process requires time, and that the healing process would be no exception: Time doesn't heal, but healing takes time.

By the end of the first year of chiropractic care, I actually felt better than before the accident. In light of the days, weeks, months, and years of oppressive pain and discouragement, words couldn't capture the gratitude I had to feel like myself again. I could savor normal activities and little routines—like going for a walk, tying my own shoes, or making love without the distraction of agonizing pain. I could work again and even play pickup hockey. I enjoyed every . . . single . . . moment. Thankfully, that sense of appreciation remains to this day.

Big Bang to Beautiful Beginning

Months into the healing regimen, Dr. Moore was reviewing my X-rays and progress when he stopped and said, "Steve, you may not know it now, but you are a chiropractor." He explained that everything that happens in life has a purpose, and my car accident was actually a wakeup call—a call to my purpose for being.

This left me with a mix of both doubt and a glimmer of inspiration. I obviously appreciated chiropractic care, but in terms of academic qualifications, my psychology degree seemed irrelevant, and my science background almost nonexistent. I'd so focused on playing hockey with dreams of the NHL that I hadn't taken academics seriously. Becoming a chiropractor would mean going all the way back to high school for math, followed by a slate of university courses in pure and applied sciences— just to apply for four years of chiropractic college. Seven years—*whew!*

How could I invest that much time? How would I pay for all that education? Could I even do the work? Would a career as a chiropractor be worth such an investment?

Yet something remarkable resulted from the accident, struggle, and healing which made my chiropractor's admonition undeniable. When that spark of inspiration ignited the fuse of my divine purpose, I knew in my soul that he was right.

It was humbling to be back; it felt long, and the work was hard. But whenever the mental challenges and daunting length of the path started to get to me, Michelle, my school friends, and my parents offered the encouragement, wisdom, and support I needed to tackle it all. In that process I can see how we receive support equal to our challenges—if we are open to recognize it.

I Do What I Love and I Love What I Do

I have the answer to my prayer of, "Why has this happened to me?" Without my Big Bang—slamming into that granite wall at highway speed—I would not be a chiropractor, blessed to take part in the healing processes of so many people. I get to practice inspired chiropractic care full-time. I now speak to audiences about expanding their understanding and experience of life, purpose, health, and wellness, and I consult with entrepreneurs and corporate employees on finding balance and inspiration in their lives, and flourishing in their productivity. In short, I am inspired to help others heal on all levels as my contribution to this world.

It was a frustrating, pain-ridden period, but the temporary suffering became a gift. My Big Bang provided the experience, direction, focus, learning, and growth necessary for healing. All of the harbored resentment and anger toward John and Peter transformed into gratitude and love. The redeeming spiral of grace from that life-changing event continues outward, healing other aspects of my life, prompting higher learning, revealing and attracting wise teachers and mentors, and encouraging others who need healing. The short answer to that complaining prayer of mine was gratitude.

I envision a healing wave sweeping across the world to help us become all we can be as brothers and sisters in humanity. This wave begins with us becoming grateful for everything—as it is—healing through the power of love, and then sharing what we've learned with others. So, thank God for accidents.

Someday, after we've mastered the winds, the waves, the tide
*   and gravity,*
we shall harness for God the energies of love.
Then, for the second time in the history of the world,
men will have discovered fire.

~ PIERRE TEILHARD DE CHARDIN ~

Chiropractor, author, speaker, coach, and consultant, Dr. Stephen LaFay lives in Stratford, Ontario with his wife and two children. His newly published book, *Your Magnificent Life: 7 Keys to a Life You'll Love*, and companion booklet, *How Your Body Speaks*, layer personal stories, inspiring examples, contemporary and timeless wisdom, groundbreaking clinical science—and even theoretical physics—to expand the reader's understanding of health, wellness, and purpose. To order or register for Dr. LaFay's weekend intensive workshops, visit www.lafaylifelegacies.com.

Join the *Thank God I . . .*™ Community online to share your story and chat with the authors at **www.thankgodi.com**

Thank God
I Died and Learned the Secret of Eternal Life

THOMAS GATES

"I'm sorry; we've done all we can.
We're not sure he's going to make it."
Within moments after hearing the doctor's words,
I began an amazing journey that would transform my life forever . . .

Growing up in central Texas, I had the good fortune to spend long periods of time playing alone, wandering about the woods and hillsides, observing how everything in nature seemed to flow effortlessly with a natural rhythm and grace. Although I didn't realize it at the time, Mother Nature was teaching me—through simple observation and silence—great lessons of life that would later serve me in a most powerful way. Without really giving it any thought, I knew that there must be an underlying source or intelligence that supported everything happening around me.

In 1970, at the age of 20, I left my country home and moved to the Dallas-Fort Worth area. I worked as a professional musician, playing drums in concert and dance halls, nightclubs, and bars. I soon found myself surrounded by people who obviously had a very different take on life. Parts of the city were plagued by drug and gang-related crimes, with a growing sense of heightened racial tension. I often witnessed sudden outbreaks of violence at some of the venues where I performed.

One particular night, a gang fight erupted outside our club, and people began to fight inside. Chairs were flying, glass was breaking, and a young woman lay on the floor suffering from a knife wound. The chaos turned into a full-blown riot and, outside in the parking lot, a police officer was shot and killed.

After this tragic event, the stress and strain of living in such an environment took its toll. My health suffered; I became increasingly depressed, and I felt isolated from my friends. It was difficult to relate to this whole scene anymore, and I longed for the inner peace and silence I had known in my childhood. I spent the next two years searching for some sort of answer. Not finding it, I sank further into hopelessness.

After the steady urging of my sister, Barbara, I learned a meditation technique that she'd practiced for a couple of years. Immediately, I experienced an incredible deep silence. I was thrilled that this could be the key to help me reclaim what I thought I had lost. Even so, nothing could have prepared me for the intense experience I was about to go through.

Just one week after learning to meditate, while visiting my parents, I collapsed in pain. I was rushed to the hospital, where doctors quickly diagnosed a severe case of appendicitis. As they prepared me for surgery, I recall a doctor saying, "Don't worry. It's a routine surgical procedure. You'll be home in about three days if all goes well."

It did not go well.

Those three days turned into a month-long struggle for my life. The surgery turned out to be more complex. The doctors discovered a large tumor in my colon that had to be removed immediately. This would ultimately lead to major infection throughout my body.

When I regained consciousness after the surgery, the pain was unbearable and the doctors kept me heavily sedated for several days. When my body temperature soared to 107 degrees, I heard the doctor announce to my father, "I'm sorry; we've done all we can. We're not sure he's going to make it."

Within moments after hearing those words, I witnessed the process of emptying out of my body, and looked down from somewhere just above. At first, I didn't recognize it, and then realized *that body* was *me*. Or was it?

How could that be me, when I'm up here—looking down at that tiny, empty shell?

In that moment I realized that nobody really dies . . . "Nobody gets out of here dead!"

The view of my body gradually faded away, and I found myself expanding—like molecules of air, filling up a vast, empty space that unfolded before me. I was released from all attachment to the life I had known before. From that point onward, I had no past and no future— there was only the present, moment by moment.

I moved through an expansive tunnel and a brilliant golden light appeared in the distance. The magnetic quality of the light gently drew me towards it, until finally I entered into it. This exquisite light had a pure healing essence and warmth that completely absorbed me. I felt a sense of timelessness as I became one with the light.

I eventually moved beyond the light into a seamless continuum of deepening silence. Finally, I crossed over an invisible threshold into . . . nothingness . . . beyond time and space. There was nothing to know, nothing to do, and nothing to be. No thought. Only the potential for everything. Yet it was unmanifest in its silence. It was the Pure Unmanifest Source of all creation.

The next thing I knew, I crossed back over that same invisible threshold, heading back in the direction from whence I had just come. It was only then that I recognized Source for what it was—the eternal Source of my existence. I experienced my own consciousness as inseparable from absolutely everything in creation. I had no need, no desire, and not a single trace of fear.

All was one and all was well.

Perfection.

Little did I know that I would soon be returning to the world and the body I had left behind.

Then I had the sensation of moving faster and faster. Reaching an intense rate of speed—I was suddenly slammed back into my body. I opened my eyes and looked around, but I had no memory of ever having been in this body before, and no memory of the world around me. I didn't know who I was, where I was, or even what I was. But that didn't matter. I had the memory of the incredible journey I had just taken, and the truth of my own eternal existence.

The slate was clear.

One life had ended and a new one had begun.

The day I left the hospital, it was a completely new world. Even from the confines of my wheelchair, I felt an overwhelming exhilaration by what I saw, as I passed through the hospital doors to the outside; the sunlight, the air, the sounds, the smells, the colors, the spring blossoms, the birds, and the human beings—lots of wonderful human beings. I viewed everything as connected and inseparable, the unique expression of the same eternal Source. I'd had absolutely no idea that any of this was going to be here and it was just fantastic. It was good to be alive.

It took a year to physically recover, but it took many more years to integrate fully into this new life, and to understand the ultimate purpose of my experience. Over time, I shared my story with others, and noticed that people often had spontaneous transformations, simply by listening. Hearing the story tickled the memory of the eternal Source within them, and they experienced more wholeness in their lives. It was becoming clear that the revelations of my experience were not for my benefit alone.

I soon perceived a growing presence of the golden light in my physiology, and discovered that I had acquired healing abilities through it. Simply by being present with this light, I could enliven a person's natural healing processes. In addition to the release of physical pain, illness, and emotional trauma, individuals experienced a deep, peaceful silence, along with an expanded state of awareness. This expanded awareness enhances one's ability to experience that unbounded Source.

My purpose is now clear and I understand why everything in my life happened exactly the way it did. Every day I am thankful for the blessing of these experiences. My mission is to share all this with others, and to help them live with joy and inner peace, knowing that infinite, eternal Source within. This is my life's work—and the journey has only just begun.

❤   ❤   ❤

Thomas Gates, international healing facilitator, author and speaker, is the founder of Healing Spectrums for Health and Wholeness, and creator of the Destination Wholeness Workshops and WorldwideHealings.com. Audiences across the nation have been inspired and empowered by Thomas's healing workshops, training programs, and personal consultations. He is committed to enlivening the experience of unbounded consciousness in others, and accelerating their natural physical, emotional, and spiritual healing. For more information, please visit www.WorldwideHealings.com or www.DestinationWholeness.com; e-mail: thomas@WorldwideHealings.com.

Thank God
I Saved My Life

ANNABELLE BONDAR

I am 57 years old—and I am in the prime of my life.

Imagine at 57 years the joy of experiencing the "prime" of life.

It was only eight short years ago that my life was threatened with breast cancer.

As I child, I watched both my mother and father being poorly treated by traditional medicine in hospitals. Based on these childhood experiences, I mistrusted traditional medicine and disbelieved doctors.

But I had to find a way to save my life.

Growing up, I remember being a bit of a tomboy. With the boys, I loved to play games like baseball and football. But of all the memories that shaped and impacted me, there is one that uniquely stands out. My dad encouraged me to groom and ride a pony at the stable I used to visit frequently. My friend, Debbie Hector, and I would spend entire Saturdays at the stable—grooming, laughing, and riding. At first, the horses seemed so large and intimidating, but slowly something magical

246

happened. Through these magnificent horses, we began to trust that they would take us where we wanted to go, and we experienced the freedom of the outdoors. At first, I remember trusting the horse to walk, then to trot, and eventually to gallop. We would sway and rock. Over time, we learned to blend our bodies into the rhythm of those beautiful animals. It was a feeling of true confidence, of love and trust for the horse and my riding skills.

As this trust grew, events spun around me that created a strange but true reality. I grew strong within myself—while mistrusting the outside world.

I watched my grandparents, aunts, uncles, and so many of my family grow old. How could they be so vibrant at home—and just wither away in a hospital?

One thing became very clear.

I knew intuitively at a very young age that there was much more to true healing than just the physical care offered by traditional medicine.

My mom was sick and in the hospital for many years. High blood pressure was uncontrollable in those days. In the fifties, children were not allowed to visit in the hospital, so I watched and waved to her from the window. There was little connection with patients, and hospital room settings were cold.

Sometimes there was no sunlight.

There was little movement.

In this atmosphere, there was only physical healing. It was the weakening of the mind and soul that developed in that scenario that continued to plague my mind. *What would happen when people were sent home from the hospital? Who would help them, then? How would they feel? How would they manage in a weakened condition?*

I developed mistrust for doctors and hospitals as I watched certain things happen over and over again. Things were done without any interaction or feeling of connection in those white, sterile hospital rooms.

I knew in my heart there was a better way to heal.

When I was seven years old, my beautiful mother passed away. I remember her clear skin and lovely hair.

My dad was lost without her.

The passing of my mother was very hard on him, yet he tried to keep my life as special as possible. For a long time he kept all her pretty shoes and clothes in the dressing room. We had moved to a gorgeous home, as he thought that might help her recover.

Exactly one year after my mom's passing, Dad started having problems with his throat. When he discovered that he had cancer of the throat, he searched for the best medical advice, and had his surgery in Rochester, New York.

He went alone.

He didn't want to worry my brother and me.

I stayed with my next-door neighbors for a few days at their cabin in Windermere.

When Dad came home, he lived with a higher mind and spiritual practice. He developed healthy eating habits, breathing exercises, a ritual of massage, and high self-esteem. He was outgoing, loved to dance, and became a master.

My dad lived well for 30 years following his experience with cancer.

He loved life as a gift and a blessing.

In January 2000, my dad developed congestive heart failure. He was in the hospital, alone, in a room with a machine by his side. It was a new procedure to remove fluid that kept building up in his lungs. He had that positive attitude, again, ready to go home—but the weakness this time was too much.

Finally he became dehydrated—but was sent home too early.

I watched his relapse.

He could barely walk because he was so weak. He went from a strong, vibrant man, to being weak, frail, and dependent.

I remember him looking in the mirror and having difficulty recognizing himself.

I was terrified every time I went to visit him in the hospital and saw all the things that were happening to him. He was so weak. He said he was all right, but he felt my fear, and as his rest was mandatory, I could only stay a few minutes at a time. He did *not* want to be hooked up to all the machines. He did his best to pull through. He wanted to be at home; Marcia Powell his caregiver—who I am still in touch with every year—was wonderful to him. She helped him cope through the final stages of his life with love, dignity, healthy food, a little sunshine, and hope. I know he looked forward to her coming each and every day to look after him.

One year after my dad's passing, in January 2001, I was in the gym and started to panic as I could not do my sit ups. There was no problem the day before. I thought I was in the best shape of my life. Physically I was, but inside—after all those years of worry and internalizing—tests showed cancer in the right breast.

The shock of the news was hard.

I waited in a little dark room for the results of the biopsy.

I knew I was in for a big wake-up call when more and more mammography pictures were required. A false hope came from the biopsy technician with assurances—"Everything is fine." Do you know how devastating it is to think you *may* or *may not* lose a breast?

Instead, the surgeon said, "Until we get in there we cannot be sure."

My healing journey began that day.

I went through traditional cancer treatment, but knew I needed more healing. Not having a regular doctor to go to, I did not know where to turn. I did not want to be involved in groups for "sick people" because as I did not "feel" sick. I had a cancer experience, which through the messages from society often took me to *what do I do now?* Inside, though, I knew things were okay.

I was working out again, but not seeing results. It takes a while to come back from cancer; after all, cancer does not happen overnight.

The lady at the vitamin store told me about Dr. Hoffman. I was interested in what this woman had to say, and made an appointment, which has taken me to new levels of wellness in all areas of my life.

There was something very different about Dr. Hoffman's Centre that I had not experienced before. I remember looking into a room with people sitting in comfortable chairs surrounded by a library of books.

They were having IVs for detoxifying the body of heavy metals—things like mercury and lead. Dr. Hoffman was casual and welcoming, and he wanted to see every piece of information about my health.

I remember answering questions about my health that I did not even know mattered. For instance, there is a seeming correlation between teeth and disease. There was an *aha!* moment where I could see that the root canal I had many years prior was perhaps directly related to my breast cancer. This is today's medicine. It is cutting-edge knowledge.

Trained in both traditional and complementary modalities of alternative medicine, Dr. Hoffman dedicates his life to his patients. He is a master in his field. Patients understand what their results mean and learn what the optimum levels of health are, as he charts their progress with each appointment. He is thorough and raises the bar on wellness in today's world.

When I went to review the first set of blood test results, I knew I was in good hands. It was not by chance that I discovered Dr. Hoffman. It was a blessing. Do you know how special it is today to have a doctor who *listens* to you, who *knows* from his vast study of all the modalities of integrative medicine *which* areas to apply? Together as a team, we committed to a protocol, and followed it from beginning to end. With each visit, I became a little stronger and had a little deeper healing.

Dr. Hoffman helped me save my life.

Today, the results of my blood work are the best they have ever been.

I feel that I am in the same place as I was as a child—riding my pony, galloping freely for hours in the open field. Sun, rain, and snow—it didn't matter—I wanted to ride that pony.

Over the last several years at Dr. Hoffman's Integrative Health Centre in Calgary, my doctor and I have explored almost every area of healing. I continue to study and read the books of many alternative practitioners. I visit the best wellness spas, and incorporate all of it into what I call *harmonic health*.

I have discovered the beauty in healing.

Recently, I decided to take a break for a week, for total self-care, and to surrender to the things I am grateful for in my life. I am especially grateful for my mission, and dream to be the spokesperson of *harmonic health*. With hope, authenticity, and certainty in helping others discover there is true beauty in healing, I am grateful I can share my heart experiences around the world.

Today I visualize my body in perfect harmony—from the cellular level to the spiritual level.

It has been a magnificent journey of transformational healing.

I thank God for my mother and father.

I know in my heart that I was to have all these experiences in order to take me to this special place of mastering my health, and sharing all the blended ingredients of wellness with those who want to live their lives to the fullest.

❤   ❤   ❤

Annabelle Bondar was born and raised in Calgary, and now spends her time sharing her personal journey through lectures based on her book. Annabelle is the director of It's Me Annabelle, Inc., a not-for-profit organization dedicated to raising awareness of complementary cancer care. She hosts It's Me Communities, which offer support and education to those with life-altering conditions. www.learningtolovecancer.com

Join the *Thank God I...*™ Community online to share your story and chat with the authors at **www.thankgodi.com**

Thank God
I Lost My Child

LOUIS IANNELLO

From April to October, I played eight to nine games of softball per week, five of them on the weekends. Baseball came above all else. I didn't have time for girls, until I met Margaret in 1978. We married in March of 1982—before baseball started!

Nothing changed in my sports world, except for the addition of fantasy football, which took up my Sundays from September thru December. Family functions had to happen after a game. I wouldn't miss a game for *any* reason.

Our first child arrived on July 23, 1985. Bryan's christening didn't take place until after baseball ended. Then Michael arrived on September 16, 1987.

Michael's birth went well, but later that day they told us that Michael's blue coloring was a symptom of a medical problem needing immediate attention. That night he was transported to a facility specializing in pediatrics. Margaret stayed at the hospital and I rode in the ambulance with Michael. Hours later, the doctor told me that Michael had a condition called transposition of the great vessels. That means a reversal of the pulmonary artery and the aorta going and coming from his heart. In laymen's terms, oxygenated blood flowed to certain parts of his body and unoxygenated blood flowed to the rest. They performed a temporary procedure called *ballooning*. This opened a valve in his heart so blood and oxygen could mix throughout his body—a temporary measure until he could withstand open-heart surgery.

They performed open-heart surgery in April 1988. I held Michael's hand as they wheeled him to the operating room. At the door he cried when I let go of his hand. Our hearts ached for him, but we knew he was in GOD's hands now. The operation took six or seven hours, which seemed like weeks. Finally, the doctor came out and said everything went well.

Seeing him in the recovery room was the saddest sight I'd ever seen. He was hooked to a respirator, a heart monitor, an IV, and they affixed a gadget to his finger to track the oxygen level in his blood.

The sedation wore off—and Mikey opened his eyes.

We felt such happiness anticipating his recovery. After a day or so, the doctors weaned him off the IV to start bottle-feeding, but he was unable to suck on the bottle. The medical staff assured us it might take a few days for his body to recover from the trauma, and they restarted the IV.

After several weeks, he still couldn't suck on a bottle. In fact, he couldn't do anything that a six-month old should be doing. They placed a feeding tube through his nostril and into his stomach. Margaret stayed with Michael during the day, and I would take over after work. She stayed overnight on the weekdays, and I stayed on the weekends. The schedule wore on us. After a month, and with training for his care, we brought him home. To Margaret's credit she did a wonderful job.

The Michael that we brought home was not the same child we took in. He couldn't move around or sit up. As his first birthday approached, he laughed when we played with him, and he tried to talk the best way he knew how, but it wasn't at a one-year-old level. He would either sit on our laps, or just lie around on the floor or crib. He didn't walk, talk, sit, drink, eat, or anything else we all take for granted. Because he'd bite down on his tongue so hard—which ripped it to pieces—they removed his teeth so he wouldn't bite off his tongue. There were times he'd cry for hours. The doctor diagnosed colic. By now we suspected that either the doctors had no idea what was wrong or they weren't telling us.

Months passed and we did the best we could to keep Michael as comfortable as possible. By his second birthday, he had endured 10 more hospitalizations. His temperature spiked to 104 to 105 degrees for no apparent reason. A spinal tap to check for meningitis was negative.

During this time, we were unable to give our eldest son, Bryan, the attention he deserved. Many times, he wanted to go out and play, but Michael's needs made it impossible. He didn't understand. His grandparents took Michael a few days a week so we could spend some time with Bryan.

Michael's face became raw from the tape securing the feeding tube in his nose each day, so they surgically inserted a tube directly into his stomach. Michael came back from the operating room still sedated on a respirator. Over the next several days, Michael's condition didn't improve, and he still breathed through the tube in his throat. When the time finally came to remove the tube, we knew that if his throat swelled, it would cut off his air supply, and they would have to do a tracheotomy. He returned to the hospital room without the trach, which gave us some relief. As the minutes ticked by his heart monitor beeped, indicating his throat was closing.

Back to the operating room for a tracheotomy.

How could this be happening?

It was a nightmare.

But we didn't give up hope, knowing that no matter how bad things appeared, there was maybe someone who had it worse—like the kid in the ICU who hadn't had a visitor in two years. We knew Michael had the love and fight from our families and friends.

He stayed in the hospital for weeks because the insurance company wouldn't pay for in-home nursing. I calculated the home nursing care charges compared to the hospital charges—a savings of about $200 to $250 per day. I wrote to the insurance company outlining the pros and cons of Michael being home with his family, and the savings they would have. They denied my request. Several calls later to my surprise, I was on the phone with the vice president of the company. By the end of the week, we were on our way home.

We learned CPR, how to replace a trach if it fell out, and how to replace the tube stitched into his belly. The 24-hour nursing care gave us a newfound freedom, the first in almost two-and-a-half years. We'd even put our vacations on hold to care for Michael.

Michael was comfortable with the nurse we hired. He turned three; Bryan started kindergarten. You could see the relief in Margaret. Then one day I received a bill from the hospital. I called my insurance company, only to find that our agent skipped town with the money we paid each quarter. The bills from doctors, anesthesiologists, labs, and hospitals totaled $450,000. I didn't have that kind of money. I pleaded financial hardship and was able to get some of the bills reduced. People, amazed with how we held up, asked how we did it. My response: "The easiest thing to do in life is give up." When you have two boys who are counting on you, giving up isn't an option.

Shortly before Michael's fourth birthday, his temperature spiked to 105 degrees, and they performed his fourth spinal tap. Afterwards they told us to take a vacation for a much-needed break, especially for Bryan's sake. We left Michael in the care of the nurse, and left for our first vacation in four years. We arrived on a Sunday in Orlando, Florida, feeling strange being away from Michael. Two days later, I phoned my mom to ask her to give Michael a kiss for us. She said, "We rushed him to the hospital in cardiac arrest!" I didn't know what that meant, but I knew it wasn't a good thing. As we packed, Bryan overheard about Michael. To our amazement he drew a get-well card to his brother.

At the hospital, I felt the air sucked from my lungs when the doctor announced that Michael had no brain activity. Our son was dying. All the long hard work we put into keeping Michael alive and comfortable was about to end. The doctor wanted our permission to take him off the respirator. We held his hand, kissed him, and looked for any sign of life—a tear or a twitch, anything—to prove he wasn't leaving us. Our selfishness to keep him with us was strong, but we knew in our heart his time had come; knew it was best for Michael to let him go. It was the hardest decision I ever made in my life.

At one point the staff encouraged us to go home for a while to rest, as we were exhausted from the flight home from Florida. Just after midnight the call came. Michael had passed away. The next day we made his funeral arrangements. That night, surrounded by our families, we sat at home without our Michael. It was surreal. It was then that my mother and brother told us that the nurse caring for Michael didn't call 911, but instead called my mother's house. My brother Scott rushed Michael to the hospital, while the nurse administered CPR to him in the back seat. The heavy traffic going over the bridge to Manhattan delayed the medical attention Michael needed. I believe Scott still feels bothered by the events of that morning. But to us he is our hero. I cannot thank him enough for what he did for us that day.

Margaret and I arrived at the funeral parlor before anyone else, and saw Michael without tubes, trachs, or heart monitors attached to him. He didn't have to suffer anymore. When the rest of the family arrived, I told them, "Don't cry. You'll see Michael finally free of pain. He's fulfilled now."

For two days, hundreds of people paid their respects. To my surprise, some of the visitors were my biggest rivals playing ball. Their presence taught me that friends matter. From that day forward, I no longer had rivals. When the chips were down, they were there at my side.

My outlook on sports took a backseat to family things. We took vacations in the summer no matter the game schedule or the playoffs. I knew the game would be there when I got back. I tried to live as if it's the last day I would be here on earth.

On November of 1995, we found out that Margaret was pregnant. This naturally frightened us, as we didn't want to put another child through what Michael endured. It was a long nine months, but I knew GOD had a plan for us. Shaun was born on August 1, 1996. The relief we felt—after the first night when nothing went wrong—was like having a ton of bricks lifted from our backs.

Two years prior to Shaun's birth, my dad found he had throat cancer. Over the next four years, he also developed liver and colon cancer. One day he said to me, "I go in for chemo, and I feel like garbage for four days. Then after only one day of feeling good, I have to go back for more treatments. Today I'm telling the doctor to stop all treatment." We watched as he whittled away to nothing. He died at home on Sunday, September 27, 1998.

It was at that time that I realized I no longer felt love and affection for my wife, and hadn't for a long time. Margaret and I separated in February 2000, and our divorce finalized in 2001. It broke my heart to leave my boys, but I knew they would be a big part of my life and they are.

I worked in the World Trade Center, and on September 11, 2001, I was a block away when the second plane hit the building. My sister and brother worked with me as well. I tried to get to the building, and then tried to call from my cell phone, with no success. I knew GOD had a game plan for me. So far each day had been a challenge. Both Melissa and Wayne were late for work that day and avoided the "tragedy."

In July 2002, I met Lisa. We hit it off immediately and have been together ever since. She and my two sons get along well, and my family loves her. The nice thing is that I get along better with my ex-wife now than I did when we were married. Lisa suggested that we include Margaret at holiday functions, so she can enjoy those times together with our sons, instead of staying home alone.

I make it a top priority to get away from the everyday grind by taking vacations each year with my boys, just Lisa and me, and with Lisa and Shaun. Bryan, now in his early 20s, vacations with his buddies. I'm able to do that more easily now because of my profession with World Ventures. I get to travel at wholesale rather than retail, and that saves a lot of money, so I can go on vacation three times a year.

My priorities changed drastically over the years because GOD sent me one of HIS angels, Michael. If I had to do it all over again, I would welcome it with open arms. I would rather have Michael for those four years than to know life without him. I thank GOD I lost my child because it showed me the real meaning of life. I thank HIM for giving my family and me the opportunity to enjoy Michael for the short time he was here.

♥   ♥   ♥

Author Louis Iannello worked the floor of The New York Board of Trade for 28 years; 13 of those years he was an active floor broker for L & I Commodities. He's now entered the world of electronic markets, trading via computer. An entrepreneur, Louis represents World Ventures, a company that offers discount travel at very affordable prices, and Ambit Energy, which specializes in supplying electricity at a discounted rate. Visit his travel website at www.dreams4you.biz and his Ambit Energy website at http://dreams4you.rovia.com/.

Thank God
I Am an Adrenaline Junkie

DAVID GULICK

All the signs are here. The shakes, red eyes, dry skin, nose drip, sleep deprivation, achy muscles. Only one thought fills my mind—but it's just a way to pass time before the next fix.

Most won't understand.

I don't expect them to.

I'll try to describe the feeling.

Close your eyes and picture this. Time stands still, no sound exists, the walls are closing in, but my mind is free. I haven't been this clearly focused on anything in my entire life. Everything in this moment is perfect. I am one with God. I am the master of my surroundings—and nothing can stop me. I can feel my soul blend into the cosmos. There is an amazing inner peace; I live at the edge of my nerves; there is an overwhelming sensory overload, as I take it all in at once; total awareness of everything around me, and yet I'm not even there, man.

I'm not even there—I am gone into a whole other state of being.

Yes, I have it.

I have it.

I can see myself in a month, week, or even a day from now, standing in the basement of a little church coming clean to a group of fellow addicts, "My name is David Gulick—and I am an addict."

There . . . I said it.

But as much as I might need it—I don't ask for help.
I have no desire to be cured.
This life chose me; I didn't choose it.
Addiction works in funny ways; alcohol, food, work, money . . . not now.
My drug of choice, *now*, has become *adrenaline*—and *surfing* is how I quench my thirst. I'm doomed to live a life run by weather patterns. This far transcends normal addictive behavior. This is a passion, an art, a religion, a healer, a humbler, and there is history to this noble sport of kings. I'm just doing what I was meant to do—riding the waves as they are provided.

While I don't want to take away from the severity of other addictions to alcoholism, drugs, food, etc., this addictive behavior controls me just the same—only with different hours and a better tan.
In fact, I first noticed my addictive behavior with alcohol—out seven nights a week for months on end—binging. I just called it my 20s. I grew tired of that destructive behavior, and found a new drug of choice—adrenaline—and I got my fix riding waves.
My life has not been that of a silver-spoon wave rider, or a total beach bum. In fact, as I sit here writing, I am in the midst of losing my life's savings: a real estate portfolio that has taken years of hard work to acquire, perfect credit, a retirement plan, the "Great American Dream"—GONE. Some 10 years spent behind the bar living a vampire life. Plenty of broken bones, sprains, strains, surgeries, with instant access to an easy escape from daily stress of making it in New York City—alcohol.
This surfing addiction actually provided the gateway to leaving alcohol, self-doubt, and hesitation to commit to something bigger than myself.

This addiction has proven to be the "healthiest" choice I have made—even though that was put to the test as well.

You don't forget your FIRST wave. I bought an old six-foot two-inch tri-fin at a surf shop in New Hampshire. It was beat up, but I didn't care. I took great pride in mixing the fiberglass and resin to rebuild the damaged tail, so that I could get it in the water. I waited all summer to take it out. Growing up in the suburbs, I was nowhere near the beach, but each August we took a vacation to see my retired grandparents in North Carolina. I remember Shark Week conveniently played on the *Discovery Channel* the same week we vacationed every year. I was scared shitless, but I had to watch. *ESPN* used to have something called, *Hot Summer Nights,* and every Tuesday they would show SURFING.

It was written in the sand that the ocean would somehow control my life.

First day—August 1994, Emerald Isle, NC. I paddled out and caught my FIRST wave—and stood right up! I had watched it so many times on TV—it just felt right, but now here I was in the ocean, standing on a surfboard. The feeling of walking on water was the biggest thrill I had ever experienced, and I wanted that feeling again and again.

Now that I had found surfing, I knew that life wouldn't be the same . . .

Fast-forward a few years to my first real tube. South side of Scripps Pier, San Diego, California. It was late in the afternoon. The sun was setting. The surf was a few feet overhead on the sets—and clean—and I was riding my six-foot eight-inch Merrick rounded pin. I dropped in late on a right, and the whole thing started to wall up. I raced it high. Instincts took over as I was running on pure adrenaline. The lip came over me, and I was covered by the moving water for just a moment, before I snuck out the doggie door to avoid getting crushed.

For that brief moment I was in the energy of the wave—and time stood still.

I couldn't hear or feel a thing.

It was pure magic—that little room that only existed for a second—and then was gone. That little space existed only for me. I would now dedicate a good portion of my life to finding the perfection in that moment—when all the elements came together and time stood still in the tube.

This search took me around the world: Sydney, Gold Coast, Bells, Margaret River, Bali, Lombok, Sumbawa, Java, Rio, Ireland, Costa Rica, Baja, Puerto Rico, the list goes on . . . trying to fill my passport before it expired.

What a glorious life, right?

It comes at a price.

To start, I quit my career as a mechanical engineer. I recall missing weddings, funerals, birthdays, and major holidays, blowing countless relationships, job opportunities, and savings accounts, and I avoided committing to anything that meant a possibility of missing waves—all for the sake of surf.

What an asshole—right?

I'm so fortunate to have parents who put me through college. I repay them by . . . quitting my job to surf. Its like, "Hey, Mom and Dad, thanks for working your whole life to pay for a degree that I won't use!"

I didn't care about anything other than making enough money to afford the next plane ticket.

I couldn't control it.

When the forecast called for surf, I had to be there—no excuses.

When times got tough, I retreated to the ocean. The ocean was my healer. When things were falling apart, good waves would make everything better.

It was my time.

I could be in my own little world.

Of course the fix was only temporary, and often the lack of responsibility that came with hiding out in the ocean made things worse. How could something that has given me the greatest memories in my life, also cost me so much? People, who loved and cared for me, worried when I went incommunicado for weeks—and sometimes months—in some hard-to-reach corner of coastline.

I felt like I let so many people down.

Every addict has to hit bottom before they are willing to change. My bottom came when I flew over the handlebars of a motorcycle in Bali. The first day of a six-week surf trip ended in a flash.

I was very lucky.

I snapped a collarbone.

With a quick surgery, some stitches, a bunch of lost skin, and a few months rehab, I would be fine. I would heal, but the neglected relationships would require more. My carelessness with other people's feelings carried over into my own safety—and I paid the price.

I was no longer invincible.

The accident was all the wakeup call I needed.

I hadn't missed waves before—and now here I was stuck in a hospital bed in surf heaven, while my buddies scored the best waves of their lives. Not only was my big surf trip ended, but also the life I had lived through most of my 20s.

Back home was no better. With two months recovery plus rehab, I couldn't work and couldn't surf, my friends were all at beaches getting waves somewhere, and my life savings was running out.

Not what I planned . . .

Ten years in the water.

Ten years of selfishness.

Was this my payback for all those I hurt and ignored when there was surf?

A chance to reflect, to mend some of the damage I did to every other area of my life.

I thought about quitting.

I moved on to my next addictions with partying, and then again with work. The same patterns with a different focus. Relationships suffered; it was still all about me.

My addictions serve me well.

While some areas of my life would suffer, I learned to honor where they gave me success. I became grateful. Yes, I was addicted, but surfing was the healthiest thing I could do. *The ocean calls: the rhythms of her movements mesmerize me.* This addiction has saved me.

When my health was back I chose to surf.

The addiction needed a home—and the ocean was it.

Looking back, I wouldn't change a thing. For every relationship I've lost, a new one—if not hundreds of new ones—have begun. With these new relationships have come countless new opportunities. Thanks to a lack of commitments (a.k.a. flakiness), I have been able to take advantage of them. The world has become a much smaller place, and I have become a global citizen with good friends scattering the globe.

For the education I chose not to use, I have received an even greater one as a student of the world, learning about different cultures by immersing myself in them.

I realize just how strong my parents' love for me is, and that they haven't judged me—as I judged myself. I am grateful they let me make my own mistakes. I have been fortunate to give them the gift of travel, as they have been able to see the world through my eyes.

I value all the relationships I have been able to keep, and the lessons that I have learned. I maintain balance by having learned to work hard and play hard—when the times are right. I maintain excellent health, and feel as fit as I was at 18.

Surfing is something that I won't "master," and for that I'm on an endless quest for knowledge and experience in every area of my life. I see clearly where my values lie and, after years of drifting through life with no real plan, I have found my purpose.

Instead of traveling the globe to get away from it all, I travel to share knowledge. I'm not telling the world to drop everything and take up surfing. What I *can* offer is that when you are fortunate to have found your mission, and can live from a place of love and inspiration, everything else will work itself out.

The family now understands.

So do friends.

Flakey is a word that sometimes fits. I like to think of it more as *committed*. "Cause' when da surf's good, nobody works!" (Turtle, *The North Shore*)

Timing is perfect.

It matters.

It really does.

Miss the wave and you've missed the ride. But it isn't done. The next wave is right behind waiting and growing.

The perfect wave.

God doesn't send one chance for you to get it right, and then dry up the possibilities. The next one is on its way. Life is about the ride—the bigger the wave, the bigger the reward—and the bigger the wipeout.

Making the wave isn't what matters; it's that you went when it came.

Ride it!

Go as hard as you can. Enjoy that experience, and take it for what it can offer you. It will be over soon—and then there's another coming—just paddle out there and let it take you . . .

❤   ❤   ❤

Dave Gulick currently has seven surfboards, five wetsuits, roughly 25 pairs of board shorts, a few travel bags—and that's just what's in his small New York City apartment. He's fortunate to work full time with *Thank God I . . . ™*, traveling the globe doing so. An entrepreneur to the core, he has done many businesses, including having a website, investing in real estate, and trading options. He will surf as long as he lives. His pet project within *Thank God I . . . ™* is to create a *Thank God I . . . ™ Surf* book—and use it as a way to help save our oceans and beaches for future generations. Contact Dave at davidg@thankgodi.com and please join the "Thank God I Surf" group in the Online Community.

Thank God
I Was Adopted

NANCY PARELLA

My name is Nancy Parella—and I am adopted.

I was born in 1969. My parents tried to have a baby the conventional way, but had several miscarriages and decided to adopt. Meanwhile, a 16-year-old girl was pregnant with me—and abortion was not legal. With the help of her parents and a lawyer, the arrangements were made.

My parents awaited my birth, and then brought me home just five-days old.

Growing up, I knew I was adopted—even before I knew what it meant. I had friends who were adopted, as well, so I did have people to talk to who could relate to how I felt. We would talk about things—like who we looked like. We wondered if our original parents thought about us, and if they were even still alive.

People of course had questions for me because they didn't understand. Sometimes it was annoying; sometimes they would say insensitive things because they just didn't know any better.

At times it was hard being different from most people.

The good thing was that if I didn't want to tell people—they didn't have to know.

In high school, my friend and I decided that when we were old enough, we would search for our birth families. It wouldn't be easy because when I was born—everything was different. My records were sealed—and I had no rights to them. They didn't have "open" adoptions, then. I could not even find out my medical history without consent. I didn't have any information to work with. I did have friends who had a name that they could search.

As I got older, I wanted my medical background, which is why I began my search. I could *only* have the records released *if* there was a signed consent by my birth mother. Since I could not find her, I could not get that consent.

Now that I had my own family, I realized how hard it must have been to give up a child.

I am grateful for that selfless act.

Even though I remember other kids saying I was a "mistake" when I was young, I realize that I was "meant" to be here. These 16-year-old *kids* were meant to bring me to my parents to help fulfill their lives with the child they had wanted but couldn't have.

I grew up with lots of love and everything I needed.

I had a good life, one I might not have had if I were not adopted. I became very busy with my family, and stopped pursuing my search.

Although, sometimes, I still wondered.

And yet I was at peace with the fact that I may not know more.

Fortunately for me the story does not end there.

Before I stopped searching, I had registered on different adoption search websites. I had only my birth date and the lawyer's name to submit, but I figured out how many baby girls were born on the same day as me, and were adopted from Pennsylvania. I received an e-mail about a year later, asking me if I had any new information, or if anything changed. I answered back that my address had changed, but that was it. This man who ran the website voluntarily replied, and said he thought he had a match.

I was skeptical but played along.

We went back-and-forth for about a week, exchanging information and photos. He then passed on our e-mail addresses—and left the rest up to us.

It was exciting and scary all at the same time. I let her make the first move, and soon received an e-mail from my birth mother. We decided to write the courts, and have them release our information, since they had our consent now. I received a copy of my final adoption papers.

It was official—and I found her.

After weeks of "catching up," I knew the things I had wondered about for years. The next step was to meet. I had found out that she had stayed with my birth father, and that they married two years later, and two years after that had a son.

I had a full biological brother!

All of a sudden, I had this whole other family.

My mother wanted to come with me to meet them. We set out on an adventure that not too many people can say they've been on. I am thankful to have a mom who supported me through all of it, and was so grateful for me that she wanted to thank them.

I felt truly blessed to have so many people who loved me.

There were many different emotions I felt.

I am still in touch with my birth family, although my mother *is* my Mother. She is the one who raised me, and that is what a mom is. Being a mother, I now know that. I am raising three beautiful children—and it is challenging. I can't say it is a bad thing to have more people care about me in my life, though. My children have many more family members who love them as well. I don't know how deep their understanding is, but I know they enjoy seeing them.

I am grateful to have found them, and to know what I knew all along: they gave me up so I could have a better life than they could give me at the time.

As a parent, I know what a great sacrifice that was.

I am thankful for being adopted because I now understand how much I was wanted, and how blessed my parents were to have me. I also appreciate how blessed I am to have three healthy children of my own. I am trying to raise them truly to appreciate life, and to be grateful for what they have.

I am thankful for the way my story turned out, and that I could have the closure I now have.

❤   ❤   ❤

Nancy Parella lives in Lynbrook, New York, with her husband and three children. She has been home-raising them for the last 15 years. She is going back to school to become a personal trainer, and hopes to start a career in this field. It's her interest in health and nutrition—and her enjoyment of helping people—that leads her to assist people to get healthy.

Thank God
My Sister Died

BETTIE BLECKE

The day my sister died, I began to live.

Sounds strange doesn't it?

Dying is simply an emotion that becomes a reality in ones mind. There doesn't need to be a focus on dying or on living, only on the present moment. Being that we only have the *now*, there is no need to waste our emotions on anything less.

Growing up in my home was challenging. There was yelling, screaming, arguing, and fighting going on. With three children, you would think this was normal—except that the above activities were between my father and mother.

Dad was just plain mean and vicious.

Mom tried to keep things going, but eventually became very mean as well. In spite of the mental and physical problems she endured, she still did the best she could.

In the middle of this "family" were my brother, my older sister, and me. My sister had the burden of taking care of us.

I cannot say if things were different before I was born, but my earliest recollections were of my parents fighting, and seeing my mother being hit, beaten, or pushed out of the way. Dad frightened all of us. He didn't treat us like human beings—but like animals. I do not remember a single moment during our time with him when I wasn't scared. He loved to belittle us—and would go out of his way to hurt us.

My sister had a challenging childhood. Being the oldest, my mother depended on her basically to raise my brother and me. Mom sewed unbelievable costumes for us to enter any athletic arena. She may have been secretly fulfilling a dream she wasn't allowed to pursue during her youth—dancing, singing, acrobatics, and swimming to name a few. She would cart us around like there was no tomorrow, and my sister remained on top of things.

Jealousy and envy grew between us.

My sister was becoming both my mother and my dad.

Mom was feeling the constant abuse, mentally and physically, and she seemed to get progressively worse. Dinnertime was more of a knife-throwing contest.

I really believed that my father was the devil.

There were many things that we were forced to do, but one of the worst memories I have was to eat my own vomit—not once, but twice. That was to enforce upon me the need to eat what was given to me!

As time went on, we learned what to say and do around both of them. We had our own signals that we would use to prevent us from getting a beating or another type of punishment. Mother, becoming more and more frightened of Dad, would secretly leave with us at night to go to someone's house to stay.

We all started to speak in whispers.

Mother taught us how to sneak in and out of the house without making a single sound. Being so young, I didn't knew what was going on, and I began to think and act just like my mother. I was already becoming sick like she was—without even knowing it.

After Mother and Father separated, I thought things were going to be better.

I was wrong.

We moved countless times during that 10-year separation. We believed we had all been "brainwashed" by our father—now Mother was there to see we remained that way. She had taken a full-time job, so my sister had the tremendous burden of still raising us, and had complete jurisdiction over us. My sister had been abused and beaten by my father as well, so her thinking patterns were naturally on that same path. My brother, though one year younger than me, was growing past both of us in strength and size, and he—being from the same troubled family—was slowly showing his dominant side. His actions were much like my father's, and his thoughts like my mother's.

Soon after the divorce, the future only declined for us.

From old to very young—it didn't make much difference—Mother started dating any man who would have her, and accept her three children.

Her sexual behavior was no secret.

After the third or fourth husband, my sister left home. I remember being crushed when she left. It was soon after her 17th birthday, and the years that followed were totally insane. It would be four years before I would see her again. My life without her soon spiraled downward. We kept in contact by letters, but that was all. My mother hated her so much she made sure there was no contact between her and me, or my brother.

Meanwhile, my mother pursued yet another two husbands—the last one being the one who turned me inside out.

He was a creature from hell.

He had a woman in every town—and boasted about it. His overture of sex with me was kept secret—but destroyed me. I didn't have my sister to talk to anymore, so I was left with the choice of either confronting my mother—or remaining silent. I chose a path that confronted my mother—and it was the last time I remember talking to her.

The two or three years that followed are blurred to this very day.

My clearest memory is of my sister and her new husband coming back to find me in a bad way—and seeking help for me. She offered to take me in and take care of me, again. She also had the distasteful decision of seeking help for my mother. In those days, there were no facilities like there are today. Mentally unbalanced people were put directly into lock-up wards and administered shock treatments. The thinking at that time was that shock treatments would bring the patient back to the state of mind where the trauma began. That meant bringing her back to her childhood, literally erasing her entire life up to the age of five. I don't know how my sister found the courage to proceed with the decision, but it was the best decision she would ever make.

I did graduate, found a job, and thought I was doing okay, but soon learned that I was not "all better." I had nightmares constantly, and soon began to experiment on ways to end my own life. I was putting my sister through hell and, true to the fashion in our family, ran away.

There I was—alone at last.

I was making just enough money to find a small apartment close to my job. I contacted my sister a few months later. We were like bookends for almost five years. I kept my private life a secret, though, even from my sister.

I started going down the same path my mother took with relationships. It would go from bad to worse. I now understand that I was seeking out men just like my father. That is the only type of man I knew. The worse they treated me—the better it was.

As for my sister's marriage, it was following the same path. We all know in life that things change. My brother-in-law was becoming more like my father, and the jealousy was more dominant—or, perhaps, I was at a stage in my life where I could see it.

It was happening all over again, but this time with my sister instead of my mother. The beatings and the lying were all present, along with a newly acquired taste of alcohol. They both started drinking like there was no tomorrow. My sister became boisterous and overbearing, and my brother-in-law became mean—mean enough to kill.

I began straying away from them, but was there when my sister needed a place.

I was now watching out for *her*.

Many frightening nights followed with my rescuing her from one place or another. Her home life resulted in a smashed face, bruised arms and legs, burnt clothes, and broken doors and windows. One night I picked her up on a deserted street, only to have my brother-in-law come charging at us with his car, and then smashing the window in to get at both of us!

My once strong, once powerful, once loving sister was becoming an alcoholic right along with her husband—and there was nothing I could do to help her. I didn't know the signs, and by that time I had married, and had my own responsibilities. I was becoming a fly, again, in that trap. I certainly was not free from my own demons, and I had no experience in this new area. I did what I thought was best at the time— and supplied her with liquor

I also started to find liquor soothing and mellow.

We had stopped communicating for almost two years, when I learned that my sister was dying of lung cancer.

That news was too much for me to handle.

I remember screaming to my husband, "My sister, my sister was . . ." I then drank myself into a stupor.

My sister was told she had six months to live—and she died within that time.

Her last wish was for me to stop drinking.

After her death, I felt anger, despair, guilt, hate, remorse, self-pity, and very little love for God. It would take me another year before I could face the reality of her death and of my drinking.

Then, help was sent to me.

Not in the way you would think.

Through some powerful spirit—that being God—and my love for my sister, I was able to ACCEPT help, and FACE her transition and my drinking problem.

It would be my first time to live life on life's terms.

My sister's death brought me to a place in my mind where I was finally able to devote time to myself. She instilled in me her courage and her wisdom, and I thank God that she was in my life.

Dealing with death at any level is confusing and unsettling.

I know now that she didn't die.

She lives with me now—in my thoughts and in my prayers.

She taught me to survive no matter what.

Her death gives me life.

I am no longer saddened by her death; I am an extension of her life.

Thank God my sister died.

Getting to know me . . . Not one person can be read by one snapshot, nor can one person be described simply as being "a kind person." Our lives are intertwined in a vast arena of what has happened to us in the past and in current events. My aspirations in life are to help others seek their own individualities, and to instill a passion in them they had lost—or possibly hadn't known they had. My love for music, my thirst for knowledge, and my "don't-give-up" attitude are all very much a part of me. Minding the store within *is* top priority. I have spent much of my life living as someone else—and I am now learning how to live as *me* and, yes, I am a different person than I *was*, and that is the greatest gift I have received. Bettie Blecke, BeeJay Management, LLC, www.wealthybeyond.ws.

Thank God
. . . for Disillusionment

IT TEACHES US TO DANCE
WITH THE INVISIBLE

DR. SUE MORTER

As with everything else in Life—disillusionment serves. Every experience serves our ultimate empowerment—our awakening to the realization that we are powerful beyond measure. It eventually happens for each of us during the course of our lives in one form or another. The key is to recognize it "as it is happening," in order to manage the effects consciously.

As a doctor caring for patients—for what was then nearly two decades—perfectionism had served me well. It remembered details; it had me doing all the right things, focusing on being a good doctor and being a good person—helping others even beyond caring for myself.

It served in so many ways . . . right up until it didn't.

Things got done.

The hallmark successes were reached in my career and social life. But I had the proverbial empty feeling in my heart that comes along with such *outside-in* efforts.

"Follow the rules and you will win" wasn't working for me, somehow.

So, I did what everyone does, I found a Guru. Okay, not everyone does this in the traditional sense, but most of us do in one way or another. We find someone or something that teaches us an alternate perspective to what we have been seeing. We may even abdicate our personal power to them, thinking that they have something that we do not.

These new teachings offered many answers toward a deeper understanding of my purpose here—and a conscious avenue inward—that I had not known prior. And because it was enlightening in many ways, I committed my time, my focus, and my financial support even more fully.

I traveled to India to serve and to learn.

I raised money—lots of money—to build kitchens in small villages where people were cooking on dirt floors. And I attended as many gatherings as possible to sit with this teacher—to listen, learn, and absorb all that I could. The more my conscious mind integrated this way of looking at my life experience, the more I committed to doing everything as "perfectly" as I could, to ensure that it all worked the way it was "supposed to."

I followed all the rules—and there were plenty to keep me busy.

If you are familiar with the Guru path of teaching, you know that there are many inexplicable, seemingly illogical ways of providing circumstantial learning experiences for the student. This was a feeding frenzy for my perfectionist, stressed out mind, and a perfect setup for what was to come.

Initially, I thought it was due to my "do-good" orientation—and my willingness to go the extra mile—that I was taken in very closely and very quickly by the leader of this teaching. Later, I realized that it was simply my destiny, if I were ever to relax. But at the time, I thought that it had to do with my attention to detail and capacity to get the job done right, so I leaned in with everything I had. I turned up the juice on my willingness; after all, I was learning so much, and I was so grateful that I tried even harder at every assignment and at every request.

And so of course the requests came on strong.

I found myself with multiple, simultaneous assignments, often tedious and seemingly ridiculous. They demanded my efforts well into the early hours of the morning, with little or no sleep many nights in a row—during the gatherings that the organization put on—and still the jobs could not be completed, no matter how hard I tried.

My perfectionism was at serious risk.

And as for the practice of meditation and the application of the teachings, I was creating a spiritual rash over trying to get it "right."

Prior to this time in my life, I had not meditated, and here I was with many who had been very devoted to it for 30 years or more. I sat peeking out of the corner of my eye to see if I was sitting right, holding my chin just right, breathing right, even Om-ing right! It kind of defeated the entire purpose—if you know what I mean.

I held a record-breaking tension in my body with the entire concept.

One day, after many months of this pattern, and three specific sleepless nights in a row, I found myself frustrated, exhausted, and "over" the slave-driving service concept. I gave up in the middle of my tasks, and surrendered to the Main Hall—where everyone else at the event was enjoying beautiful music, chanting, and engaged in peaceful meditations. Disillusioned by the fact that all this service wasn't making me feel any better than what I had been doing for all those years prior, I was compelled to honor something else that was happening inside of me.

I sat down—or rather fell down—and began trying to learn the chant. I was too tired to worry about doing it "right" this time. And I knew that I was "breaking the rules," so to speak, by not doing what the Guru had asked of me—but I realized that I had to *do* something *kind* for myself.

With this decision made, I felt my heart start to fill from a deeper place than words can describe.

It was my core—and it was immense.

My breathing had to slow down considerably in order to hold the tones as long as the chant went. My mind focused on one thing—the simple words that were Sanskrit names for God and the Divine.

Then it happened.

In an instant—after several verses of the chant, breathing slowly and being intensely focused—I was instantly in another place, or rather in another dimension of the *same* place. I experienced my self as *me*—but not in a body.

I was a pure shaft of Light.

I could see 360 degrees in every direction—the same as in front of me. I could sense the earth beneath me, small and far below, but I was connected to it, embedded into it up to what would have been my knees.

The Light was so magnificently bright it seemed 10 times brighter than the brightest day in the desert that I had ever seen.

Most importantly—I felt complete.

There was the most beautiful sense of Well-Being present—far greater than anything that I had ever imagined.

I did not want for anything.

With each breath, I could see a tremendous and magnificent rise and gentle fall of a beautiful pink Light, translucent and iridescent, and in the form of a blanket that stretched to the horizon in every direction, and seemed to be soothing the planet beneath me.

I had a knowing that it was Love.

In some way, I was connected to breathing Love to the planet— sounds crazy, I know. Especially for a doctor trained to see things tangibly and objectively, and trained to know that these things do not *really* happen. Yet it was more real than anything I had ever experienced. In fact, the difference between that dimension and this one is like the difference between being present with an actual person verses seeing a photograph of a person. The latter seems flat.

Since that moment, there has been a much deeper vision of Actuality for me.

It changed me forever.

It awakened me, again, to the invisible.

As a child, I was able to see energy fields and auras around objects and people, but I abandoned my ability when I saw that my talking about it made people uncomfortable. I had tried many times to "get it back," but couldn't.

Now it had returned.

Likewise, after this experience, my body began to heal a lifetime curvature in my spine—which now is completely resolved. And most importantly, I came in contact with the True essence of my Being. I dropped the need to measure from the outside what would determine my value, my experience, or the perfection that I am.

Further embodiment of this miraculous event came later, when I learned that many of the things I thought this Guru stood for were not a reality at all. Not the teachings themselves, but rather the application via community projects, etc. Many of the projects that we worked on, the monies that I collected and donated personally, the special grants and honors that she had been given by other spiritual organizations and teachers—were in large part not real.

Therefore, most of my respect and devotion were based on something that existed in theory only.

Another disillusionment? Yes.

Did it serve? Of course it did.

I now know that I have the power within me to determine the value of any event in my life, and therefore to determine the impact that it has. I learned that to trust the way I feel in any given moment is the only guidance I need. I realized that when things don't feel as they should, they probably are out of balance with the Universe—and appreciating and redirecting that is all we need to do.

No attachments.

There is something far greater for us just on the other side of what we see. The most profound aspect of *human* life was made available to me in the moment that I stopped trying so hard, and simply chose to *love* myself enough to engage in an act of self-kindness—even when it broke the rules. Through that frustrated, disillusioned moment, I am now able to dance again with the Invisible and a deeper version of Truth.

I am forever grateful.

Now *that's* Perfection.

Today, when I recognize that things are not working as easily as they could, I begin to manage the situation consciously by allowing there to be a "bigger" picture than I thought possible just a moment prior. I see the magnificent Beauty just beyond . . . and I share that with others. I immediately focus on consciously trusting the Actuality that exists beyond what we may see as "the rules" on the surface of life. It is, in fact, invisible and inviting us to dance.

This is the work that I teach in Intentional Living, an internationally celebrated body of wisdom that is the evolution of this experience. I travel all over the world and teach the concepts that I recognized in those moments—in live workshops, tele-seminars, and on radio and Internet television—seemingly without any effort on my part. Instead, people are being served more by my simply "Being"—and being integrated into the space that I reached that day.

My intention is to assist that awakening in anyone interested.

May you Bless and Love yourself enough to have that dance.

❤ ❤ ❤

Dr. Sue Morter has been speaking, teaching, and training for the past 20 years—both nationwide and abroad—on the concepts of user-friendly quantum physics, bio-energetics, and their application to evolving human consciousness. She illuminates how old belief systems that were established early in life often contribute to habits and dynamics that interfere with our lives today. By understanding the relationship between human energy fields, our conscious thoughts, and our subconscious memory, audiences begin to see how *change* is a natural flow, a Universal Law, and an opening to freedom. She shows us how we self-sabotage but, more importantly, how we can end this cycle to become, again, who we really are.

Dr. Sue hasn't taken an antibiotic for an illness of any kind. She shares this possibility with others in her Focused Care Treatment Programs, revealing the power of conscious self-healing.

Known as "one of today's messengers with tomorrow's message," Dr. Sue is known for her high-impact energy, and deep, guided meditations in seminars and workshops presented worldwide. To arrange or register for an event, or to schedule treatment sessions with Dr. Sue, contact Morter Health Center at 877-I AM THE 1 (877-426-8431). www.drsuemorter.com www.morterhealthcenter.com

Thank God
Mom Escaped Life Support

STAN GRINDSTAFF

Insight

If you are reading this . . .
   you are not in a coma.

If your body moves . . .
If you see around you . . .
If you are conscious . . .
   you are not in a coma.

Mom was in a coma for two-and-a-half weeks.
While comatose, she used me as her portable consciousness.
On her behalf, I visited people and places.
When she desired, she used my eyes to *see*.

Beneath the still surface Mom lived.
Silently we conversed.

Telepathically, intuitively, she shared her creative process with me.

Life support—in this instance—kept her from moving on.
This is Mom's story of ultimate victory.
Not history.
Her story.

Hindsight

Think of *your* mom. Smile as you recall the lovely, kind, make-you-feel-safe, cause-you-to-giggle kind of things.

Now think of *my* mom. Keep the joyful thoughts and feelings about *your* mom—the qualities you love—then picture the short, cheery, plump, sweet and kind-hearted Good Fairy in *Cinderella*.

My mom, though, didn't need a magic wand. *She* was the magic. Everything she touched came alive. Stardust sparkled around her and girlish laughter danced in her eyes.

Mom was a simple woman without earthly riches. She took care of her parents' family instead of graduating from high school. She didn't own a car or learn how to drive. She mended used clothes and made quilts out of scraps. In order to pay for toys for my younger brother and for my piano lessons, she babysat. She loved cooking without recipes—using whatever was at hand.

Foresight

Mom loved the truth of love.

She taught me to have a kind heart, to be loving and strong, and to care for my world and those in it.

She said, "Be thankful and you won't be bored."

She developed my sensitivity to spirit, encouraging me to trust intuition.

Mom said there is no such thing as "dead" life. Forms of life may change so butterflies, for example, can fly free. Ice may turn to water, then to steam, to clouds, rain, and finally to deep pools of crystal clear water. We don't have a funeral because a baby "form" is left behind as the adolescent emerges—nor do we mourn when an adult "body" replaces that.

Death is an illusion.

Life is eternal.

Mom shared how there is no distance or geography in spirit—how you are just as close in heart no matter the miles. As a natural healer, she showed me how to use my hands so I could *feel* the energy of loved ones anywhere on the planet. Each evening, she would get cozy in her flannel robe and fluffy "slippies" and, sitting with a meditative mind and prayerful heart, she blessed many she cared for all over the world.

When she first met you, Mom would call you close for a hug. You would feel "home"—maybe for the first time. Total appreciation. You would remember how she first used her sleeve to wipe away any cookie crumbs, little bits of pine nuts, or cinnamon that might still be on her lips. And her soft voice would bless you—whispering in your ear, "You are safe in my heart."

Then your world would spin around and spiral down into a cup of warm herb tea in her small cottage in Southern California.

Oversight

I remember the last chat I had with my mother.

Phone in hand, I gazed at California Redwoods out of my second-story window in the Oakland Hills, watching a squirrel open a shelled peanut from a neighbor.

Mother was unusually intense and insistent.

"I really think you need to be more compassionate and patient with the elderly."

As a grown man in my hurried world—this irritated me somewhat. Older people were okay in their own way, but I dreaded sitting around hearing the same stories over and over and over.

I knew she had triggered something in me, but I couldn't put my finger on it.

Sightless

A week or two went by—and then I felt strange, ill at ease, and restless.

A long-distance phone call said Mom was injured. She fell and was taken by ambulance to the hospital.

Fell?

Hospital?

I needed to fly south.

I tried to tune into my mom—to feel her smile.

Nothing.

I tried intuitive skills she shared with me to connect with people— again, nothing.

I closed my eyes and tried to breathe deeply.

Panic.

Sight for Sore Eyes

I drove myself to visit Mom in the hospital.

Feeling numb I drove into a void.

I could hardly breathe or think or feel.

Was she already dead?

I finally found the drab concrete hospital, the crowded parking lot, an empty space that wasn't for the handicapped, the cluttered entrance, the faded map to the ward, the scratched elevator button, the floor, the sleep-deprived nurse on duty, the long hall with dreary linoleum tile and an echo of voices—and finally, finally her room with a faded muslin curtain pulled shut.

Why pulled shut?

I parted it and floated in.

I felt smothered by the muffled sound of machinery.

Somehow I had entered the wrong room.

Motionless in bed was a stranger with a wrapped, pale, bruised, and puffy head, with straggly gray hair, and a pipe down the throat, and tubes taped everywhere.

Oh, no.

My stomach lurched.
The motionless stranger was on life support—in a coma.
I felt claustrophobic.
I felt helpless and nauseous—then stopped breathing . . .

breathe my boy breathe
see past what you see

What?
I turned around and then back.
What was going on?
A voice inside my head?
No. It was my imagination. This hadn't happened before.
And yet—I couldn't doubt it.
I felt magic to the core of my being.
How was this possible?

share my smile
love you son

It was *Mother.*
I started to breathe again.
Feel her love again.
Know her spirit again.
Tears slid down my face.
I tried to smile.

grateful you're here

I wept.

son
i see thru your eyes
rest in your smile
dance in your heart

Blind Sight

open your eyes son
let me see son

I wiped my eyes—and felt compelled to look at her prostrate body. I found my gaze being controlled, my head turning first to her toes tucked under the hospital blanket, then up the blanket to the mangled gray hair of her head, and then around the room—bright energy burning through my eyes.

In my mind—or heart—I asked, *What happened?*

sweeping singing whistling dancing
carried box upstairs

i left my body

looked
down

body
fell
down
down
stairs

I gulped.

head
hit
stone floor

flew back to body

paramedics came too soon

At First Sight

visitor coming

I felt my eyes scanning the bed, again, vividly seeing every detail, every fold—assuring decorum and modesty for my mother.

your job honey
calm her down
need to chat

I greeted the visitor, held her hand, helped her settle down and get over the initial shock of seeing her life-long friend in a coma—replacing any disgust with trust, and any pity with a sense of connection.

thank you love
bye for now

I found myself propelled out of the room . . .

Later, the lady shared her amazing experience of communing heart-to-heart with my mother—the same as me—enlivened and brightened by her spirit.

Many more encounters would follow the same pattern.

Not By a Long Sight

As her son—encouraged by her to honor the creative process in all things—I felt I was the key to bringing my mother out of the coma. Surely, by increasing the life current I could bring her to consciousness, again.

Mom, I sang in my heart, *I can bring you back.*

no son
please!
brain damage
it's my time son

Okay, Mom . . . okay . . .

now please . . .
get me off off off life support

I was summarily informed that the medical establishment was in the business of "saving" lives—not "ending" them. They would fight me in court if necessary. Once machines are hooked up and breathing for a person, family declarations and statements—or wishes of the comatose—mean nothing.

I felt a cloud of heavy responsibility surround me.

What could I possibly *do* to help Mom escape life support?

Down the hall from my mother, I called my older sister on the public pay phone. She was appalled at the idea of "pulling the plug."

As I hung up, Mom said:

it's okay honey
i'll find another way

Instantly the weight on my heart lifted.

Now—instead of letting go to the Light—Mom rallied to get better . . .

In the next week or so, the doctor in charge finally agreed to take her *off* life support *IF* and *WHEN* she could breathe on her own— "Not very likely," she added.

Sightseer

In the meantime, I visited people and places my mother wanted to see.

Near her home, many of her closest friends and I joined hands and closed our eyes in a circle celebrating Mom's life. Suddenly my eyes opened and my head turned—as what felt like an outpouring of fire focused on each one in the circle—then my eyes closed again.

Another time, she turned my head to the front of a house where we used to live, intensified the life current through my eyes for a second or two—and that was that.

Sometimes she just wanted to see flowers.
Sometimes the sky.

Out of Sight

One morning, standing in the trailer where I was staying—after several days of no communion with Mom—she communed . . .

> *hey there*
> *been workin' deep*

Where do you go? I asked in my heart/mind.

> *come on*
> *i'll show you*

Suddenly flooded with golden-yellow light—the room disappeared. Transported through more radiant light, we were joined by what can only be described as hosts of heaven—light beings, many of whom I sensed I knew from my past—Father, Grandpa, Auntie, friends of the family.

Mom was the tour guide.

Timeless harmony reigned supreme.

Transition from this earthly state to higher frequencies became clear.

Life celebrates itself at all levels.

And then just as quick I was back—with the room and everything around me snapping into focus.

Sight Unseen

> *your inheritance son . . .*
> *my chinese checker set . . .*

(Mom had coached me: "Just jump marbles and have fun!")

> *. . . and my compassion for the elderly*

(Afterwards, I was genuinely surprised to find how easily I connected with those more mature than me.)

After two-and-a-half weeks in a coma, transition was close. *Mom, I can spend the night here at the hospital with you.*

you need your sleep
go home love
i'll wake you . . .

The next morning at 7:20 I was awakened by the warmest hug—

. . . bye honey

—and promptly fell back to sleep.

At 7:30 AM the doctor called.

Finally, she said, my mother had gotten strong enough to breathe on her own, was taken off life support—breathed heartily for a couple minutes, then all body systems quickly reversed—and she expired in peace.

"Yes! Yes! Thank you so much. We are truly grateful."

After hanging up, my cheer was loud and long.

The butterfly was finally out of the cocoon.

Sight

After she transitioned, a hand-scribbled list of over 70 names of friends from around the world was found in Vivian's little home. Smiling each night with eyes closed and heart open, she had brought balance and inner peace to each *beloved one*.

❤   ❤   ❤

Stan Grindstaff is a drama teacher, author, and editor. He is inspired to help create the *Thank God I . . . ™* Community as part of the Core Team and, as Chief Editor, to polish stories in this book. Stan holds an MFA in Theatre; he has used his considerable experience to create and lead dynamic self-presentation seminars all over the world. His experiential coaching empowers participants to speak in front of an audience with *light* instead of *fright*. Stan is also a master of energy healing with over 50 years experience. With his wife, Lori Dawn, he helped create their company, Hope Springs Eternal. Together they clear negative subconscious memories, trauma, and habit patterns in couples and individuals for personal renewal and self-discovery. To benefit from Stan's editing services, professional self-presentation coaching, or energy clearing, e-mail: stan.grindstaff@gmail.com or stang@thankgodi.com.

Thank God
I Had Postpartum Depression

DR. SHOSHANA BENNETT

It was over!

A dream fulfilled.

A wonderful marriage, a new house, a career teaching Early Childhood Development to college students—and now I was a mother!

The hours of childbirth classes, the planning of the nursery—even the long labor and delivery ending in a C-section—were done.

I had my baby—finally.

All the wishes and dreams about having a child had come to fruition at exactly 8:00 PM on November 22, 1983.

And now in the operating room all eyes were on me.

My husband Henry was watching me intently for signs of excitement; the doctor smiled at me through his surgical mask; and there was an eager, expectant look on the nurse's face when she turned toward me holding Elana—my newborn.

As I lay on the delivery table, the nurse held my baby next to me.

I heard myself uttering the appropriate, endearing baby-talk words to Elana. I was hearing the words as if they came from someone else. I felt like an actress. I was performing—this wasn't real . . .

The pressure was immense—I had to do the "right" thing.

All my dreams suddenly shattered.

Henry and I had eagerly anticipated the birth of our first child. I had conceived using a particular system, read the right baby books, consulted with appropriate medical professionals, and taken the suggested Prenatal Exercise classes. I taught Early Childhood Development classes.

Why was this happening to me?

I may as well have been shot through the heart.

BAM!

I became sick to my stomach when I realized the awful truth about myself—I was *not* a normal person, and I wasn't able to be a "good" mother.

A good mother wouldn't feel the way I did.

I was supposed to be fulfilled.

I should feel "love" for my baby.

But no—*not me!*

I was numb and detached.

I felt nothing.

Empty.

A shell of my old self.

I couldn't tell anyone my horrible, shameful secret. What would they think of me? I became overwrought with fear, self-loathing, and inexplicable guilt about my poor, innocent baby, who ended up with *me* as her mother.

Little did I know that this emotional state would last for years.

The first few nights after the birth, I barely slept at all. My anxiety was through the roof. I slept on the floor next to my baby's crib, afraid that if I fell asleep—I wouldn't hear her if she stopped breathing.

If I did sleep, I'd awaken with a full-blown panic attack a few minutes later, gasping for air, believing I was having a heart attack and dying. I became so sleep deprived that I started hallucinating and having delusions that everyone was out to get my daughter.

My paranoia, panic, depression, and scary obsessions kept me prisoner in the house. Every day when Henry left for work, I pushed the moveable living room furniture in front of the door to prevent a violent intruder.

I had thoughts and feelings I didn't think a mother ought to have, and didn't have the feelings I thought a mother should have.

What was left of my hair after delivery (hormones plummeting can make hair fall out) went straight, instead of having the natural curl.

I enjoyed flavors of foods, but now eating had become just another chore—and everything tasted about the same.

The lighting in my world had become dim, and objects literally appeared in shades of gray without much color.

I couldn't bond with my infant.

When she'd try to engage me, I couldn't muster the emotional energy to get eye contact with her. I had no energy or motivation to do anything. Getting off the couch was sometimes impossible. It was like I weighed a thousand pounds. Having taught Early Childhood Development for many years at the community colleges, I knew intellectually how my behavior must be affecting my sweet baby girl.

But I was too ill to help myself.

The embarrassment, shame, and guilt were overpowering.

Shouldn't I—of *all* people—be able to control my behavior enough so it wouldn't damage my infant? I was smart and educated—I TAUGHT this stuff. What was my problem? Why couldn't I snap out of this, and treat my daughter normally? I didn't deserve to be a mother.

I was horrible.

To others outside my family, I continued the good actress performance. They didn't guess that there was anything wrong. When anyone asked me how I was, I answered, "Fine." If they really knew what kind of a mother I was, they would have taken my baby away. At one point, I started collecting names of adoption agencies—since anybody could be a better mom than I am.

I was surrounded by ignorance.

It wasn't anyone's fault; they just didn't have the information. The judgment and criticism from others came from lack of knowledge— not meanness. My mother-in-law was a postpartum nurse for 35 years and a mother of five, and she criticized me for being selfish and self-centered. In all her years of nursing, no one had ever taught her about postpartum depression. My husband—listening to his mother—was impatient and frustrated with me.

My own mother did her best, but she didn't understand what I was experiencing.

Women have been having babies for thousands of years—what was my problem?

There was nothing but doom and gloom. I felt like my life was over. I was a burden to my family. Clearly, my husband and baby would be better off without me. On two occasions, I seriously considered suicide.

I chose to stay because I had a duty to perform—the joyless job of being a mother.

I wasn't going to kill myself on purpose, but I do recall thinking it would be fine with me if I didn't wake up the next morning—or if I got hit by a bus.

Why didn't anyone have answers for me?

Why was I suffering so?

Elana was two-and-a-half years old when my hair started curling again, when I started tasting my food, and started seeing in color instead of shades of gray. My chemistry was returning to normal. I started to feel like my old self again.

Looking at her one day, I thought, *Maybe I can be a mom.*

We decided to have another baby . . .

Once I delivered—I again immediately plummeted into the well of despair and anxiety. Within two months I became suicidal, again, convinced I was the worst mother who ever walked the Earth. Had someone tried to tell me back then that everything happens for a reason, I would have dismissed it as a ridiculous and callous joke.

When my son, Aaron, was almost one, I caught a glimpse of a TV program where a woman was describing exactly what I had been suffering off-and-on for years. I was riveted. I sat there staring at the TV and bawled.

This was an illness.

And it had a name: Postpartum Depression. I had no idea that I had been experiencing almost every one of the Postpartum Mood and Anxiety Disorders—simultaneously. All I knew was I had lost myself completely. I was both relieved and upset. If this disorder, called Postpartum Depression, was so common—where was the help?

Why had my family and I been allowed to suffer horribly for so long?

Still sitting there, an indescribable feeling of intense desire and determination filled my body in a huge way. It was as if I didn't have a choice—I had to do something about this unnecessary devastation. I knew it was my mission, but I had no idea where it was coming from. In my head it made no sense—I was still deeply depressed, but yet I was supposed to go out and educate? HOW? I was a terrible mom, but I'm now going to be in charge of helping other mothers? I vacillated between the excitement that I could channel my energy into this new mission, and confusion about why and how this was to be accomplished.

I vowed to myself I would not let another mother and her family suffer from this illness.

That was the second I began to find the purpose for my suffering. I began to laser-focus this enormous new energy and started taking action. I just knew I had to do this. It was a deep knowing and yearning, and it felt healing. I could think of nothing else.

Still very depressed, I started reading everything I could get my hands on from all over the world about postpartum mental health, and started knocking on the doors of hospital administrators, asking if they wanted me to train their staff or run a support group. They answered, "Shoshana, it's a nice offer, but we *rarely* see this problem here." Of course they were seeing it *all* the time—they just didn't know what they were looking at.

These same hospitals now hire me to train their doctors, and routinely hand out my brochures to new mothers.

I posted two flyers—one at the pediatrician's office and another at a grocery store. The word spread like wildfire. Each week my living room was filled with between five and 15 women. They were driving many hours to join me. For a few months, there were two women who flew to California from Hawaii to participate in the group. When therapists today ask me how I got my group going, I'm almost embarrassed to say how effortless it was. I hadn't done much of anything—and the women started showing up. I understand, now, God's hand was guiding this work, and helping it all happen, but back then I didn't give it much thought. I just accepted—no, I *knew* that women would show up. I didn't think too much about how or why I knew—I just did.

I now fully understand why no one could help me out of the darkness for all those years, why no one had answers. They weren't supposed to help me—*it wasn't time yet.* Twice I needed to walk through the horror, so I'd learn firsthand what I needed in order to help thousands of others. The moments when the deep truth of this hit me, I was in utter awe. What had felt so meaningless and random, I now regarded clearly as brilliance. When this understanding broke through to my consciousness, I wailed long and hard from relief, acceptance, and humility. I got it. There had been a divine plan for me all along.

Women understand I've "been there," and can sense I've not only fully recovered—I'm better than ever. They intuitively know I appreciate them unconditionally and have only love and compassion for them—no judgment.

I owe the richness and abundance in my life to the fact that I almost lost it.

As devastatingly painful as it was, I wouldn't alter a thing. I understand now that I was meant to experience the postpartum illnesses in just the way I did, in order to provide hope to others and help them recover—which, with proper help, they certainly will.

My understanding of God has deepened over the years and, as it has grown, so has my state of gratitude. Now, daily, I wake up feeling blessed about those hellish years I spent at the bottom of the well. Daily, I ask God to help me reach as many women and families as possible. I am in awe of this magnificent process, and I'm quite clear that the work

I do saving lives isn't my work at all—it's God's work. I understand my purpose and the job I was put here to do. I thank God for choosing me to get the word out.

I can't think of a more gratifying assignment.

❤   ❤   ❤

Shoshana Bennett, PhD, ("Dr. Shosh") is the author of *Postpartum Depression for Dummies,* and co-author of *Beyond the Blues: Understanding and Treating Prenatal and Postpartum Depression.* Her latest book is *Pregnant on Prozac.* Guided-Imagery audios help moms take care of themselves. National TV shows—including *20/20* and *The Doctors*—feature Dr. Shosh as the Postpartum Expert, and news stations consult her. Several publications, including the *San Francisco Chronicle* and the *San Jose Mercury News,* have written articles on Dr. Shosh's work. She's interviewed regularly on national radio and television, and has been quoted in dozens of newspapers and magazines, such as the *Boston Globe, Glamour, Psychology Today,* the *New York Post, Self, Cosmopolitan, USA Weekend,* and the *Chicago Tribune.*

Dr. Shosh is a pioneer in the field, and considered the "go-to" expert for postpartum depression. She is a survivor of two life-threatening, undiagnosed Postpartum Depressions. She founded Postpartum Assistance for Mothers in 1987, and is a former president of Postpartum Support International. She has helped over 18,000 women worldwide through individual consultations, support groups, and wellness seminars. As a noted guest lecturer and keynote speaker, she travels throughout the US and abroad, training medical and mental health professionals to assess and treat Postpartum Depression and related mood disorders. She has earned three Teaching Credentials, two Masters Degrees, a PhD, and is a licensed Clinical Psychologist. She is working to pass legislation that helps reduce the incidence and impact of Postpartum Mood Disorders. She can be contacted through ClearSky-Inc.com.

Thank God
My Daughter Has Down Syndrome

JAMIE WILLIAMS

It was Thursday morning, February 7, 1991, and I was in my eighth month of pregnancy with our third child. The sonograms showed we'd be bringing another beautiful girl into the world.

I felt a little out of sorts that morning. I had a backache and some dull cramps. It seemed a bit unusual, but I dismissed it and went about my business. I didn't have the morning sickness with this one—and didn't feel the kicking and movement as much as with our other daughters. This pregnancy seemed different, but every time I would hear that little voice saying, *Something's not right with this baby*—I would dismiss it. Many times I would think, *What am I doing pregnant again? My two girls are seven and nine, and now here we are starting again with another baby?*

This pregnancy wasn't planned.

But life happens.

The backache steadily got worse and the cramps got stronger. It didn't occur to us that I could be in labor. But when the backache and

301

cramps became more intense, we called my doctor. A close personal friend, he told me to come straight to the hospital.

I honestly didn't think I could be in labor—but I knew something wasn't right.

We went immediately to the exam room. He said I was indeed in labor. We were very surprised—being four weeks premature—but we were excited, too.

Things then became very busy. Because the baby was to be premature, my doctor called in a neonatologist, and asked some student doctors and nurses to be present. The atmosphere was pleasant. Mike and I were excited; the labor wasn't too bad, and my good doctor friend was delivering our baby. I blew and pushed; we laughed; the students observed; my doctor kidded with me.

"We have a girl!"

She was so tiny it was amazing.

My doctor then quickly handed her over to the neonatologist. Everyone was congratulating us. Laughter and joy filled the room.

The neonatologist was very quiet for several minutes, and then the words he spoke, "We have a problem. I think we have a Downs . . . " resounded in my head like a canon going off.

Then everything fell silent.

Mike squeezed my hand—my doctor's eyes got wide as he looked up at me—the students and nurses stopped and listened to the specialist speak.

I don't know that I heard anything.

I remember feeling as though I was falling into a deep dark well, and those words just kept echoing in my head . . . *"I think we have a Downs . . . "* It was the most extreme shift in emotions that I had ever experienced. I went from the highest high of euphoria for given birth to another beautiful daughter—to the deepest depths of shock and despair.

My husband and I looked at each other in disbelief—but we couldn't speak.

I couldn't believe it.

It wasn't possible.

I couldn't accept it.

It had to be a mistake.

What did this mean? How would we tell the girls? Our family? How would this change our lives? How could this happen to us? How would we handle this? Why did God do this to us?

Everyone in the room was at a loss for words.

The students left.

My doctor told us not to panic. "Do you have a name for her?"

"Casey."

Then they whisked her away.

I was cleaned up and moved to my room—to my *cave;* a deep dark cave that I didn't want to leave. All I could do was cry. I was sad, depressed, and just unable to confront the fact that I now had a child with Down syndrome. It wasn't real to me. I couldn't accept it. I just couldn't get out of this state of mind I was in. I knew my life and my family's life—as we had known it—was over.

It wouldn't be the same again.

My Father—God rest his loving soul—went back to his office and wrote Mike and me this letter. He delivered it when he returned that night.

My dearest Jamie and Mike,

It is the 7th of February. . . . I now have my seventh grand-daughter and I'm proud to be 'Papa' to each of them, and to be in 'Love' with each of them.

I would like to share something with the both of you insofar as an experience I had in a time of my life before WWII for a period of about 5 years.

When I went into High School in 1937 I had my first serious (I thought) romance, such as one can have at the age of 14. I fell in love with a girl named Barbara. . . . This was the first and perhaps the only experience I had of contact with a child with 'Downs.' When Barbara told me about her sister . . . I think she was apologizing for her . . . . The child, when I met her, was about 10-11 years old and I gotta tell you that there was a love in her eyes which consumed me. We became quite close and we called each other "Pumkin"! . . . Until I went into the service, I had a great deal of contact with her, and I must say it was a loving experience. We conversed and played silly games and had fun.

Don't misunderstand what I am saying here. I don't mean to imply that to raise 'Casey' will be a piece of cake, but I will say that acceptance of what 'is' is going to make it easier as long as you do not blame yourselves or beat up on yourselves for something you have no control over. What you do have control over is your ability to give 'Love' in keeping with the individual needs of all three of your beautiful children. What you get in return will be multiplied sevenfold.

I, as a Father, bleed when you bleed, I laugh when you laugh, I'm happy when you are happy, and I'm sad when you are sad. Remember that happiness is a direction, not a place or a thing. Anger is like acid. It can destroy the object which contains it as well as the object on which you place it. There is no such thing as a problem without a gift for you in its hands. We find problems because we need their gifts. What the caterpillar calls the end of the world, the wise man calls a butterfly.

I love the five of you very, very much. All of you are SPECIAL IN YOUR OWN WAY. Love wears many faces and is the most enduring 'Thing' that exists on this earth or elsewhere. One can NEVER give all of one's Love, because the more you give, the more you receive.

Thank you for being here for me . . . . I affirm your well-being and my Love to you and yours (OURS).

Love always,
    Dad

A few months prior, we had been introduced to Scientology. Auditing is a Scientology practice performed with a trained auditor, meaning "one who listens." As a minister of the church he/she works one-on-one with an individual to help locate, confront, and handle areas in life causing emotional travail. It's very specific to the individual being audited, and the result is a release of the charge—and of the negative feelings and emotions—associated with moments of physical pain and traumatic emotional upsets.

When my auditor, John, learned of the situation, he came to the hospital the next day to see me. I was depressed and despondent. I really didn't want to see or talk to anyone. He was there to give me an "Assist" to help me work through the incident. I was less than enthusiastic, but I agreed. He put a "DO NOT DISTURB" sign on the door, made sure I was comfortable, and we began.

The process involved two questions. The first was, "Tell me what happened."

I answered the question with tears, grief, blame and shame. I ran through everything—the first cramp that morning, the delivery, shock, disbelief, and on and on. It took some time to get through it. The tears and sobbing wouldn't stop.

He thanked me, and asked the second question, "Now, was there an earlier beginning to that?"

I thought about it, then went back earlier in the pregnancy, and talked about an earlier incident, again with much tears and sobbing.

He thanked me. *Then* he repeated the first question, "Tell me what happened." And so it went. He would ask—I would answer.

Each time I recounted all the events leading up to the birth, my emotional state improved. Tears became less; grief subsided; and my ability to confront the situation strengthened. Finally, I experienced laughter, joy, and love for my child and my family.

The only words that come close to describing what occurred, here, would be "Miraculous Transformation." I came completely and utterly out of my depression and, by the end of the session, was laughing tears of joy—and couldn't wait to hold my baby. And that was it:

four hours. I haven't looked back; haven't dropped "down" again. All of the grief and emotional charge associated with her birth and her handicap were GONE. I can't thank John enough for getting me through that.

Well, that amazing session was a blessing, and brought me back to where I needed to be to confront everything that was ahead for my family and me. I was inspired to write a letter to our friends to help them understand where we were with the situation, and to make it easier for them to be able to communicate with us.

Dear Family and Friends,

As you are all aware by now, on February 7th we were blessed with a new little girl to our family. She was born four weeks early and was a whopping 5lbs, 15oz and 19-¼ inches long.

Because she was four weeks early, a neonatologist was present for the delivery. After four minutes of joy and excitement, he performed a brief examination on our new baby and reluctantly informed us that there was "a problem." He said that she appeared to show some signs of Down syndrome.

After the initial heartbreak and many, many tears, God's Hand touched us as we hadn't felt it before.

Our baby is special, yes, but in a wonderful way. She was given a real challenge with her life and will have many obstacles to overcome. As her parents we are determined to help her meet every challenge she faces to the very utmost of our and her ability. Our goals for her are no different than the goals we have for our other two children; to be fulfilled and strive to be the very best that they can possibly be.

In the few short weeks that she has been part of our family she has filled us all with so much love and joy. She's a beautiful, alert, and very joyful baby. Her two big sisters love her very much and play with her and help us quite a bit. My newborn is off to a great start and, with God's help, is going to do very, very well. . . . Believe us, there won't be any avenue unexplored when it comes to the help and support we want to give this child.

We know it can be awkward for friends and relatives right now, not really knowing just what the right thing to say or do is. We understand, but would like to help you out a little bit here by saying, "Don't worry" about us or our baby. We're okay, really. Please feel free to ask us any questions you may have. We welcome and are grateful for your sincere concern, your prayers and your Love. We hope that you will love and accept our baby, as our other children, without pity or reservations.

Through God there is hope, and where there is hope, we find miracles. Together, through God's Grace, we will all witness the miracle of our new daughter, Casey, as she grows to be a strong, beautiful, healthy and fulfilled individual.

Thank you for your love, kindness, and prayers. God Bless You!

Love,
　　Mike and Jamie

The years that followed with Casey tested our strength and our resolve. Casey had two heart defects. One was a ventricular septum defect (VSD), and the second was a cleft in her mitral valve. She had two open heart surgeries and numerous hospitalizations due to congestive heart failures, pulmonary distress, and pneumonias. She was required to be on oxygen most of the time, needing breathing treatments, along with speech, physical, and occupational therapies. We participated in the Doman Program, providing many therapies to assist her development ourselves. We administered a strict nutritional regimen for her, including many nutritional supplements. After her second open-heart surgery at four-and-a-half years old, Casey's health got better and better. Eventually there were no more constant doctor visits, hospitalizations, oxygen machines or breathing treatments. She was well.

Casey is 17 years old now. She is healthy. She is a loving, beautiful young lady. When I look back at all we went through with her in her young years—as difficult as it was—we learned, loved, and grew as a result. Casey is indeed a special child; a very special being. She exudes love unconditionally and has a hug for everyone. Casey has a knack for softening and bringing out the love in others. This child, who came into my life with sadness and despair, made me find strength I didn't know I had. She has taught me unconditional love. I appreciate the life experiences this beautiful being has taught me, and I say, "Thank God I have a child with Down syndrome."

❤   ❤   ❤

Jamie Williams holds a BA from the University of South Florida in accounting and finance. Upon graduation from college, Jamie obtained a Florida real estate license. In her 28 years as a Florida real estate broker, she has owned and operated a successful brokerage with multiple associates. Her previous experience includes residential and commercial sales, procurement and management of investment properties, and development of several commercial properties. She has owned and managed other successful businesses, including an equipment leasing company and a multi-specialty health clinic. Jamie currently specializes in private investments and funding for large projects. Although a very busy business professional, Jamie is a caring mother of three girls.

Thank God
I Left My Kids

MABEL KATZ

When I received the invitation to write this chapter, I first checked to see if "spiritually" it was the correct thing to do, and of course I wanted my children's approval. This is a delicate subject—and I wanted to be sensitive to their feelings. As it turned out, my oldest son Jonathan, then 24 years old, responded, "Mom, if this will help create more opportunities to share your message with people—go ahead. I'm okay with it." Lyonel, who was 19 years old, said, "Mom—it's sad. But go ahead. I'm okay."

So I'm taking this opportunity to share with you how some things that we may consider "wrong," "incorrect," or "bad" can be *right* for our loved ones and us—even if we don't know it until after the fact.

When I separated from my husband back in 1998, he wanted to be the one to stay in the house with the kids. I'd never heard of any woman who had done such a thing. The mother and children usually stay in the house, and the husband is the one to leave. I was outraged and extremely upset. *How could he propose such a thing?* I'd been fair

309

with him, supporting him so that he could do and be whatever he chose and, since I made a good income as an accountant, I always helped him financially.

Fear-filled, I left my marriage of more than 20 years, leaving behind my husband and my children.

I started a new career and signed a lease, taking on a huge financial responsibility without backup funds. My faith and confidence in myself allowed me to act in spite of my fear. An inner voice told me that I could do it, but this security did not come spontaneously. I acquired it by working on myself—reading books, taking seminars, and daring to face and accept the things that I needed to change. By trusting in the Universe I was willing to feel the fear of the unknown—and do it anyway.

Fortunately at the time, I was already practicing the ancient Hawaiian art of problem solving—Ho'oponopono. Ho'oponopono teaches us how to "clean" and "erase" old memories or programs that attract things that don't work for us, allowing what is right to come at the perfect time in our lives. But often "we don't know that we don't know." As soon as I began my "cleaning" and "erasing" regarding my husband, the following thought came to me: *He's actually helping me. He doesn't know it consciously—but he's helping me. I need to be by myself in order to do what I came to do.* At the time, this was a novel and scary thought but, because I was doing my "cleaning," I trusted and decided to let go and let God.

Prior to my leaving, the kids fought and put each other "down" constantly. After I left, they started being more responsible and their relationships grew. They became good friends who cared for each other. They were also closer to their father and a great source of companionship to him. In fact, they helped him through a difficult transition. In the end, my decision to leave was best for everybody—even though I didn't know it at the time.

When my mother came to visit from my birthplace, Argentina, she asked, "Mabel, I don't understand. Are you *abandoning* them?" My response was, "Mom, I know this is not what we learned as the 'right thing' to do, but don't you see they're fine?" Her reply was, "Yes—but

I don't understand. Don't they suffer?" She was also worried because they didn't call me. I told her, "Mom, that's a good thing. It means they're okay."

I never set up visiting days or times with my sons. I gave them no guilt trips. They saw me only if they could and if they wanted to, and they always called me if something was wrong. I would ask them, "Does this work for you?" This way they learned to ask that question of themselves and of others, and I let them know that I loved them no matter what. I told them that love doesn't depend on what they did or didn't do—or on their behavior. It didn't depend on whether or not they got a college degree. These statements surprised them. They looked at me with wide-eyed wonder as though I was telling them the strangest thing that they had ever heard in their lives.

At the time I left, I could never have imagined a relationship like the one we now have. My oldest son, Jonathan, calls me every day to tell me that he loves me. He says I'm on his best friend list. By my actions, I taught them it's not selfish to put oneself first. I showed them that by being themselves they would find happiness in who they are. Without self-love we cannot love anyone else. By refusing to accept this, we deceive others and ourselves. It is essential to learn to love and accept ourselves exactly the way we are. It doesn't work just to do things for others. If something doesn't work for us—it won't work for anybody else.

Especially as mothers we tend to believe that we must relinquish what is important to us—and sacrifice for our children. However, the best gift we can give them is to love ourselves. With our example they can learn to love themselves. When we are in the correct place, we allow others to be in their correct place. The more we try to obtain love by doing things and behaving in certain ways for others, the more we distance ourselves from the possibility of experiencing the very thing we so desire.

When we dare to follow our dreams and go through our fears, we reach the other side of the tunnel and see the light. We then recognize truth. We feel triumphant and present with ourselves, and can look back and see that the journey wasn't as terrible as we had imagined. When we stop attaching ourselves to the result and stop worrying about situations, when we abandon the need to have opinions and pass judgment, and when we become aware that we know nothing and surrender and accept the process of life, then—and only then—can we experience the flow of the Universe. It is at this point that things start to happen in the easiest way. I often tell my children that their job is to be grateful. When we are grateful things just come to us effortlessly.

Before I started my self-transformation process, I lived my life trying to measure up to everyone's expectations. When I left my kids, for the first time in my life I was able to love and accept myself just the way I was. Love for our own being is the most powerful tool of transformation. Love begins with us. It's useless to look for it elsewhere because we can only experience it if we have it within. Unless we love and accept ourselves unconditionally, we cannot love truthfully. If we don't allow our children to be themselves, we love possessively—and they become slaves of our thoughts, opinions, and perceptions. I was raised in this "old tradition" and became a "people-pleaser." I needed to know that people liked me. I now know that if I hadn't had enough self-love and trust, I would never have been able to make the decision to leave my family. I would have put other people's ideas and approval first and, although unhappy, I would have stayed married. I would have become an angry mother and made my kids' lives miserable. Fortunately I faced my fears and chose the path that taught my kids to follow their hearts and be themselves.

In my case, it was essential to show my sons how a person can change—no matter their age, sex, or religion. When we started taping my TV show at home, my son Lyonel would help. He often came to me and said, "Mom, I am so proud of you." What else could I have asked for? Many people say our kids are our gurus. I believe that we have been with them in other lifetimes, and they come to give us another chance. They give us the opportunity to take 100% of the responsibility. Our children come to teach us something—not the other way around.

When situations are present in our lives, it's very easy to see them as problems, tests, or punishments—instead of blessings and opportunities. Usually, the first thing we do is judge. We have opinions and tend to think that we know what is "right" and what is "wrong." Through my experience with my family and countless others, I have learned that

God knows what is right for us, and that if we get out of our own way, we tend to "miraculously" be in the right place at the right time.

In Ho'oponopono we use two very important tools for transformation. These are "thank you" and "I love you." When we repeat any of these, we erase, clean, and let go of the memories that don't serve us anymore, and allow inspiration to enter our lives with the perfect ideas and solutions to our problems. The best thing is that while we are erasing and cleaning, whatever is erased from us is erased from our families, relatives, and ancestors as well. That is why things start changing without you having to be present. We definitely affect relationships in ways our intellect cannot understand.

Remember: our kids don't listen to us. They observe us and learn from our example. My sons saw the differences between their father's path and mine, which gave them opportunity to see and decide what works for them. My decision to leave my kids helped us all grow in ways that I could not have imagined. Our judgments and opinions of situations and events have to do with our own insecurities. Our fears do not allow us to know who we are or to understand the power we have to create and manifest in our lives. When we trust and believe in ourselves we recognize that every moment is perfect.

> *Your children are not your children.*
> *They are the sons and daughters of Life's longing for itself.*
> *They come through you but not from you,*
> *and though they are with you, yet they belong not to you.*
> *You may give them your love but not your thoughts.*
> *For they have their own thoughts.*
> *You may house their bodies but not their souls,*
> *for their souls dwell in the house of tomorrow,*
>   *which you cannot visit, not even in your dreams.*
> *You may strive to be like them, but seek not to make them*
>   *like you.*
> *For life goes not backward nor tarries with yesterday.*
> *You are the bows from which your children*
>   *as living arrows are sent forth.*

The archer sees the mark upon the path of the infinite,
and He bends you with His might
that His arrows may go swift and far.
Let your bending in the archer's hand be for gladness;
for even as he loves the arrow that flies,
so He loves also the bow that is stable.

~ KAHLIL GIBRAN ~

Mabel Katz is the author of *The Easiest Way. Solve your problems and take the road to love, happiness, wealth, and the life of your dreams.* Her inspiration is sharing the power people have inside themselves to change their lives. She hosts her own TV show, *Despertar* ("Awakening"), and travels around the world "awakening people's consciousness" with her lectures and seminars. Mabel is president of Your Business, Inc., where as a business consultant she helps others create successful businesses. For more information, please visit www.mabelkatz.com or www.businessbyyou.com.

Thank God
I Am an Entrepreneur

Varant Majarian

I was born in Lebanon, and my parents brought me to America when I was two years old.

While still a young child, I knew the meaning of perseverance.

My parents wanted the best for their child, and directed me towards skills and behaviors they believed would lead me to success. Their plan for my life was to obtain a college education, then join the work force in a secure job, with a dependable salary and good benefits.

My father stayed on top of me constantly to pursue a quality education.

Obediently, I set my mind towards a high academic goal.

I was an only child—and very gifted—so my parents expected the best with whatever I chose to do with my future.

I studied hard in high school, and qualified for the honors program.

I was so achievement-oriented that at age 16 I attended community college part time while still attending high school.

College was a revelation. My strict background helped me see that with a college education, I really could "make things happen."

But there was a price to pay.

My parents were very strict during that part of my childhood, and did not allow me to participate in any social gatherings. Not having a social life made me cry at times, especially when I saw all my friends having fun. I stayed home to study, while my friends attended parties, sports activities, and dances. My only outlet consisted of serving as Student Council President for three years.

I was a "nerd" as I focused on my education.

The momentum towards my goals filled my days with challenges and pressure. At age 18, I attended college full time, and embraced my father's vision of getting top grades and honors, as I worked towards two degrees—one in computer science and the other in business.

At this time, another opportunity caught my attention—an opportunity that went against everything my father expected me to do. I watched those who turned their backs on traditional work opportunities, and instead tried to figure a way to make money from home. This piqued my interest and, being a computer whiz, I turned to a "new" career advisor—the Internet. An entirely new world opened as I scrolled from site to site taking it all in.

My first endeavor was selling Beanie Babies online. My parents indulged me, as long as I continued my studies towards a real "job."

But the entrepreneurial bug had bitten me.

On my 21st birthday, I took my parents to dinner, and happily announced that I'd decided to start my own home-based business, which I planned to run from the comfort of our home. As soon as I announced this, my father's anger flared and his face showed his deep displeasure at my decision. He told me I needed to look for a government J-O-B with great benefits, so I could earn paychecks weekly. My father believed that the path I wanted to follow was not honorable or financially secure—calling it a "pyramid scheme."

Stunned—as the knowledge hit me that he considered me a disappointment—I thought, *Why?*

Why is my father saying this?

My emotions hit bottom. At the young age of 21, I felt like a loser and gave up. My dreams and excitement crashed to the ground.

Then one day I went to a coffee shop that had been a hangout since childhood. I sat in deep depression. Mr. Doyle, an older gentleman I knew, sat next to me. He said, "Varant Majarian, what has happened to you? You look very sad and alone."

I responded, "My father doesn't want me to start a career. He wants me to get a J.O.B." I trusted the man and allowed my mingled emotions, sorrow and hope, pain and determination to show. "Mr. Doyle, I really want to start my own business."

Mr. Doyle understood my vision and purpose, as he himself was a successful entrepreneur. He achieved much success owning commercial properties and houses, and was able to retire without a pension at the age of 52.

During the conversation, Mr. Doyle said something that struck me emotionally and physically. He said, "It's GREAT that you love your parents, and that your parents love you unconditionally, but sometimes you have to stand up to the challenge, and do whatever is right for *you*."

Mr. Doyle was absolutely correct.

I took his words to heart, and was determined to start my own journey.

I approached my dad and told him that I knew what was best for me, and that he needed to let me take on the challenge.

My dad wasn't pleased—but I stood firm.

My first year in business brought many challenges, and I wondered if perhaps my father was right after all. But I didn't give up; I kept my chin up. My father was amazed at how determined I was to get this going. However, the first two years became a downhill road, and I didn't make any money.

To my surprise, my parents saw that this was my vision and purpose—and my father backed me financially. I didn't anticipate how challenging a business start-up could be. I couldn't sleep, and tossed and turned all night. I felt guilt deep in my stomach.

But I didn't give up.
I had a vision in my mind.
I really could do this.

Things started to roll in my third year in business. My adult entertainment business kicked into gear, and I achieved the success I worked
so hard to find—and found financial stability. In my fifth year of business, I connected with a nutritional company called Liberty Health Net.
I wanted to help individuals both with their health and to earn money
from home. That was one of the best parts of my success—helping
others.

After that my father and mother told me, "Thank you for not listening to us. We see your success in all you're doing and accomplishing.
We're very proud of you, son."

I felt their sincerity.

Now at age 31, the *Thank God I . . .* ™ Book Series Team
approached me to share my story. I realized that I could actually teach
and inspire individuals. I joined this project in a heartbeat. I'm grateful
that the Universe loves me, and I believe that if you keep on moving
forward, God will bestow all kinds of gifts and rewards with education
and career.

Because of the strong expectations of my parents, I knew how
to prepare myself, how to keep a work ethic, and how to persevere
through my challenges.

Because of what they instilled in me, I am a success.

I see many young kids out there who don't have parents like mine
to guide them into a secure future. I've had the privilege of speaking at
schools and teen groups, encouraging them in pursuing their studies,
developing a work ethic, and just sticking to whatever it takes to make
something of their opportunities. I tell them how I followed my inspiration. My goal is to inspire them to do the same.

I'm also a financial speaker and teach money management. I tell
them to find inspiration in their work, belief in their future, and gratitude for their own stories.

At the same time I joined with *Thank God I* ... ™, I made an investment in another business, and placed several Internet machines in some casinos in Las Vegas, Nevada. These are Internet-based machines, where people can spend money they've won. Once again, I found a great opportunity to help individuals, and I'm very grateful.

As I mentioned, the Universe gives me gifts because God knows that I love to help individuals in any situation. My current project is to help people in health care. I'm currently involved with a company called Ameriplan USA. This program helps people reduce their medical expenses.

I currently earn one million dollars per year.

And now my job is to help you find your own way to success.

Thank God I'm an entrepreneur.

Varant Majarian coaches individuals on earning residual income. He is also involved in Ameriplan, www.askvarant majarian.com, where he's helped people save up to eighty percent on medical benefits. Varant Majarian can be reached through his website, webmarketingconcepts.blogspot.com.

Thank God
I Blew Out Two Discs in My Back

DR. DOUG LEHRER

*B*efore I was conceived, my mother was a professional dancer and singer who injured her lower back falling off stage while performing.

When I was eight, she became bedridden with crippling pain that mysteriously returned from the herniated disc in her lower back, along with sciatica, severe nerve pain down her legs.

There's a bit more to this story; let's go back a bit earlier.

My mother's childhood was one of sacrifice, obedience, and abuse. My grandmother had wanted to be a silver-screen star, but her parents forbade those dreams. My grandmother's arranged marriage and subsequent pregnancy—which turned out to be my mother—further closed the door on her yearning for stardom. So my mother became the obsessive object of her mother's unfulfilled desires.

By age two, Mom was wearing tap shoes and learning to dance and sing. If she didn't obey, she was verbally abused and physically punched.

I came into the world unconsciously experiencing my mother's physical, mental, and emotional pain. Later, I was to learn that *a mother's thoughts, feelings, and experiences can pass on to and program the child like a computer*. This determines how they experience life; whether they experience life with ease, joy, freedom, and prosperity, or experience life with pain, disease, misery, failure, or lack.

Leading scientists, doctors, and researchers now know that we can be neurologically and emotionally imprinted by stressful experiences in our own lives, as well as those of our genetic lineage. Simply put, negativity and judgment can be transferred to the baby who becomes the child, the teen, and the adult—who ends up reacting to life with similar attitudes and behaviors, and thus experiencing similar health issues, finances, and relationships as the parents. "As a man thinketh in his heart so is he" (Proverbs 23:7).

Then it was my turn to deal with life.

When I was born, I got the common vaccinations that are now suspected to damage the immune and nervous systems.

My mother also fed me baby formula—rather than breast milk—which most likely contributed to years of painful ear infections.

The doctors then gave me antibiotics, wiping out the beneficial bacteria flora in my stomach, which is 75% of immune system function.

When I got even worse, the doctors convinced my parents that removing my tonsils and adenoids (immune glands) was a good idea.

All this was only treating symptoms, which further damaged my immune system—but didn't treat the cause.

For years after that, I got high fevers and suffered from constipation and severe abdominal and back pain. Add in allergies, hay fever, nose bleeds, and migraines. By the end of high school, my shoulders, neck, and back became extremely tense, and I experienced frequent severe pain. My back and hip would lock up—and I would limp in pain.

By the time I graduated from high school, I was in constant pain.

A neighbor suggested I see a chiropractic doctor, which I thought was strange at the time. But I went—and it helped me feel much better. So I decided to become a Doctor of Chiropractic.

While in college, I worked for nine years in smoke-filled restaurants, and with ranting and raving, abusive bosses. I didn't really think of why I was putting myself through all that pressure. I was just doing what I thought I was supposed to do to pay my dues and become a doctor. As the stress on my mind and the tension on my body accumulated in my cells, I noticed the pain would come more often, and go away less easily with the chiropractic adjustments I would get in our college clinic.

I was relieved when I quit the restaurant business, graduated, and started my own chiropractic practice. Within a few months, I felt this terrible pain explode in my back and rip down my leg. The doctors took X-rays and did MRIs, and found two herniated discs (rubber-like pads between the vertebrae that cushion spinal bones and protect nerves that come out of the spinal cord, controlling many cells of the body) in my lower back. The diagnosis: one fragmented disc, totally destroyed, pretty much bone-on-bone, and the other disc protruding into the spinal cord.

Ouch.

It hurt to sit, stand, bend, twist, go to the bathroom, and even have sex. I remember crawling to the bathroom and pulling myself up upon the toilet in pain-torn tears. Chiropractic adjustments made me feel better, but the pain came back within 24 hours. The orthopedists and neurologists gave me pain pills, which made me feel sick, and they suggested back surgery. I knew firsthand that surgery was ineffective because I was treating people who had surgery and most were in a worse condition.

So surgery wasn't an option for me.

All those long, tough, hard years of "working my tail off" studying and slaving in restaurants, bending to the whim of whoever told me to do something—and now I was "damaged goods."

I felt beaten up, put down, dragged through the gutter, and backed up against the wall of my life.

My body collapsed and my emotions were overwhelming.

I didn't know what to do.

I felt all alone, helpless, degraded—a chiropractor with a seriously bad back. I was totally embarrassed; I felt ashamed and out of integrity because I would often scream uncontrollably as I leaned over to adjust a patient's spine, sometimes scaring the heck out of them!

I didn't give up—yet.

I tried acupuncture, physical therapy, cranial sacral work, massage, and osteopathy. I studied Tai Chi and meditation. But nothing really worked—and I was getting worse.

Now using a cane to prop myself up—as my legs weakened and movement became more excruciating—I thought my life was over.

I wanted to quit chiropractic—and I did.

I became depressed.

Then came the migraines and Irritable Bowel Syndrome.

At this point—I prayed that God would take me, please.

When that didn't happen, I changed my prayers, and a gem I learned in chiropractic school came zooming into mind, "The body has the power to heal itself of any condition." It was my only solace.

I asked deeper, "What was stopping my body from healing?" I had instantly updated my consciousness with that question, and I further asked, "What would it take for my body to heal and feel better?"

It was so simple, *Ask the "right" question and thou shalt receive the "right" result . . .*

Blessedly, after suffering for two years, I met a brilliant doctor who told me my body was in "survival" mode. That I couldn't heal because negative subconscious memories were stuck in my body, interfering with my natural healing power. He had developed a form of energy medicine that released years of trauma, negativity, and genetic memory from my body.

The first time this doctor treated me and balanced my brain and nervous system, the pain down my leg disappeared—and didn't come back. I was mightily impressed.

With further treatments, my back pain went away, and my discs healed, as did my depression, Irritable Bowel Syndrome, and migraine headaches.

This healing transformed me—and my life. I began to master energy healing and energy medicine—the art and science of applying quantum physics, the law of attraction, and soul consciousness. I began to understand deeply that my body, mind, and emotions needed to be treated simultaneously to heal my body. My past emotional stress and genetic cellular memory of trauma needed to be cleared in order to heal my heart, soul, and physical body so I could truly transform and restore myself to health and vitality.

Lifetimes had come full circle. I learned how my mother's negative experiences had programmed my body with feelings of abuse, fear, and powerlessness which I, in turn, attracted in my life. Being teased by other kids, being hit by my mom, yelled at by my father and bosses, I made choices based on my software programs of fear, guilt, and shame—even creating the same injuries as my mom.

Over the years, my healing skills shifted and transformed. I became a greater conduit of healing energies, trusting my inner voice and inner vision, as my intuitive abilities heightened, facilitating more release and healing for others and myself.

I found myself renewed with new enthusiasm and joy for life, as I empowered people to heal themselves and become more conscious and aware.

I learned the lesson that we are no longer destined to repeat the mistakes of our past or of our family's history. We can let go, and resolve the negative feelings and beliefs programmed within us. We can have truly healthy, fulfilled, prosperous lives free of physical and emotional pain.

I know firsthand that we can heal; we can change; and we can transform.

I've facilitated thousands to do it.

Released from the suffering experiences, I now find ease, joy, and glory in life. I live in the freedom of choice, in a healthy, youthful body, with awareness of how I create my life in every moment. I understand how we can transform our world by completely loving ourselves first. In the words of the great Mahatma Ghandi, "Be the change you wish to see in the world."

So I ask you, what would you like to be, do, and have in your life?

What would you be choosing, if your subconscious memory wasn't refusing it?

What would you heal, and what would you receive in life?

Today I get to have so much fun, knowing I'm making a huge difference in the world by empowering others to heal the past, and live in the greatness of who they undeniably are. I love guiding others to uncover and emanate the light of spirit within, the light that I had read so much about—but can now truly BE.

Thank God I blew out two discs in my back.

❤   ❤   ❤

Dr. Doug Lehrer is an internationally known doctor, speaker, author, and radio show host. A master of energy healing, board certified in *Quantum Medicine™* by the American Naturopathic Board of Medicine, chiropractor, and Access Energy Transformation facilitator. Developer of *Dr. Doug's Symbiotic Quantum Nutrition™* to remove safely environmental toxins that affect everyone by destroying the detoxification, digestive, hormonal, brain, and immune functions. Find out about Dr. Doug's Transformational Wellness, Relationship and Consciousness Seminars, Retreats, and Nutrition Programs, and check out Dr. Doug's *Total Body Wellness* CD/DVD and Belly Fat Burning Nutritional Programs. To learn more, please visit: www.drdougwellness.com.

Thank God
I Got a Divorce

JAYNE DRESSOR

*I*f anyone had told me five years ago that I would be writing a story about hope and gratitude, I would have thought—*For what could I possibly be grateful?*

My divorce was not what I expected.

The man I thought I married *didn't exist.*

The feeling of total hopelessness, abandonment, and isolation would paralyze me from head-to-toe for days on end. My heart ached from deep inside my soul, oozing out from every pore. I felt lost and very alone. How can anyone be grateful when the pain is so deep that your entire being feels numb from the shock of what your reality has become?

There are no words to describe what I was feeling while this was all happening.

I felt like someone took a razor to the middle of my heart and gutted it. How can anyone describe how that huge hole in my heart felt and my only thoughts—my most secretive thoughts—were of death.

The worst part was the fear of not being able to tell anyone how I really felt, worried that I might yet, again, lose the only part of me that was left, the most precious part of me—my child.

Somewhere along our 15-year marriage, I had lost my true self.

I knew I should have left years prior, but I "loved" him—and had gone through such lengths to have this child. I had four years of infertility—and longed to have a child. I was considered to be a high risk, and was put on bed rest for 16 weeks, followed by a scheduled C-section.

When I thought it was all over, I got very ill and was hospitalized for 10 days.

I knew, then, my baby girl was a miracle and a blessing.

I wanted to keep the marriage together—for all the wrong reasons—but it seemed I was the only one trying. I became bitter, angry, verbally abusive, and self-righteous; in other words, I felt justified in my behavior. Pain and emptiness consumed me, but the pain I felt for my daughter was nothing in comparison to my own.

Becoming a mother changed everything for me.

But now—after I had the one thing I wanted—someone was trying to take her away. I wanted to protect her from any emotional hurt, but I knew I couldn't. I couldn't make her pain go away; I could only love her through it.

How can anyone go through such conflicting emotions of wanting to die?

Why would anyone who has such horrible thoughts want to live?

At that moment, I had only one really reasonable thought for needing to live—not wanting to live, but rather not wanting to die.

I just wanted to feel fulfilled again.

I wanted my daughter to play and be with her friends. Being shipped back and forth between the two of us was taking its toll.

The pain was so overwhelming that entertaining even one fleeting thought of wanting to die was extremely dangerous. Had I possessed a gun—or any other means to stop the hurt by ending my life—it wouldn't have been a hard decision.

Suddenly, I realized, *No, I must live for my daughter.*

It was that simple.

Nothing could be that horrible to end my life and ruin hers forever.

I thank GOD for his gift to me—my precious child. She was—at that very moment in time—the only reason I could justify staying alive. I realized GOD gave her to me to give life. I had not realized, in doing so, God gave me back my own life.

Feeling like a lost soul, I stood there in the kitchen, feeling lost, alone, abandoned, humiliated, and emotionally stripped to the bone. With nothing else to lose, I began to know I was *exactly* where I was supposed to be.

I realized I had to experience all of it. I had to be left with nothing; I had to see who I really was.

I would not rest until I did everything possible to ensure my daughter's stability. I didn't care if I had to spend all of my spousal support, house proceeds, or whatever else I had to do in order to protect her.

I knew my purpose.

I had my reason to live.

I knew from this moment on it could only get better; my eyes were opening to the beginning of endless possibilities. Opening my eyes to who I had become was humiliating—but believing this was a new beginning made me want to see more of me. Changing my thinking helped me see the things I didn't want to see. It is so obvious to me, now, that everything happened to me for a very specific, GOD-intended reason.

GOD's world is completely different from the world where we live. Appearances are not necessarily actualities. I didn't know at the time I was being prepared for something great. That wake-up call opened my eyes to a new vision, a new way to perceive the events and people around me.

I needed to grow up.

I needed to have those experiences, hardships, and heartache. I needed to change my way of thinking. Wanting to make a change—and actually taking serious steps towards that change—is when the real work begins. It gets real; it gets hard; but most of all, it hurts more than I can describe.

Being in and out of court for two years felt like a lifetime. I knew, eventually, justice would be served. But at the time I felt "dead" on the inside. To be stripped of everything familiar—all at once—made me feel like I was in a bad movie that had no end in sight.

It has been three more years, and the past two have been incredible.

I knew it was temporary; I knew I would be more successful than I ever imagined. I didn't know how, but I felt it in my gut. Verbalizing a belief in something we cannot see is an amazing task.

It was just the beginning of my journey.

It was something I had hoped for; I was learning to cherish every moment. In order for me to understand why, I had to endure all of it; I had to walk through the pain, walk through every hurt, shedding thousands of tears for this very purpose.

I saw my life unfold.

I needed to change my way of thinking and my way of looking at different situations. I needed to be stripped down to nothing in order for GOD to reshape and re-mold me.

I swear I won't judge another human being as long as I live.

You don't know whose shoes you might end up walking in. The awareness that came over me swept away all doubt. I knew God counted every tear, blessing me beyond my wildest expectations. I have become a better human being, and an example of grace and dignity. I haven't given up my hopes and dreams.

The blessings we have received have been more than I could have hoped for—and they keep on coming. I know I was brought into this world for a reason, and I know what my purpose is. I have become a great mom, friend, sister and—most of all—a better human being.

I feel honored and blessed to have the opportunity to share this with you, and I want to encourage those of you who are smack in the middle of whatever is haunting you, please be assured, *it is only temporary.*

There is a light at the end of the tunnel.

Look within yourself.

You are stronger than you think.

Changing your outlook on your experiences will affect the way you see your future.

Be fulfilled, encouraged, and hopeful.

Most of all, know that you are loved and that you are not alone.

You have the power to transform anything.

It is that simple.

Life changes daily, and there is the need to embrace these changes with inspiration, hope, and gratitude. Jayne Dressor is a single mom, full of life and energy. Her teenage daughter is her inspiration. She says, "I feel blessed having been given the opportunity to raise this awesome child." After discovering her purpose, Jane wrote this story. She hopes that sharing this story may change the outcome of at least one person, affecting their thinking and perhaps changing their life forever. Having had a great role model herself, Dressor proclaims old school values, being a woman of GOD, and a woman of integrity. She says, "I love life and everything it has to offer. I decided that I was going to be successful; so here we are at the beginning of my success."

Thank God I Died

THE THIRD TIME IS THE CHARM

JULIE ANN COHN

I've often heard the expression, "The third time is the charm." Little did I know that it would apply to dying or, as I am often reminded, *nearly* dying.

Of course, I would not still be "renting" this body *if* it died *completely*.

I have lived through three near-death experiences.

The first two were preparing me for the third—the one that would forever change the course of my life. I've known fear, pain, depression, loss, and denial. I've come to know gratitude, joy, health, love, harmony, and abundance. I've been blessed with success to counter hardship.

Death is *not* a hardship, but—at times—"living" having known the "peace of death" *is* a hardship.

The first time I crossed to the "other side"—the place where time ends, spirit resides, and I left this body of mine—was when I was 19.

Like many at my age, I had taken a break from college to experiment with the hippie culture. I met a man named Osiris. He had long hair, golden skin, and a beautiful smile. It felt as though I had stepped out of the book called, *My Life,* and into a fantasy of love, music, and drugs.

At first we lived in a penthouse apartment in West Los Angeles. Life seemed grand. He worked for a school supplies business, and I was a salesperson at Judy's.

Then we moved to the Valley in Southern California—and lived in a trailer. Along with friends we ran a health food restaurant. It was there that he got addicted to nitrous oxide—also known as laughing gas. We had tanks of it in the back for baking.

One time Osiris brought one of the tanks home to the trailer. He started sucking on the gas. At first this just relaxed him and put him to sleep.

Then one night—out of the blue—as he was doing his usual gas, the tube started whipping around out of his mouth.

I reached over to turn it off and—*BAM!*

Osiris grabbed a knife, cut me twice, threw me out of the trailer, and left me for dead on the ground, bleeding.

I have no idea how I managed to get myself into my car, drive back over the hill to my parent's house, and then fall on the horn in their driveway. My white silk shirt was drenched in blood.

I was watching myself from above.

I remember seeing my father move me into his car, saying, "I hope this taught you a lesson," and drive me to a hospital.

From that point on I was *gone.*

I did not have an awareness of light, or any of the things I experienced later the third time I visited "beyond." In fact, it seemed to me that I was just floating . . .

. . . until the "knowing" came.

I woke up in the hospital *knowing* I had been through something very powerful. Contrary to how it was all perceived, I felt like I had received something wonderful. Of course no one understood, and many tried to point out the awfulness of the situation.

But I knew I had walked in the Light—if only for moments (hours actually): life was amazing.

After recovering, I went back into "my life" at college—a bit wiser, and a whole lot more curious about metaphysical, spiritual things.

The second time I journeyed "beyond" was when I was 35.

I had been working in advertising moving up the ladder. One of the perks I used to get was Kings Hockey tickets. I mean—great seats. It was the third period of the Stanley Cup Playoffs. The game was tied.

I went to the bathroom during a break. While there, a woman sprayed hairspray all over the place.

As I returned to my seat, I began losing my air.

Although I didn't know it at the time, I was having a severe asthma attack. I was wheezing, coughing, and screaming for the Kings.

The man sitting next to my now ex-husband—then husband—kept nudging him, saying, "Maybe you should get her out of here."

When I heard this, I proclaimed, "No f---g way! This is a playoff game."

By the time we got to the car—I was not breathing.

White light was surrounding me.

There was an unsettling inner peace that came over me—unsettling because I felt afraid.

I felt stuck.

Then I fought to come back. I wanted to live. I wanted to breathe. I wanted to continue.

We went to the hospital, and I know from what they tell me that they had to put a shot of adrenaline in my heart to get it started again. I was pumped full of steroids to open my breathing passages.

Again, I experienced a sense of floating.

My "return" this time was different.

It felt like an abrupt interruption—for all of a sudden I felt my body again, heart pumping fast, grasping for air.

I knew I had just experienced something extraordinary.

I was aware of every breath I took.

The gift of life was in my breath.

I awoke with a great appreciation for air, for color, and for those who loved and supported me.

I understood that life is precious.

I was so grateful to be alive.

Now fade to black.

I am 39.

It is a beautiful day.

I am at the top of my game in advertising, loving life, and having fun. I had become a typical Type A personality—an achiever. My employees referred to me as their "Hippie Boss" for my unconventional management style. I loved what I did.

It is three days before the third time I died.

I had four of my most trusted staffers in my office speaking about the company's insurance policy, and I said, "Someday, I want to do what I love, without having to think about money." I knew that my career was not who I am, and I wanted to *do something* that reflected more of who I am, even though it may not be as financially rewarding.

We all mused at this notion, and all expressed a sigh of, "Oh well," at the passing thought.

Three days later, I decided to leave work a bit early at 4:30 PM. It was September 18, 1998. I was driving my hot black '96 Corvette south on 405, going about 30 miles an hour in traffic.

All of a sudden—*WHAM!*

My car spun out of control into on-coming traffic.

Then again—*WHAM!*—as the same black car hit my car, spinning me in the opposite direction.

I thought, *Oh my God, that guy just hit me!*

I tried desperately to control my car.

But my brakes, airbag, and seatbelt *all* failed.

I felt my fingers rip off my hand . . .

My car landed head-on in the center divider. My blood was everywhere. My spine was severed, and my lower back was broken. My fingers lay on the freeway. My arm was broken, my leg destroyed, and the seatbelt ripped across my stomach.

I screamed my last words, "I have insurance!"

A doctor stopped on the opposite side of the freeway and picked up my fingers, taping them to my hand. Five women in a white SUV stopped to call 911. There was so much blood . . . *and I was gone.*

I remember being surrounded by that familiar white light.

My younger brother—who died of AIDS at 30—was there, healed and whole. My grandparents were there—and my cat . . .

All of them perfect, welcoming.

I remember beautiful, vibrant colors.

It was warm, safe and beautiful.

I was shown pictures of my life. Still shots. And only one question was asked with each picture I saw, *What does this have to do with love?* I was not aware of the horror I had just been through. I was only aware of that single question, *What does this have to do with love?* It is not as if I were answering, rather just knowing that *love* is what my life was and is about.

I had no concept of time.

I remember feeling like I didn't want to leave this place.

Then the *voice* came to me. It told me in no uncertain terms that I had to go back and heal the world—in exchange, I would walk with angels—and be able to return whenever I wanted.

The next thing I know—I'm back in my broken, bruised, pain-riddled body.

All I know is horrific pain.

Then the drugs. Morphine, Methadone, and so many others—all designed to distance me from the pain, depression, fear, anxiety, and despair of my circumstances.

I thought my life was shattered, that my dreams were gone.

I was at my lowest low ever.

Doctors told me the worst: "You will never walk again; you will never be out of pain; you may not have the same use of your hands."

And then there were surgeries. Some 20 procedures to correct the nerve root damage in my spine. Only to be followed by the news, "The damage is non-repairable. This is as good as it gets."

Wow.

To look at me today—except for a few scars—you may not know what I lived through. You may not know that I *do* have pain in my body 24/7—even though I don't use drugs. You would not know that it took two years of working with a team of doctors, physical therapists, and alternative medical modalities to get me where I am today.

You would not know that I struggled in denial trying to recreate my old life, only to find that I was not the same.

You would not know that I sunk so far into pain that I tried to die again—just to get back to that place of inner peace, tranquility, and love.

You would not know that I went through major drug withdrawals.

To look at me today, you would not know the anger I harbored for years, before appreciating: the hit-and-run driver who left the scene; Caltrans for not capturing the accident on the cameras poised over that section of the 405; the lawyers who advised me not to sue GM—because I would run out of money before they would—giving them the opportunity to counter-sue for malicious prosecution; the doctors who could not cure me, and who only "practiced" medicine; and of course *me* for having left work early that day and getting into the accident in the first place.

To look at me today, you would not know that I choose life every single day.

To look at me today, you would not know I studied, reinvented myself, and found my way back to loving life.

To look at me today, you would not know I am a miracle of love, light, faith, and perseverance.

Today you would look at me and wonder, *Where does she get that amazing energy?*

She is so filled with love and light; her smile is so bright.

Today I live in and reflect gratitude. I am not just thankful for my life, but for everything I have been through. Yes, I am doing what I love—without thinking about money. I am a living example of *Be careful what you wish for—stay conscious all the time.* I am so grateful I know that life/love/spirit and my work move *though* me and are not *of* me.

I became a master transformational healer, a teacher, a life coach, and an author. I am still a marketing wizard doing consulting even today.

I'm blessed.

I know God and spirit, and walk with and see angels.

I know the magic of life, the wonder of each blue sky.

I am not who I used to be—I am better.

Thank God I died—for it gave me life.

❤   ❤   ❤

Holding BAs in English and Theatre from UCLA, Julie Ann Cohn also graduated from The Royal Academy of Dramatic Arts in London with a Master's in Theatre. She holds many spiritual credentials, including: Usui Reiki Master, Magan David Life Energy Master, Doctor of Metaphysics (PhD), Sufi Reiki Master, Shaman, Crystal Resonance Therapist and Minister. Julie still consults in marketing today and, in addition, has spent recent years as a transformational healer, teacher, and life coach. Julie has a Chakra Meditation CD on the market called, *Transformational,* and a book she has written, *CASH-Creating Achievement and Success Harmoniously*—both available on her active website www.lightmindsthinkalight.com.

Julie is also founder and co-creator of *The Blend™,* and is an active partner in Silver Unicorn Spirit Gifts. Founder/chairman/CEO of Techmorrow, Inc., Julie has worked for major ad agencies such as DDB Worldwide; Western International Media; McCann Erickson; Davis, Ball & Collombatto; Chait/Day; Telmar Group, Inc.; Donnelley Marketing Information Services; D&B; and Response Technologies. Julie has regularly been a guest speaker for the National Association of Database Marketing, the Advertising Research Federation, UCLA Extension, Loyola Marymount University, and the University of San Diego. Julie Ann Cohn has *brand equity,* and is world renowned in her healing and teaching work—serving clients in Israel, London, Brazil, and Australia.

Join the *Thank God I...™* Community online to share your story and chat with the authors at **www.thankgodi.com**

Thank God
I Was Tongue-tied

KEITH LAGGOS

For much of my life I have fought hard to conceal—and to compensate for—the fact that I was born totally tongue-tied. I did not receive corrective surgery—which is usually done now for an infant—until about the fourth grade. Because of the older age that I received this surgery, I was left with what is termed "a lazy tongue."

My tongue was thick and its muscles were undeveloped.

Years of speech therapy still left me with an unusual way of talking.

To this day I dislike the smell of peanut butter because for years I was forced to lick it off the roof of my mouth as a tongue exercise. I still remember many of the tongue twisters I had to practice. Today there are still certain letter combinations I have difficulty pronouncing.

Teachers and grown-ups seemed to understand, but children were much less kind. Many were even cruel. Kids often called me the "la-la" kid—and much worse.

Some groups treated me as a social outcast because I spoke "funny."

When I say that I have fought to compensate, I mean it more than just a figure of speech. It has been my version of Johnny Cash's *A Boy Named Sue* song—where a boy was named Sue, so he would learn to be tough in order to defend himself.

As children brutally made fun of my speech, I could not effectively communicate a verbal defense because of the speech defect they were mocking.

A frustrating silence built as time went on.

As a young boy, and later as a teenager, I learned to silence my verbal abusers with my fists. Of course, I am not claiming my physical response was justified because of their verbal abuse. Right or wrong, it was the only response I found that worked effectively.

I have been blessed many ways in my life.

Yet in retrospect, this one relatively minor handicap seemed to have a greater influence in my life than all my blessings. For example, I was blessed with a high IQ, but because of my speech impediment, I could not express myself—and was often perceived as an idiot. I have been told that this led me to strive for academic achievements to demonstrate my intelligence. I simply applied myself to academics, where performance was not judged on socialization skills.

It worked.

Achievement felt good—and getting good grades became easy.

If it were not for this, I may not now hold multiple Masters Degrees and a PhD.

As a young boy I felt that I had to defend myself from the ridicule that I received for being tongue-tied. I worked out and learned how to fight larger opponents, and how to fight several opponents at a time.

The country was suddenly thrust into racial uproar during the 1960s when I was a teenager. My family did not run—as did almost all the other white families—when the neighborhood turned from middle-income, Anglo-Saxon, to an impoverished lower income neighborhood.

The fighting skills I learned from defending myself saved my life many times. A blessing in complete disguise, I was attacked simply because I was white. On a couple of occasions, several of our black neighbors and a few of my black friends placed their lives in danger by defending my family.

I learned many blessings from this period of my life.

This includes, obviously, that prejudices know no color boundaries. People will make judgments on anything different from themselves. However, my black friends didn't made fun of my speech. I learned that right and wrong knows no color.

I also learned that I did not want to live my life impoverished.

As a young adult, many often asked me if I was from Boston; that is, everyone except those from Boston! Bostonians had no clue what my "accent" was, but they knew it was definitely not a Boston accent. I learned that it was much easier just to say yes, I was from Boston, rather than try to explain that I was born tongue-tied, and still had a speech impediment.

I was also blessed with good looks—at least in my youth. I was strong, intelligent, and athletic. If it were not for my "strange speech," I could have easily become a womanizer. Instead, I was more modest and introverted. I found it difficult to communicate and "sweet talk" women. Instead, I preferred a close relationship with one person who understood me, and who realized what I had to offer in spite of my speech problem.

I got married as a teenager and started a family. Marrying at a young age allowed me to move to a safe environment, and helped me focus on my future.

This probably saved my life.

Because of my lack of confidence with words, I became more comfortable with numbers. I majored in math and computer science in college. I became an inventory manager and a systems analyst. After I received my first of three Masters Degrees, I taught math and economics at high school and college levels, while working on my PhD. I felt so much more comfortable teaching courses that depended on numbers rather than words.

This eventually gave me confidence to speak in public on any topic on which I have a firm grasp. I have now done public speaking to groups of 10,000 or more. I have appeared on television and on radio programs.

I am still, however, more comfortable with a pen. Because I was born with a "disability," I have become a writer and an author.

I believe I had a "minor" disability. I was fortunate. Even though I had the corrective surgery later than I should have, it was a disability that I could overcome. I cannot say that I am a totally compassionate person. I am certainly not a patient man. Anyone who knows me would agree with that self-analysis. However, I have learned to be more understanding of the challenges faced by those with disabilities. As a result, I have created a concept of enabling the disabled. I have written a column on that subject and outlined a book of that title. I have also assisted the World Association of Persons with Disabilities to introduce direct sales to the disabled.

Would I have done this if I had not been born tongue-tied?

We won't know for sure, but quite likely not.

Certainly, my life today does not center itself around the experience of being born tongue-tied. However, simply to say that I am what I am today because I was born tongue-tied may be an understatement, too.

Before being asked to write my story down, I hadn't realized how much of my life became the way it has because of the way I was born. I doubt my immediate family has ever considered it either. After all, being tongue-tied is not a serious disability. Yet, it has made me work hard most of my life to compensate for this disadvantage. I no longer feel compelled to try to conceal the fact I was born tongue-tied.

In retrospect, I can honestly say, thank God I was born tongue-tied.

I cannot say that someone with a severe disability can or should give thanks for their disability. Perhaps, though, those who find the fortitude to overcome the challenges that a severe disability creates can thank God for giving them the will to meet and conquer those challenges.

Their stories inspire all who hear them, including me.

I have also learned that those who have been fortunate to have lesser disabilities and disadvantages have a choice. You can use your particular problem as a challenge to overcome so you can be successful in life. Perhaps it is really true that the disadvantages and disabilities we have define who we are *more* than the blessings and abilities we are given.

It is, after all, easy to thank God for our blessings.

Could it be that *only* when we can thank God for our challenges, we truly become blessed?

I would have to say in a voice full of confidence—and with just a hint of an accent—"YES!"

♥   ♥   ♥

Keith B. Laggos, MA, MBA, PhD, began his career in the Direct Sales Industry in 1971 as an Amway distributor, and was a consistently high producer in his affiliations with several Direct Sales companies. In his 30-plus-year association with the Industry, he has been a management and marketing consultant to dozens of Direct Sales companies, as well as to other sales and distribution companies outside the Industry. Keith serves as keynote speaker for Direct Sales annual meetings, trainings, and special events. Keith is dedicated to acting on his mission to empower entrepreneurs globally. He is co-founder, president, and publisher of *Network Marketing Business Journal®*. Entering its 24th year of publication, it now serves seven countries in seven languages, and has a monthly readership of over a million-and-a-half worldwide. Available shortly, *The Sixth Sun* is Keith's latest fiction book—a DiVinci Code type thriller centered on the 2012 Mayan prophecies.

Thank God
... for Toxic Parents

LINDA CROSSLEY

My life turned upside down in the spring of 1996 when my marriage—and my reality as I knew it up to that point—shattered.

My husband had created a situation that forced me to stop in my tracks.

It rocked my world, and sorely tested my number one core value of unconditional love.

It was only when my own marriage reached this breaking point that I began to realize how much my parents' divorce created deep emotional charges that controlled my life.

I was a workaholic and took responsibility for everything. I could not say, *No*, to anyone because I was driven to "please" everyone.

I was an emotional eater—only eating after meeting everyone else's needs. I was driven to work hard by the fear of being hungry again—like I was when I was a child—and I was determined not to be hungry again.

I was truly exhausted from my fears of rejection—and loss of control—and the need to prove my worth and value in this world. I believed if I worked as hard as I could, I could prevent my past from impacting my future.

Instead, I created an environment that almost facilitated history repeating itself.

As I worked through my marital issues, it became clear that my behaviors did not demonstrate to my husband that he and our life together were my number one priority. I used my work to fulfill my needs that had not been filled during my childhood. Through a great deal of work, I came to realize that what I experienced as a child— chaos, addiction, conditional love, manipulation, and rejection—were the tools I needed to redefine who I really am. These tools were the best gifts my parents gave me because they helped me find the child that got buried at the age of nine, when my parents got divorced.

In the divorce, my mom got custody of us three kids, and we moved into a two-bedroom apartment. It was at that point that the family roles got reversed. Little did I know at that time how much this change in roles would impact the rest of my life. Taking on the responsibility of my mother's emotional needs became an all-consuming chore for me.

Her needs were many and deep.

The day that my parents separated—although I did not know it then—was the day my childhood died.

I became the adult, taking responsibility for things like paying bills, counseling, and working so I could buy clothes and food. I began babysitting when I was 11, some nights until 3:00 AM—and I would run home because I was so scared. I didn't tell anyone how scared I was because I knew how much we needed the money.

My mom would go over the money situation with me—how much was coming in and how much was going out—and there didn't seem to be enough. Food was something that came in behind paying the rest of the bills, so many nights we would go to bed hungry. We would visit my father every other weekend and we looked forward to it because my dad provided food. We would eat the whole weekend, knowing that when we got back home, we might not have any food.

We also had to listen to him criticize our mom, telling us she was greedy and selfish. Then when we returned home from our visits, we had to listen to our mother criticize our dad about being cheap and selfish. Both of them were so focused on themselves and their own pain, they were incapable of recognizing anyone else's needs or seeing how much pain we were in. They both focused on money—mom on how to spend *more* of it, and dad on how *not* to give mom money, so she couldn't spend his money on herself.

My "parents" used us kids as *pawns* in their personal "war"—as if our affection was a prize for them to win.

I was constantly torn between them because I loved them both.

I walked on eggshells, being very careful about what I said to avoid hurting them—or making them any angrier than they were already. I learned to ignore my own feelings and stuffed my emotions down. I tried to be the perfect daughter, putting everyone's needs before my own, doing whatever I could to maintain the "peace." When we were with my dad, we agreed with Dad, and when we were with my mom, we agreed with Mom.

This emotional tug-of-war continued for nine years—with money being the weapon of choice in their confrontation.

And when I turned 18—that weapon was turned on me.

My father "disowned" me as his daughter. I didn't even know what that meant, and I certainly didn't know what I did to deserve it. I had to resort to writing letters to ask him what I had done to cause him to reject me because he would not take my calls and he would not speak to me.

In my letters to him I poured my heart out.

I was not prepared for what he wrote back.

In his first letter, my father accused me of siding with my mother in a lawsuit against him for child support—after I had worked so hard *not* to take sides, after all those years of battle.

He basically said he no longer loved me—and thought I was greedy.

After reading that letter, the pain felt like someone had punched me in the stomach.

I could hardly breathe.

I could not believe my own father was saying the things he put in that letter, especially when I had nothing to do with the lawsuit my mother initiated. The pain was so bad that I could not write back for several months.

Then the holidays came around, and I wrote to him at Christmastime—trying to respond to the painful things he had written me.

I was once again devastated by the words written in his response.

He indicated that I "used" to be his favorite child, but "now" the pendulum had swung—and my sister was his favorite child!

At that point, I knew he wouldn't respect my feelings, or even attempt to hear what I was so desperately trying to convey. Even today, when I read those letters from him, my mind still has a hard time comprehending that a parent could write such hurtful things to a child.

Through a great deal of self-inquiry, I discovered the sources of my emotional charges—fear of rejection, fear of loss of control, manipulation, and a belief that to be worthy I had to work hard to get what I deserve. The symptoms of my emotional charges—suppressing my emotions, anger, my unhealthy relationship to food and money—all were rooted in conditional love. I truly viewed food as a "comfort," filling an emotional void. The overly responsible child in me, along with the feeling of unworthiness, made me into a workaholic—seeking approval from my superiors and employees, since I did not get it from my parents.

Being a workaholic was what finally made me seek professional help.

My counselor explained that I had "toxic" parents, and that they "robbed me" of my childhood.

She also explained how saying *No* is a gift to be given. I really thought about saying *No* as a gift—and tried it out. This tool—in of it itself—has provided me such freedom—freedom to explore my own needs and define boundaries.

My next step was to look deep into my heart, and think about my husband and my marriage in the light of unconditional love. At this point, my mind and body had gone numb from the pain, but I knew I needed to make a decision. And I knew this decision would be a defining moment in my life.

Do I follow in the footsteps of my parents—and get a divorce—or do I practice what I preach, and work our issues out?

Do I love my husband and our life together enough to do the "hard" work necessary to heal myself?

This light of unconditional love uncovered a deep well of gratitude.

I really began to feel this unconditional love and gratitude fill me up, warming my soul to the greatest depth. I had so much in my life . . . so much to be grateful for. From this place of gratitude, I was finally able to connect the dots . . .

My father's greatest gift to me was to teach me the lessons of "conditional" love, so that I could root my life in "unconditional" love. His "disowning" me launched me on my journey of self-discovery, so I could uncover the truths residing in my heart. The beauty in the pain he caused is so clear, now. The lesson I learned is the ever-present unconditional love available *to* me and *in* me.

Thank GOD my father loves conditionally.

I will be forever grateful to my father for his love, and when I speak with him today, I come from a place of love—instead of obligation and fear.

Through my mother's gift of a chaotic life—and the resultant fear I harbored of losing control of my life—I have been able to explore the underlying causes of my being a workaholic—and save my marriage.

I learned that I do not have to work hard to prove my worthiness and value in this world. My work no longer defines my identity, and is no longer my source of approval and acceptance. My work is no longer needed to numb the hurt and pain that stemmed from my unfilled childhood needs. I have been able to look at my addiction, see it for what it was, and truly release it from my life.

Thank GOD my mom loves to spend money, and create chaos in her life from this activity. It is a reminder of the lesson I learned—to love and appreciate all things as they are at all times, and to know the inner peace that comes with this lesson.

I can truly live a balanced life and trust that I am worthy of the abundance the universe has to offer.

I have come to realize that the pain from my parents' divorce—including fears of rejection and loss of control, addiction (both food and work), and the needs for acceptance and approval—actually served me very well. On my journey of self-discovery and healing, I have been able to identify the abundant wealth in all areas of my life:

- Mentally—clearly defined values
- Physically—a healthy relationship to food
- Spiritually—a clear connection to spirit maintained in a yoga practice
- Financially—self-sufficiency and a trust of the universe's abundance
- Family—healthy relationships with all family members
- Socially—the capacity to value diversity
- Vocationally—a healthy work ethic with balance

I am truly grateful for my parents, and for experiencing their divorce.

And thank GOD my husband rocked my world so I could discover my heart's truth. All my life experiences make me who I am today. And dedicated to my yoga practice and teachings, I am able to say that I am proud of myself, and love who I am today—and remain joyfully married to my husband.

❤   ❤   ❤

Linda Crossley has spent the majority of her professional life working in the health care field as manager, trainer, educator, and consultant. She earned her BS Degree in Business Administration from Rider University and, at St. Joseph's University, an MBA in Health Administration. In 2002, she discovered the healing power (inside and out) of yoga, which inspired her to become a yoga teacher; she is now a *Registered Yoga*

Teacher (RYT®) at the 500-hour level with *Yoga Alliance®*. She is inspired about sharing the benefits that will naturally develop in students as a regular yoga practice is embraced. She gets a great deal of satisfaction from assisting students on their personal journeys toward self-acceptance and unconditional love. She truly believes yoga provides a vehicle to attaining balance in life, as well as enhancing a student's physical, mental, emotional and spiritual well-being. With their two dogs (Eclipse and Mocha), Linda and her husband of 20 years, Randy, live in Huntington Beach, California. She is a partner in a yoga co-op, there, and teaches yoga classes—both private and group—as well as workshops and teacher training. Please check her out at www.cloudnineyoga.com.

Thank God I Was Molested

SUSAN CONTREAS

You know, whenever I meet someone new I often hear, "Wow, you're such a fulfilled person."

I'm often asked what the secret to my fulfillment is.

My answer is usually, "I meditate a lot"—which I do every day.

But after I get to know someone—and we begin to share our stories—I hear, "Susan, how can you be such a fulfilled person all the time? I wouldn't have guessed all the things you've been through."

Well, I have been through many experiences in my life, starting at a very young age. However, I have learned to take something away—or rather become aware of what I needed to learn—from each experience, to help me grow spiritually, and to become the very best person I can be.

When I was a child of around four years old or so, some very important people in my life began to abuse me verbally, physically, and even began to molest me. I couldn't stop the unwanted touching, fondling, and sex acts I was forced to perform. I felt ugly, unloved, unwanted, and so very confused. No one would pay any attention to me—unless it was in a sexual manner.

I tried to tell my mother what was happening, but she only scolded me, saying it was not right for me to make up such lies.

I wasn't listened to or heard.

I began to ask questions like, "God, why have you chosen me to be born into such a horrible life? As a child, what did I do to deserve this type of life? Why did I see other kids around looking so full of joy? Why was I supposed to be unloved and miserable?"

My life often consisted of either being left alone with my sexual abusers, or being taken out to the onion fields—where my parents were migrant workers—to work long hours of hard labor, on weekends and all school vacations. While the other neighborhood kids where at swimming pool parties, I was in the onion fields; when other children where having sleepovers, I was going to bed early because I had to work in the morning.

I would try to get a good night's sleep, all the while fearing that someone fondling me in the middle of the night would awake me. I learned quickly that my life was very different from other children, and that made me different, too. I began to believe that the only reason I was on this earth was to suffer—but I still couldn't understand why.

The older I got, the more often I would ask God why I was doomed to live such a life, but somehow I knew that when I was an adult, things would be much better for me—because they couldn't possibly get much worse.

By the time I was 12 years old, most of my siblings had moved out to be on their own, and I was left at home with my brother, who was only a year older than me. I grew tired of my father's alcoholism, and his constant physical abuse of my mother.

Apparently, so did my mother because she moved us to a small city an hour away, where she rented a tiny bachelor apartment above an appliance store, where we literally lived out of our suitcases.

This was a difficult time for me because I was still enrolled in school in my hometown, and I was dropped off in front of the school hours before the school even opened, so my mother could get to work. I then would have to wait for several hours after school for my mother to pick me up when she got out of work, sitting in front of the school by myself—with the home where I grew up only a few blocks away.

During that summer, I went to work with my mom in the onion fields to help pay for our expenses, but I was often left alone at night with no phone, television, or radio. I made friends with some of the local kids, and it was nice to have somewhat of a fresh start with people who didn't know my past, and who didn't pass judgment on my working out in the onion fields.

I just couldn't stop feeling homesick.

It wasn't long before my parents reconciled, and we moved back to my hometown. I was inspired to be home—but all of my nightmarish fears of sexual abuse came back, too.

My self-loathing and anger slowly began to increase, and it was starting to show, now. I would stay in my bedroom when I was home, trying to forget about everything beyond my bedroom door. I would lose myself for hours at a time in the lyrics of just about every genre of music I could find.

Soon I was doing drugs to numb my pain and in an attempt to forget my ugly past.

My parents began fighting, again, so I left the house as much as I could because I didn't want to hear them anymore. I started drinking with my friends so I could escape my troubles at home.

Then, at 16, I was raped. I became pregnant by a 23-year-old who had known me since I was a toddler, and who told me that he remembered my past sexual abuse, and felt it was okay to act off of those memories.

My parents sent me away because they felt I was a disgrace to our family.

This is when I learned that my parents believed that any young girl who was taken advantage of sexually deserved it—because she was "asking" for it, and had encouraged it . . .

I was eager to leave.

After my son was born, I spent nine months with him, before my mother decided that she was better fit to raise him, and my son was moved to her house—and I was kicked out to live on the streets.

I again began to ask GOD why this was my life, and if my heart-aches would ever stop. I tried to exist—only now I was a full-blown alcoholic.

At 17, I met someone who I cared for very much—and who I thought cared for me. Although we didn't marry, we lasted eight years together, and four years into our relationship our son was born. My mother let my oldest son come live with us. We were an instant family—but I was still an alcoholic, who still had a lot of rage inside. This caused many physical altercations between us, and I realized that this was having an effect on both my sons, so we ended our relationship.

I met, fell in love, and married my husband one year later. He accepted me and my two sons, my alcoholism, my ugly past and all. We have a son and daughter together.

My oldest son could not put up with my alcoholism, so went back to live with my mother.

I began to realize that the relationships I had with men—even my own son—were very strained because of my sexual abuse years before. I was still dealing with my alcoholism, when my husband and I had an extremely violent physical altercation in front of the three kids. I realized that the pattern was still there. I could change the people I allowed in my life, but I would still revert to the same behavior with men, unless *I* made some changes to *ME*.

So my journey began.

I was determined to make my life better—for my children and me. I didn't want my children to hide in their own home for fear of being abused—or seeing abuse—ever again.

I overcame my alcoholism and studied hypnotism. I became a Certified Clinical Hypnotherapist, and learned to meditate. During my studies, I learned about psychology and behaviors. It helped me to understand my abusers, and get through the pain that I carried for so long. I was finally able to appreciate my abusers—but most of all I appreciated myself—and realized that I was not responsible for what had happened to me.

Slowly, my confusion dissipated, and I finally understood true love for the first time. I wanted for everyone in the world to know this awesome feeling.

I began to thank GOD for all the experiences of my life leading up to my being able to experience such overwhelming joy and love for the first time ever.

I have overcome so much, and I am now a true survivor.

I am learning that this type of abuse is so much more common than I could ever have imagined growing up. I want to get out there and help those who are dealing with these issues right now, especially teens who have enough to deal with just growing up. I know that if I had had someone to talk to as a teen, someone who understood the anger, the pent up frustration, the need for release, then maybe I could have been spared some heartache as a young adult, and been spared making some of the bad choices that I made.

My goal is to help as many teens as possible get through the tough times in their life, and to deal with some issues many may still consider TABOO.

I want for them to know that there are still people in this world who care, and who want nothing but the absolute best for them, and help them understand the importance of family and true love.

I understand, now, that I needed to experience everything I went through first hand, so that I can now assist others through their trying times. I can now help them become the best people they can be—and be fulfilled doing it.

❤   ❤   ❤

Susan Contreas has lived in Southern California's Santa Clarita Valley for over 35 years. She has been involved in supporting many community programs, such as the Food Pantry and the Domestic Violence Center. Santa Clarita's teen population has benefited from her being a former volunteer and mentor for the Teen Mom Program at the Child & Family Center. She has been joyfully married to Steve for 14 years, and they have two wonderful children together. Susan also has two outstanding older sons. Susan has been a Certified Hypnotherapist for nine years, and is currently working on Meditation CDs for self-improvement—with Steve contributing his beautiful musical talents. You can find out more about Susan and what she is working on by visiting her website at www.positivewonders.com.

Thank God
My Dad Died

MARC RABINOWITZ

*W*hat attracted me to this book was not the title alone. It was what would came out of it. Believe me, folks, the death of my father had a tremendous impact on me.

However, there were positive factors that balanced out the negatives.

I was 17 years old when my father died of a sarcoma cancer that spread from his right quadriceps muscle to the rest of his body. He ignored the pain, thinking it was a "Charlie Horse" from jogging. So, when he finally gave in and went to see the doctor, a biopsy confirmed it was a malignant tumor that had been growing for some time in his leg. My father was told he had to have his leg amputated—or risk the spread of the cancer—so he chose the amputation.

He chose the amputation for his children. He thought being alive for us—even to risk a limb—was worth it. This showed his real love and genius. But most importantly, it revealed his true courage.

My father was a religious person and, as a Jew, kept kosher. However, after the cancer spread, the pain became constant. He was constantly sick from the chemotherapy, and he was angry with god. That is when he took his first bite out of an un-kosher meat. It was a whopper, literally. My father was so religious before his cancer, he once made my friend, Mathew, eat his ham sandwich out on the porch— instead of eating it on the inside kitchen table.

To me—my father didn't really die.

He only changed in form.

I had to find the new form of "Daddy." He just was not in my immediate, evident, present state. When he died, there was an insane denial that it happened.

Then actuality sunk in.

This made me stronger because I took his place here in the universe. I became more responsible, more productive, and more authoritative. I had to be the new head of the family. I had to accept *actuality* when it stared me in the face.

I had to become a *man*.

I had to receive my destiny—embrace it, love it, treasure it, and represent it. It's only when you love someone for who they *are*, who they *were*, what they represented, and what they dominantly believed, that you can fully understand "destiny."

My father believed that nothing was impossible—that impossible was really nothing—as long as your perception believed it could be.

He made me swear that being born with a deformity would not be an excuse *not* to become a success.

He was right.

Born with a muscle deformity, I didn't once let it stand before me as a reason not to be successful.

I wish he could see me now. He taught me not to give up. In actuality, he can see me—because I am part of him . . .

He lives on in me . . .

He wanted me to be a doctor, a lawyer, or a surgeon. In essence, he wanted me to be *me* . . . whatever I turned out to be.

After his death, I started seeing his traits in other people. I've seen some traits of him in my mom, my sister, my friends, and in myself. In my friend, Bob, I have seen the trait of comedy, selflessness, and love. In my sister, I have seen his stubbornness, and in me I can see courage, leadership, honesty, and productivity.

People don't really die—they only change in form.

Freeman Dyson once said, "Consciousness is a cloud of charged particles of light."

Energy cannot be created nor destroyed, but only change in form.

We are holographic entities.

When I close my eyes and meditate, I can actually visualize my father and speak to him as if he is standing next to me.

I am now in his place, starting my new life with my new family. His death brought the family together. It started me on a new mission and vision to be an inspired person, father, businessman, and friend. I now had some new incredible energy to want to do something and become successful in my life.

I started my own company called Hollywood Satellite. My company was started with a $5,000 credit card, backed by love, wisdom, and certainty. I had failed for months trying to sell customers satellite dishes, but I heard my father: "Don't give up. The most successful people in the world failed. You're going to be one of them!" he shouted.

After a year in business, I had made one million dollars in sales.

I became a mentor to my friends and co-workers.

Now I own a few companies.

Not only has his death helped me become wealthy, but I have also graduated college—the first Rabinowitz ever to graduate college. I received my degree in Health Science. I wanted to study how cancer is created and cured.

What I discovered was that cancer really comes from your psyche.

You create it.

The word *disease* broken down is *dis*-ease—or stress.

You create your own cancer by not loving.

Whatever you don't love, you create, attract, or become—until you learn to love it.

What a challenge it was to take on a death of a loved one, especially the death of a father at the early age of 17. All of a sudden, there were bills, responsibilities, taking care of my mother and sister, sacrificing hanging out with my friends, going to college, and graduating.

I started to learn how to be an entrepreneur. I knew I had it in me to become a success. I had a lot of support and challenge in my life, which helped me in the growth process of my mind. I learned every time I helped someone with something, it helped me to grow as well. It simply is one of the laws of the universe.

What started as one of the most devastating and limiting events in my life has now reversed itself—and has served me far, far more than I could ever have thought.

My father died.

By finally appreciating his death, seeing his traits in the loved ones around me, and seizing upon his energies, I have allowed the event to serve me. It unlocked the resources within me. It provided the perseverance, the intense energy, and the patience needed to let the universe unfold before me.

Now through this story I share the gift of my experience with you and thousands of others.

❤　❤　❤

Marc Rabinowitz was born May 20, 1973, in Canarsie Brooklyn. While his family was not wealthy in terms of money, he knew a wealth of love—and found growing up in Brooklyn memorable.

"As long as you can become wealthy doing what you love, I guess it don't matter what you really do for a living," said his father, who died from cancer when Marc was 17—changing his life mentally, emotionally, spiritually, and financially.

Marc graduated with a degree in Health Science—but did not love this subject enough to devote his life to it. While it took years to discover, Marc was an entrepreneur salesman at heart. He finally sold everything from pots and pans to satellite dishes. He discovered that if he had a product, then he could provide the service. He was 26 years old when he made his first million dollars. Marc has constantly honed his sales skills through education in seminars and by surrounding himself with the most successful people in business.

"The wealthiest people in the world fail the most. You must save—and continue to save—and incredible opportunities will come to you. It doesn't really matter what you make—its how you manage what you make."

In a later volume, Marc will be contributing another story: *Thank God I Sold My House.*

Thank God
... for Accidents

FINDING GRATITUDE IN THE ALTITUDE

MAISIE VULTAGGIO

"Swimmers—take your mark!"

It was a phrase I had heard many times—and rightfully expected to hear many more times during my anticipated collegiate athletic career.

I was a senior in high school, a straight "A" student, a nationally ranked swimmer, competitive, energetic and, of course, in excellent health.

Several top college swimming programs were recruiting me, thanks to my winning performances in the pool and in the classroom.

All of this success, however, came with a price.

Throughout junior high and high school, my day started at 4:00 AM, with a half-hour drive to the pool and a two-hour workout before school.

At the end of my school day, I hurried home to grab something to eat, before heading back to the pool for another lengthy swim workout.

361

Arriving back home around 8:00 PM, I ate dinner, did homework, and collapsed into bed—only to start the whole routine over again the next morning. Though I hated the sound of the alarm clock going off—I truly believed I loved what I was doing.

Swimming had been my life since I was three.

I was five-foot six-inches tall, and a muscle-packed 135 pounds. My broad shoulders and back, long blond hair, and sun-kissed skin made me easily recognizable. The years of training molded my defined arms, shoulders and legs, and allowed me to do 150 push-ups with my feet on a chair—or swim 10 miles a day.

My body was a machine—and there wasn't much I couldn't ask it to do.

People admired me for my strength and perseverance, for my cheerful nature and positive spirit.

Life was good it seemed. It held such promise for me.

Suddenly, though, everything changed—drastically and painfully—when I decided to go against my character and better judgment, and skip school to go skiing with some friends.

It had been a beautiful day on the slopes, until I hit a sheet of ice on the steepest part of a run—and completely lost control.

I couldn't stop myself.

My feet flew out from under me, slamming me backwards onto the ice, with the back of my head taking the full blow.

According to a friend—the only witness to what had happened—after the initial impact, I then tumbled like a rag doll, and spun around the slick surface, totally helpless, until I hit bottom, flew forward, and finally landed flat on my face.

I don't remember much about any of it, except for becoming conscious face down in the snow, with a friend crouched over me—thinking I was dead.

At first I lay there, unable to piece together what had just happened.

Eventually, I tried to get up, struggled to become upright and, somehow with the help from my friend, made it to the ski lodge.

After my friend brought me home a few hours later, I was determined to keep this accident to myself. I took some Advil—and actually went to swim practice the following morning. I couldn't even lift my head off the pillow, and literally had to roll out of bed in order to get up.

Unfortunately, things didn't get better.

The excruciating headaches started as a stabbing pain that went from my jaw and temples, down the back of my neck into my upper back and shoulders. I didn't want to move—because the pain would greatly intensify if I did. At my very worst, just going from a lying down position to sitting up would usually cause me to see stars, and I would black out. Standing up required some sort of assistance because the explosive pain in my head would bring me to my knees.

Soon I found myself in and out of emergency rooms and doctor offices. After all the poking and prodding, the stacks of X-rays and scan results, and numerous consultations among seven doctors and three dentists, the final diagnoses were made.

I had suffered severe skeletal-muscular damage to my neck and face, with contorted vertebrae, herniated disks, a dislocated jaw, broken teeth, and a shattered inner ear and vestibular system—which all led to a post-traumatic concussion disorder and chronic pain.

My medical and therapy bills quickly mounted into the tens of thousands of dollars—and yet nothing helped to lessen the pain.

One highly touted dentist—who specialized in temporomandibular joint disorder (a.k.a. TMJ)—stuck needles directly into my ear to flood my jaw with pain relievers, in an effort to alleviate the pressure from my dislocation and damaged inner ear vestibular system. I remember lying there in a reclined bed, watching this eight-inch needle come towards me, and hearing the cracking and popping of my skin and tissue in my ear and jaw as the needle penetrated. A pain specialist delivered yet another series of trigger point injections, with an even larger needle all over my neck and head, to infuse medication into my bone-hard contracted muscles to get them to relax. As I would be writhing in pain, they could not give me any anesthetic because they needed my response to see if they hit the most painful areas.

At 17, I was now hunched over like a 100-year-old woman. I had to have daily physical therapy to help me straighten my contorted body, and to learn how to balance myself again. I had also developed speech and memory problems, and I had little recollection or recognition of who I was with or what I was doing.

I spent many entire days in my darkened bedroom, just praying for some relief and a return to the life I had known.

My dreams had all been put on hold.

My previous accomplishments in the pool had become meaningless.

Was I going to wallow in despair, or finally was I going to try to figure out what I could salvage, what I could change, what I could do to breathe life back into myself?

I had to put away any thoughts that life as I had once known it would be restored. I couldn't go back; I needed to go forward.

It was through my darkest days of lying in bed, trying not to move, listening to my breath, that I learned what it truly meant to be in the moment.

As I was striving for high levels of success, I didn't have moments where I could quiet my mind to let God's messages become apparent to me. I find it remarkable that God knew that in order to communicate with me, I would have to be stripped of my physical abilities, become bedridden, and practically forced into meditation.

I used the power of visualization—that I used many times as an athlete—to see myself as healthy and vibrant again. I remember saying to myself that each day is a gift, and as long as I have my breath I can make a difference.

A song by Gloria Estefen often sang in my head. I felt as if she wrote this song for me:

> *Coming out of the dark, I finally see the light now*
> *It's shining on me . . .*
> *As I stand on the rock of your love.*

Two years later, almost to the day I tumbled and crashed to the ice, a miracle happened.

I woke up and realized I didn't have a headache . . .

It was so liberating to start the day without being in pain.

It was as if a veil had lifted, and I could see my surroundings with clarity.

By then I was a sophomore in college and had grown to love my new independence, not because of what I accomplished, but because of who I was. In living my life in the moment, I was no longer consumed with recording personal best times in the water or winning races. I took a job in the career-counseling center, and discovered amazing satisfaction in helping others find their inspiration and potential career choices. I also used my years of experience in swimming to volunteer my time to help underprivileged children learn how to swim.

Just as my physical ability to balance was restored, I had gained balance in my life.

What I had once considered a tragedy had become an enormous gift.

As my life fell apart around me, I'd been given the chance to put it back together better than it was before. I realized how important it is to give from a place of love—not obligation. Love and compassion are what create and sustain life. Before my accident, I was self-consumed by my efforts to please others through perfection. Balance was only achieved once I could give to others through my intention. I was less concerned with the particulars of life, and more aware of how just being truly present could be enough.

I defied the odds in my junior year, when I became a collegiate scholar athlete—when before that it looked as though I might not be able even to function normally again. I swam lifetime "best times" and even competed at Big Ten Championships, but this time around—my victory was solely personal. I was actually there as more of a team cheerleader than contributing to the team's score.

It was less about "beating" the person next to me—and more about *encouraging* the person next to me.

And I was completely fulfilled with that role.

Now I could leave swimming with a more satisfying closure. I couldn't get back what I had "lost" over three years before—and no longer desired or needed to.

I was done.

Whatever new-found success, I had came from a place of inner peace within myself, and from a love of what I was able to do, rather than from a place of feeling I had to make everybody proud.

I graduated college with honors, and have gone on to have a very successful business career.

I was no longer focused on being the best athlete I could be, but more on being the best person I could be.

Upon graduation, I went to work for a consulting firm where I was blessed to meet my husband Peter. Without the necessary shift of focus that my accident forced, perhaps I wouldn't have taken the direction that led me to that company, therefore precluding me from ever meeting the love of my life, and being blessed with two angelic children.

Thank God I had my skiing accident because my choices may well have been completely focused on my athletics. Being a successful competitive swimmer no longer defined me—or limited me—as the only great thing I had to offer in life.

❤   ❤   ❤

Maisie A. Vultaggio is a wife to an amazing husband, and a mother to two incredible little girls. Maisie resides in Peoria, Arizona, where she and her husband are founders of The LUMI Company, LLC, that provides illumination through learning. While learning professional skills, employees are gaining insights into their higher selves. She home schools both of her children, and travels with her husband internationally, while he consults with many Fortune 500 Companies. You can contact Maisie and learn about her company at www.thelumicompany.com and www.healingthroughgratitude.com.

Join the *Thank God I . . .*™ Community online to share your story and chat with the authors at **www.thankgodi.com**

Thank God
. . . for Dirty Dishes

CLAUDIA PRUETT

I stopped short of screaming—instead I prayed.
Distress became an inner peace.
My scowl turned into a smile.

With the entire family present, we'd just finished a delicious, home-made meal at the kitchen table. All five of us had laughed, talked, and ate together.

That night I arose from the table, both hands juggling dirty plates, flatware, and a glass or two. I turned the corner, headed to the sink, and found the counter covered with an assortment of empty cereal bowls, used glasses, and sticky peanut-butter spoons. The sink overflowed with dirty dishes and grimy pots and pans. If it hadn't been for the atmosphere created at dinner, the feeling of pride I felt for my kids, and the lingering sound of my youngest daughter's sweet laughter—I know I would have started yelling, "Who forgot to empty and load the dishwasher? Didn't I specifically say it had to be done before going to the gym? How come you find time to go online, but you don't find time to do your chores?"

These statements remained where they should—in my head.

Instead, I thanked God for dirty dishes.

I had just spent a great evening with my loving family. I felt grateful for them, for the roof over my head, and for my cooking talents. Most would not think that a sink full of dirty dishes could pass for "a blessing in disguise." But for me that over-crowded sink became my precious trophy—applauding my status as Mom.

In my home, we try to eat together regularly—but often someone is absent, due to sport activities, work responsibilities, or school projects. I know that nothing compares to the well-being created while sharing a home-cooked meal. Dinner does make a difference for parents and children alike. Family meals are the perfect time to talk to kids, to listen to what's on their minds, and to share stories—whether recent or of days long past. Consistent gatherings help provide a sense of stability and balance in these stressful times. They form an invisible shield that protects family members beyond the boundaries of the home.

I'm a working mother and an active community member. I'm proud of my university degrees, my professional accomplishments, and my community endeavors. However, I know that a caring maternal presence is essential in the development of children. Those important daily details that go unaffirmed comprise the fabric of Motherhood. Those time-consuming, non-ending tasks that children take for granted—until they live on their own or have kids of their own—provide a safe and nurturing environment. Cooking and feeding my family healthy and wholesome food is one of these responsibilities that I make a priority.

> *Cooking for my family is a rewarding responsibility.*
> *Eating with my family is a worthwhile adventure.*
> *Laughing with my family brings heartwarming joy.*

Betty Williams, 1977 Nobel Peace Prize Laureate, said, "Women should have the freedom to carry the torch for peace, as they carry a child to their breast." As providers of nourishment and nurturing to our families and communities, so must mothers have the freedom to be proud of their domestic endeavors, and carry the torch for family well-being.

American society neglects to appreciate the life-sustaining role of mothers. Completing the line for "occupation" should be a fulfilling moment for mothers to write "MOM"—just by itself—or perhaps "MOM & . . . (Doctor, Teacher, Executive, etc.)" However, stressed and multi-tasking mothers overlook the inherent satisfaction in doing their best in assuring the health and well-being of their families. They are disenchanted and disillusioned when their responsibilities are downgraded to "chore," as opposed to the glorified "privilege." All who do their best to maintain a sane household—while regularly cooking wholesome food for their families—should champion Nigella Lawson's appropriate term, "Domestic Goddess."

Vesta, Roman goddess of hearth and home, was so revered she was included in the first five gods of the pantheon. Her prominence inspired great devotion. The ancient hearth was sacred—providing warmth, comfort, and life.

Our present-day kitchens have lost their hallowed status and are drive-thru centers for quick snacks, brief encounters, and shallow communication. In one generation, we have destroyed the centuries-old spirit of the home. Observable effects of the kitchen's demise can be seen in the rise of obesity and illnesses in our youth.

Cooking, eating, and laughing together strengthen the family bond and elevate the kitchen to its rightful status. Enjoyable and satisfying, these activities create a foundation for family unity. They become the common thread that connects the family forever.

Fifty years ago, Meta Given, mother, renowned Home Economics Specialist, and famous author of the cookbooks, *Modern Encyclopedia of Cooking* and *Modern Family Cookbook* (JG Ferguson & Assoc. 1943 to 1965), urged mothers to take responsibility for their role as primary caregivers. She accepted that the health and fulfillment of her family was her responsibility and, therefore, spared no effort in planning wholesome meals for their enjoyment. Her creeds appear old-fashioned, but her message to use intelligence, skill, and love in preparing food—and eating it with your family—is timeless.

You don't have to be perfect to be a good family.
You just have to be together.
It's not too late to start.

I thank God every day for my family and for the blessings they bring.

I know I could rely on fast or processed foods instead of home cooking to feed my family, but I would be cheating them of proper nutrition and a basic cooking education. By combining a few ingredients from the fridge or pantry, I simplify meal preparation— leading to a relaxed dining experience. Home cooking allows me to control the quality of ingredients I use. If I don't cook for my family, who will? And do I trust them? The consumption of fast and processed foods has greatly diminished the appreciation of healthy food as nourishment, and has significantly contributed to the increase of overweight youth. Parents can teach their children the importance of wholesome food choices. Moreover, the comforting and satisfying aromas from simmering sauces and freshly baked breads are beyond compare. The wonderful smells of my mother's and grandmother's kitchens will endure in my memory forever.

Children who help prepare meals look forward to serving and eating them. At the same time, they learn fundamental life skills: responsibility, independence, and organization. The development of these key traits leads to self-esteem and improved resilience, providing strength and determination to conquer the challenges of life. Children want to spend more time—not less—with their parents. Very young ones love to play with pots, bowls, and wooden spoons; older ones enjoy helping parents cook, and teens appreciate the neutral environment of the kitchen. Teenagers can prepare delicious, healthy, home-cooked food in less time than it takes to wait in line at the drive-thru.

Feeding people is how I serve others.

In addition to cooking for my family, I frequently deliver home-cooked meals, cookies, and other tasty desserts to friends, teachers, neighbors, doctors, hairdressers, and colleagues—in short, to anyone who needs a helping hand, craves a sweet treat, or values a homemade THANK YOU. In fact, my husband is careful not to eat a fresh-baked dessert—just in case it is intended as a surprise for someone else.

And because I know it is important for many to learn how to cook, I give cooking demonstrations, sponsored by A Tavola Together Foundation (www.atavolatogether.com) at local schools. I teach basic food preparation techniques to children of all ages, abilities, and socio-economic levels—emphasizing that cooking can be easy and fun.

In terms of The Parable of the Talents (Matthew 25:14–30), God has entrusted me with the talent of cooking. I am responsible for using this resource so that it increases in value. Sharing with others my inspiration for cooking is my ministry. I am responsible to the Lord.

Every now and then I walk into my kitchen and feel compelled to scream because of the mess overflowing the sink.

But I stop myself—and recall my blessings: Thank God for dirty dishes.

❤   ❤   ❤

Claudia Belotti Pruett is a specialist in Italian cooking. At the age of five, she began helping her mother and grandmother make pasta for family dinners. Italian cooking customs—including preparing fresh pasta, making tomato sauce, and baking bread—are traditions that she continues with her family. Claudia is a busy mom and active community member. Cooking for others is her inspiration. She says, "Thank God for dirty dishes" because she knows that if her sink is full of pots and pans, she has prepared and enjoyed a great meal with loved ones. She frequently shares kitchen secrets and creations—from elaborate pasta meals to fancy desserts—with family and friends. Claudia has 20 years of professional culinary experience. She is a professional chef, a published writer, and partner in A Tavola Together Foundation—an educational organization that promotes healthy cooking and eating to school-age children.

Join the *Thank God I...*™ Community online to share your story and chat with the authors at **www.thankgodi.com**

The Power of Perfection™

Is it possible that you are already Perfect exactly as you were, are, and will be in EVERY moment?

Has it been 10 years and you're still searching for "success" or "happiness"?

Sometimes the hardest place to find a tree is in the forest. The quality of your life is determined by the quality of the questions you ask yourself. It's a lot simpler to find the Perfect Answers by asking the Perfect Questions.

Are you ready for a clear and specific technique that describes exactly how to balance any emotion and, in doing so, honor the true perfection that exists inside you?

Discover *The Power of Perfection*™—a complete education series on how to honor and love yourself, and live the life that you would LOVE.

For more information visit
www.thankgodi.com